CYBERSONIC ARTS

MUSIC IN AMERICAN LIFE

*A list of books in the series appears
at the end of this book.*

CYBERSONIC ARTS

ADVENTURES IN AMERICAN NEW MUSIC

GORDON MUMMA

Edited with Commentary by
MICHELLE FILLION

Foreword by
CHRISTIAN WOLFF

UNIVERSITY OF ILLINOIS PRESS

Urbana, Chicago, and Springfield

Publication of this book was supported by a grant from
the Henry and Edna Binkele Classical Music Fund.

Library of Congress Control Number: 2015945918

ISBN 978-0-252-03943-0 (hardcover)
ISBN 978-0-252-08101-9 (paperback)
ISBN 978-0-252-09754-6 (e-book)

This book is dedicated to Michelle Fillion. She was the primary chef for whom I supplied the ingredients, both preserved and fresh. As with much of our life together, it has been a duo performance in which each of us was simultaneously soloist and accompanist.

GORDON MUMMA

CONTENTS

FIGURES

MUSICAL EXAMPLES

TABLES

FOREWORD

CHRISTIAN WOLFF

In the essay "On the Ives Railroad" (no. 29 of this collection) Gordon Mumma provides a verbal score describing a performance he then realized at a Charles Ives centennial conference. It involves film, music using ad hoc materials (a teakettle, equipment to get it boiling, a crosscut saw and a bow), and a previously made, electronically generated tape piece. The performance begins, according to the score text, "with minimum obtrusiveness / and adjusting to circumstances" but moves on to "interrupt remains of panel discussion," first with running of the film material, then with music made up of the kettle's loud whistling joined by a "high-pitched sustained sound" from the saw, at an interval to be determined by the performer in relation to the pitch that the kettle happens to be producing. That coming together of a sound from everyday life and one that is musically produced, albeit in a nonstandard way, by the bowing of the saw (the musical use of a saw is found in certain folk musics) puts me in mind of perhaps my favorite musical experience. At the end of the first Burdock Festival concert (see essay no. 27) a group of us were doing an outdoors piece of mine that asked performers to move out and away from a base location and improvise melodic fragments, possibly in duets (not planned but picked up by ear), and to continue moving further and further away until each player could no longer hear anyone else. At that point the piece would end. Gordon set off playing his horn. In due course, all the performers appeared to be done and gathered back at the base location. But Gordon wasn't there. Then, from down in the valley, we heard a train whistle, and then Gordon's horn. Almost a mile down the road, he was playing a duet with the train.

Now back to the Ives conference. Mumma's piece ends with a playing of his tape composition "Wooden Pajamas" following the increasingly loud last sounds of the kettle and bowed saw. The title refers to Salvador Allende, the Chilean president who was murdered by the right-wing junta of Augusto Pinochet in 1973. It is a powerful piece, its politics pointed at by the title (referring to Allende's saying that they—the junta—would have to carry him out in wooden pajamas, that is, in a coffin) and expressed by a very loud, rhythmically complex wooden hammering.

So much of Mumma is revealed here. There's the theatrically striking disruption of a proper panel discussion and then the friendly and engaged participation in it. There's the use of more or less standard as well as invented and alternative media. There are the electronics, the theatricality, the presence—not direct but, so to speak, musical—of political issues. There's the interest in South America, where, as Mumma observes, musical life and political conditions cannot be separated. And Mumma's composition/performance is also very much in the spirit of the occasion, a celebration of Charles Ives.

This collection of writings, extending over more than fifty years, is a fine illustration of Mumma's remarkable range of interests and involvements, and of his particular musical personality: his energy and dedication in making music happen, in organizing and performing on horn, piano, or live electronics, or interacting and playing with others; his appetite for information about everything—music, people, social arrangements, politics, culture at large—and his sometimes surprising use of that information. He knows the classical music repertoire, especially through his piano and horn playing. I was once astounded and delighted at seeing him, as part of a piece of his, climb up on the closed lid of a grand piano and, standing there in romantic horn player stance, play something by Schumann. His performing is always carefully prepared and thought out. And while he is not an improviser, he is an alert and adaptable performer. His gestures and actions are decisive and, even when funny and outrageous, straight-ahead and businesslike. His compositions and their visual scoring are meticulously made.

Over the course of more than fifty years Mumma has worked closely with many key figures in the arts, Robert Ashley, John Cage, David Tudor, David Behrman, Alvin Lucier, Pauline Oliveros, Robert Rauschenberg, and Merce Cunningham among them, and—he's a very sociable person—he has known many more. Much of the experience of his interactions can be found in this book. And then there's Mumma the collector and archivist. Always observant, he has become an extraordinary resource with his treasure trove of carefully preserved scores, writings, recordings, and photographs. This collection of his writings is a history of an unusually interesting period in experimental music and experimental combinations of music and other arts, involving both well-known figures and lesser-known ones. This is a history as experienced by one person with distinctive perspectives. These can be different in interesting ways, for instance, in noticing the effects of David Tudor's beginnings as an organist on his compositions or in the account of John Cage, not as usual the composer or writer, but in the nitty-gritty business of performing. Included are detailed and precise accounts of technological work from the sixties and early seventies, where that technology now sounds quaint and remote. But what counts here is the spirit of it, the inventiveness springing from an independence of imagination as well as the willingness and financial necessity to work outside the given conditions of the time. Mumma shows us how that spirit is in fact crucial and, always, of essential value.

INTRODUCTION

MICHELLE FILLION

In February 1965 pianists Robert Ashley and Gordon Mumma performed Mumma's *Medium Size Mograph 1963* at the ONCE Festival in Ann Arbor, Michigan.[1] Performed at a single instrument with "cybersonic" modification of live and pre-recorded piano sounds, Mumma's work initiated a series of cybersonic compositions that would include his signature *Mesa* (1966), *Hornpipe* (1967), *Ambivex* (1972), and *Cybersonic Cantilevers* (1973). In 1960 Mumma and William Ribbens had assigned the name "Cybersonics" to their small company in Ann Arbor for the design and production of sound-editing and processing equipment for live-electronic music.[2] The technical term was related to "cybernetics," the science of automatic control by feedback principles facilitated by the emerging transistor technology. As applied to Mumma's creative work, "cybersonics" involves the live-electronic processing of primarily acoustical sounds by which some aspects of the sounds are fed back into the electronic system and modified "by characteristics derived directly from the sound itself."[3] In his experience the term also assumed a wider meaning as a social metaphor for the interactive and even theatrical process by which people, their instruments, technology, and the performance space work together, "that interaction itself being collaborative."[4] Anyone who witnessed Ashley and Mumma's performance of *Medium Size Mograph 1963* at ONCE 1965[5] was struck by its dramatic theater of two musicians working together in rapt attention over a single keyboard, their familiar actions only indirectly related to the uncommon or alarming sounds emerging, not from the heavily blanketed piano, but from the loudspeakers by way of a mysterious electronic box.

The terrain of this book is the "cybersonic arts" in the broader sense of creative interaction among artists in several media, including both electronic and instrumental music. It brings together selected essays about music for live performance, modern dance, and electronic music technology written between 1960 and 2013 by an important creative figure in American new music, the composer, performer, instrument builder, writer, and teacher Gordon Mumma. Its release coincides with his eightieth birthday in 2015. Its central thread is the power and value of artistic collaboration in his aesthetics and throughout his career across the Americas from Toronto to Montevideo, and in his prime axis of Michigan, New York, and California.

Like many in his wide circle of artistic friends, Mumma has witnessed at first hand countless events in the adventure of American new music and related arts since 1960: as a pioneer in live-electronic music, as co-founder of the ONCE Festival in Ann Arbor, as a member of the Sonic Arts Union (with Robert Ashley, David Behrman, and Alvin Lucier), as a member of the musical ensemble (with John Cage and David Tudor) of the Merce Cunningham Dance Company, as an interactive performer with such diverse artists as Anthony Braxton, Pauline Oliveros, Tom Robbins, James Tenney, and Christian Wolff, as professor (now emeritus) at the University of California, Santa Cruz, and as a writer on music and music technology. What distinguishes him from others is his energetic, even passionate commitment to documenting and communicating that experience in words and images. Whether autobiographical, analytical, or anecdotal, this book provides primary accounts and personal recollections of lived experiences from "center stage" of the action rather than from secondary research, with reference to the latter only in the accompanying notes. It also provides the foundation for a fresh assessment of Gordon Mumma's life, music, and musical thinking during this period.

This book extends well beyond the scope of a retrospective reprint. The previously published pieces, written for the most part "on the fly" between composing, performing, and teaching commitments and with limited editorial intervention, have been revised, in some cases substantially. Most have long been out of print or are otherwise difficult to access. Factual errors have been corrected, leaving the original critical perspectives unchanged. The previously unpublished items, including a 1961 essay titled "Milton Cohen's Space Theatre" (no. 2) and a journal of the summer new-music courses in Uruguay in 1975 (no. 24), were completed on the basis of manuscript drafts and journals that I located in the Gordon Mumma Collection in Orinda, California, and Victoria, British Columbia (hereafter GMC), augmented by recent interviews with the composer. This book also includes recent additions, including contributions to the Cage centenary in 2012 (nos. 16 and 20), a self-assessment of Mumma's compositional language (no. 37), and the new biographical sketch and selective list of his musical compositions that frame the book. The latter work list serves as the primary source of information on composition dates, performance history, and recordings of the works by Mumma referred to throughout the book. The sources, provenance, and editorial process of each essay are described at its opening.

My role as editor has been to assist Mumma in locating and selecting the most interesting and representative items[6] and in revising each text to tighten the prose, sharpen the argument, eliminate redundancies, expand missing details, and unify the tone. All editorial decisions were made in dialogue with the author. Obvious factual errors were corrected, but opinions representative of earlier times were retained for their historical value. Elimination of redundancy has resulted in some cases in significant cuts or reorganization of previously published material. When we determined that a certain project or event had been treated piecemeal in several sources (Cage's *Variations V* and Mumma's *Hornpipe* being notable examples), related material was conflated and placed in the most appropriate single essay to spare the reader the tasks of collating information and resolving discrepancies. Several important writings depart notably from the previously published versions for other reasons. "The ONCE Festival and How It Happened" (no. 4), for example, had mistakenly been issued in the journal *Arts in Society* in 1967 on the basis of the uncorrected first draft; this reissue is based on Mumma's corrected typescript of 1970. "From Where the Circus Went" (no. 15) restores major sections cut by the original publisher in 1975 for reasons of space, as well as additional draft materials from Mumma's projected but unfinished monograph on his years with the Merce Cunningham Dance Company. My aim has been to transform these writings from the ephemeral to the enduring, fashioning from them a cohesive document worthy of this energetic practitioner and observer of American new music and performing arts.

Mumma's essays are grouped thematically into seven parts, each with an editor's introduction supplying the context and signaling the major issues of its contents. The parts represent major themes in his creative life, beginning with "Unmarked Interchange: Ann Arbor and the ONCE Years (1960–66)." Part II examines his signature involvement in the development of live-electronic music with the other members of the Sonic Arts Union in "Cybersonics and the Sonic Arts (1966–75)." Part III, "In the Cunningham Circle," addresses Mumma's work with Cunningham, Robert Rauschenberg, David Tudor, and others in the Merce Cunningham Dance Company from 1966 to 1973 and beyond. Mumma's professional and personal relationship with Cage informs the fourth part, "Not Wanting to Say Anything about John (Cage)," while the fifth explores some of Mumma's musical experiences in Latin America. Part VI, "An American Gallery," provides short sketches of his working interactions with creative figures such as Earle Brown, Pauline Oliveros, Christian Wolff, lighting designer Richard Nelson, and the members of the Sonic Arts Union. The book closes with "Mumma on Mumma," outlining his musical aesthetics and compositional processes as illustrated in a selection of his electronic and acoustical music. Further commentary is postponed to my introduction to each part.

More than mere embellishment, the photo documentation from the GMC is an essential counterpart to the prose of this book. Many of these photos are appearing in print for the first time, with the exceptions drawn from publications now out of print or, if not, providing essential visual confirmation of key events in the text. The photos are recent additions to both previously published and unpublished essays; the cues in the text are enclosed in brackets unless integrated into the prose, with the understanding that they are new insertions. The majority are by Mumma himself. Although never more than an amateur photographer, albeit a passionate one, he rarely toured without at least two still cameras for black-and-white and color film, sometimes amplified by 8mm and 16mm movie cameras. Ever respectful of the formal performance space, he preferred to capture equipment set-ups, rehearsals, pauses, or casual moments in the working life of dancers and musicians. He even worked his roving camera during sporadic breaks in his own performance activities, occasionally drawing complaints from colleagues such as Cage or Tudor when it was seen as "getting in the way of our *real* work." Yet the quality of his candid images of otherwise undocumented events in American new music and dance of the 1960s through the 1980s and the frequency with which they appear in recent publications confirm the importance of Mumma's photographic work. Cage had evidently adjusted his perspective by 1989, when he took Mumma aside at a photographic exhibition at Fort Mason in San Francisco to thank him for having captured and preserved in his photo images the human element of life in the Cunningham milieu.

As a historical musicologist, archivist of the GMC, and editor of this volume, I applaud Mumma's heroic propensity for hoarding. I have profited immensely from his massive collection of music and musicalia, historical artifacts, programs, photographs and slides, and manuscripts relevant to this project. As his life partner, I can only add that the inestimable value of his collection as a research resource has more than offset the occasional irritations of daily life amid the detritus of the past. This book is in every sense a shared effort, a labor of love, and from my perspective a beautiful illustration of the joyful and generous collaborative spirit that has infused Gordon Mumma's life in music.

Acknowledgments

Our sincere thanks go to the many colleagues and friends who shared valuable information, insights, encouragement, and recollections with us in emails and telephone conversations or over convivial meals, especially Coriún Aharonián, David Behrman, David W. Bernstein, Brian Brant, Carolyn Brown, Richard H. Brown, Ralf Dietrich, John Driscoll, Gregorio García-Karman, Jonathan Goldman, Gisela Gronemeyer, John Holzaepfel, alcides lanza and Meg Sheppard, Julie Martin, Leta E. Miller, Graciela Paraskevaídis, Benjamin Piekut, David Revill, Jean Rigg, Julia Schröder, Volker Straebel, Paul Tai of New World Records, David Vaughan of the Merce Cunningham Trust, Klaus Wildenhahn, and John Zorn. Our special appreciation goes to Amy C. Beal for her thoughtful critical reading of the preliminary manuscript. From our first discussions of this book project, Gordon and I agreed that Christian Wolff should write the foreword, and we are very grateful that he generously acquiesced. We also acknowledge the support and cooperation of the publishers, agencies, institutions, and editors who granted permission to reprint or revise previously published material; these credits are acknowledged in the notes preceding each essay. Several of Gordon's personal friends and associates freely granted permission to use their photographs, including Harold Borkin, Jumay R. Chu, Barbara Dilley Lloyd, David Freund, Mimi Johnson (for the late Mary Ashley), James Klosty, and Aimée Tsao (for the family of the late Makepeace Tsao). Credits for all photos are included in the captions. James Klosty also contributed the arresting cover photograph that distills the vision and adventurousness of Gordon Mumma's musical and literary persona. Finally, Ezra Freeman of Twin Oaks indexing prepared the elegant index.

We especially thank our editor at the University of Illinois Press, Laurie Matheson. Her immediate enthusiasm, savvy guidance, and unfailing support for this project—along with her superb colleagues, notably Jennifer Comeau and Jane Zanichkowsky—provided wind for the sails of its voyage from first conception to realization.

GORDON MUMMA
A Short Biography

MICHELLE FILLION

Composer, performer, instrument builder, teacher, and writer Gordon Mumma was a New Englander by virtue of his birth in Framingham, Massachusetts, on March 30, 1935. His parents were Southwest pioneers: Colgan T. Mumma (1908–98) was born in Farmington in the Territory of New Mexico, and Adamae McCoy (1908–96) was raised in Tucson, Arizona. They met at the University of Arizona. Shortly after their marriage in June 1931, they moved to Framingham, where Colgan had secured a credit-analysis and management position with a major paper products manufacturer. For the first six years of Gordon's life, the Mumma family lived in the historic gambrel-roofed Stone House with its adjacent eighteenth-century Rugg-Gates House and majestic elm tree, a tourist attraction. The rustling leaves of the surrounding poplars formed one of his earliest musical memories. The poplars fell overnight in the 1938 hurricane, providing his first vivid experience of loss (to be evoked in "Poplars" from the piano suite *Jardin*, completed in 1997). These early years left Mumma with a strong sense of *place*—the New England countryside and the deserts and mesas of the Southwest, where the family vacationed.

Colgan Mumma, in his son's words, "built and fixed things." He was an innovative artisan and woodworker who designed and built two of their homes and furnishings, working on these projects with Adamae, a gifted craft artist. In his professional career Colgan was adept at motivating people to work together creatively. The lessons of making things with one's wits and hands in collaboration with others came early to Gordon Mumma.

Gordon's elementary school in Framingham included an active music and sight-singing program. The boy's precocious fascination with classical music, fueled by avid listening to the family's recording collection and opera and symphonic radio broadcasts, soon awakened parental concern, especially from his mother. A troubling sign of things to come was the 1940 family outing to the Ice Capades, where the five-year-old remained riveted on the live orchestra, barely glancing at the skaters. The family tradition of amused condescension toward its "black sheep" composer from Ohio, Archie A. Mumma (1887–1941), did not help the boy's cause.[1] Sympathetic friends provided musical opportunities, notably the occasional invitation to attend closed dress rehearsals of the Boston Symphony Orchestra. Particularly memorable was the rehearsal of Bartók's Concerto for Orchestra in preparation for its December 1, 1944, world premiere, conducted by Serge Koussevitzky.

When his father's career caused the family to relocate to Hinsdale, Illinois, in the Chicago area in 1946, Gordon played the horn in the junior high school orchestra, "the biggest interest [he] had had so far."[2] He made rapid progress, quickly moving on to the high school orchestra. When a year later they moved to Ferndale, Michigan, a suburb of Detroit, the transition was rocky. He started piano lessons, however, which he "had wanted to do for years, and that was the only thing that saved that year" for him.[3] By then he was age twelve, too old to develop the secure technique of a professional. Yet he would acquire sufficient skill as a "boisterous amateur"[4] to perform occasionally as piano soloist or in duo with such as Robert Ashley, Jon Barlow, John Cage, David Tudor, and Belgian pianist Daan Vandewalle.

Music became the guiding force of Mumma's high school years (1948–52) in Ferndale, where he continued in earnest on the horn and began composing. He performed in wind ensembles and in the orchestra, eventually widening his activities to include amateur and semi-professional orchestras throughout southeastern Michigan. Several of these included musicians from the Detroit Symphony Orchestra during the two years (1949–51) when it was disbanded for financial reasons. He also studied horn privately with Detroit Symphony regular Kenneth Schultz. By his senior year he was spending several nights each week rehearsing and performing the major classical symphonic repertoire with diverse ensembles. Meanwhile, his sister Karen (b. 1940) was likewise profiting from the musical resources of Detroit; she would develop into a professional cellist and string teacher.

Perhaps the most formative musical experiences of these years were his four summer residencies at the National Music Camp in Interlochen, Michigan (1949–52), when Mumma discovered himself as a musician among like-

minded peers. Especially influential were conductors A. Clyde Roller, Orien
Dalley, and Frederick Fennell, acoustician Roderick Dean Gordon, and pianist
George Exon, whom Mumma credits as his only significant piano teacher. By
1950 his activities as a composer were also expanding, spurred by his studies in
composition and theory with Homer Keller at Interlochen. The following year
he took first prize for his two-movement string quartet in the Michigan High
School competition, adjudicated by composer Ross Lee Finney of the University
of Michigan.

By early 1952 Mumma had outgrown high school. He was expelled following a stunning outburst of temper after he was caught playing Stan Kenton jazz
arrangements during a wind sectional for a Haydn symphony. The principal,
wise enough to recognize his gifts, arranged his acceptance to the University of
Michigan School of Music in February 1952—without a high school diploma.
Composition lessons with Finney proved contentious, however, reaching a
crisis when Finney crumpled the twelve-tone canonic trio that Mumma had
brought in for his comment and threw it out the window of his eighth-floor
office.[5] Mumma moved on to Leslie Bassett for his second year of composition
lessons, focusing with him on traditional crafts of orchestration. He transferred
to the music theory program and briefly to English literature before withdrawing
from the university in the fall of 1954, too busy with other creative activities to
complete his degree. Thereafter he continued his association with the University
of Michigan—and with academia in general—on his own terms.

In the spring of 1952 visiting virtuoso saxophonist Sigurd Rascher performed
with William Revelli's University of Michigan Concert Band, in which Mumma
played horn. Rascher told Mumma of a remarkable pianist with whom he was
touring, who played "every work as if he had lived in its time and place." In February 1953 Mumma made the long trip by train and bus to Des Moines, Iowa,
to hear Rascher, who introduced him to David Tudor.[6] The following month,
Mumma and other composition students attended the Festival of Contemporary Arts at the University of Illinois, where he first met John Cage and heard
Tudor in his March 22 recital of piano music by Pierre Boulez, Earle Brown,
Cage, Morton Feldman, and Christian Wolff. Mumma also attended the dance
recital by Merce Cunningham on the last night of the festival (March 24): *Suite
by Chance* received its premiere with tape music by Christian Wolff (his *Untitled*),
and Cage was the pianist for the revival of *Sixteen Dances for Soloist and Company
of Three*. The associations of a lifetime were forming.

Despite their personal differences, Finney welcomed Mumma as a visiting student to his graduate seminars over the following years. There Mumma
interacted with composition students Robert Ashley, George Cacioppo, Roger

Reynolds, Donald Scavarda, and others, with whom he would later develop the ONCE Festival. He also connected with the diverse guest composers whom Finney regularly brought to the University, ranging from Walter Piston and Ralph Vaughan Williams to Luigi Dallapiccola and Karlheinz Stockhausen. Stockhausen's 1958 lecture on the idea of an independent composer resonated with Mumma and Ashley,[7] who co-founded a private electronic studio early that year. Finally, in 1960 composer Roberto Gerhard (a visiting professor replacing Finney, who was on leave) proved inspirational to Mumma for his quiet encouragement to continue following his own path.[8]

Operating on the fringe of academia, Mumma plunged into a series of artistic projects involving collaboration and open exploration. He composed a soundtrack and incidental music for plays performed by the university's Theater Department including William Butler Yeats's *Deirdre* (in 1954), Rupert Brooke's *Lithuania* (1954), and Eugène Ionesco's *The Bald Soprano* (1958). In 1957 he began a long-term creative association with Ashley in Milton Cohen's Space Theatre. In early 1958 he and Ashley founded the Cooperative Studio for Electronic Music in Ann Arbor for the production of live electronic and tape music for the Space Theatre and soundtracks for independent filmmakers such as George Manupelli. His association with university carillonneur Percival Price, an expert in change ringing procedures and all things about bells, resulted in the earliest composition in Mumma's catalogue, *Etude on Oxford Changes* for unaccompanied violin (1957).[9] By 1959 he had completed *Vectors*, his first mature work for magnetic tape.

In 1960 Mumma and electronic engineer William Ribbens founded Cybersonics, a small electronic design company in Ann Arbor for the design and production of sound-editing and processing equipment for live-electronic music, film, and television. In 1961 Mumma began experiments with cybersonic compositional procedures while designing electronic music equipment for the Cooperative Studio. Mumma has defined "cybersonics" as a live-electronic feedback principle by which some aspect of the sound is fed back into the electronic process, thus modifying sound "by characteristics derived directly from the sound itself."[10] His first fully cybersonic composition was the *Medium Size Mograph 1963* for piano four hands and cybersonic console. It would become a mainstay of the Ashley-Mumma duo repertoire—along with Mumma's other piano Mographs, *Suite for Piano*, and *Gestures II*—in their ongoing touring programs titled "New Music for Pianos."

Mumma remained in Ann Arbor until 1966, maintaining loose connections with the university. He supported himself with odd jobs in local music and book stores, as an attendant in the wards and operating rooms at local hospitals, as an assistant and technical writer for the Research Department of Willow Run Laboratories, as a hornist in numerous professional and semi-professional ensembles, and increasingly as an independent composer-performer. He was also an occasional music reviewer for the *Michigan Daily* beginning in 1955, and he contributed occasional essays on film, literature, and censorship to the student inter-arts journal *Generation*.[11] His literary interests account for his lifelong activities as an unofficial documenter of the American avant-garde, while his newspaper apprenticeship left its mark on the journalistic punch of his prose.

The ONCE Festivals in Ann Arbor of 1961–65 and 1968 formed a creative nexus of his work during these years. He wore many hats at these festivals, switching off with his co-conspirators as organizer, bookkeeper, impresario, diarist, technical assistant, performer, and composer. Among Mumma's ONCE premieres were the *Sinfonia for 12 Instruments and Magnetic Tape* (1958–60), *Meanwhile, a Twopiece* (1961), and *The Dresden Interleaf 13 February 1945* (1965), the latter for 4-channel fixed media and live alcohol-burning airplane engines. Significant as well were the contacts with visiting composers to ONCE; those with David Behrman, André Boucourechliev, Feldman, Udo Kasemets, Alvin Lucier, and Pauline Oliveros would ripen into friendships. Performances with Milton Cohen's Space Theatre also continued, bringing the ensemble in September 1964 to the Venice Biennale, where his *Music from the Venezia Space Theatre* was given its premiere and friendships with Luigi Nono and his wife, Nuria Schoenberg Nono, were formed.

In the cases of Behrman and Lucier, further collaborations with Ashley and Mumma resulted in the formation of an important creative collective. The foursome performed its first shared event at the Rose Art Museum at Brandeis University on April 22, 1966, initiating a vigorous national and international roster of concerts for live-electronic and acoustic resources. Their first billing as the Sonic Arts Group was at the Winter Fest in New England Life Hall, Boston, on February 21, 1967;[12] in 1970 the group revised its name to Sonic Arts Union and remained active until 1977, with occasional reunions afterwards.[13]

Mumma's engagement with the Merce Cunningham Dance Company began in July 1966 (see part III of this book). Except for a few absences for touring with the Sonic Arts Union, Mumma was in the pit for most of the touring performances of the company until the summer of 1973, functioning as sound technician, composer, hornist, pianist, and cybersonic wizard. During these years he also expanded his performance skills on the bandoneon and the musical saw, as explored in his *Mesa* (1966) and *Schoolwork* (1970). His focus increasingly shifting from Ann Arbor to New York, he rented an apartment that Cunningham had vacated at 247 Mulberry Street in Little Italy in December 1966.

He would maintain a New York address until 1975. There his connection with the Stefan Wolpe circle and his close friendships with Behrman, Earle Brown, and Morton Feldman profited from proximity (ending, however, the vigorous mail correspondence with Feldman of the previous years). Although his circle of acquaintances widened in the heady artistic atmosphere of New York in the late 1960s, increasingly the Cunningham community provided an artistic home, more often than not away from home.

Mumma's international touring career reached a high point during these years. Besides the Cunningham Dance Company and Sonic Arts Union tours, he was actively involved in ensembles with Cage and Tudor, with Christian Wolff, and with dancers Yvonne Rainer (*Rainermusic* [1968]) and Barbara Lloyd (*I Saw Her Dance* [1970]). Collaborations with others included *Communication in a Noisy Environment* with Behrman, Anthony Braxton, Leroy Jenkins, and Robert Watts at the Automation House, New York, in November 1970.[14] Mumma premiered his *Beam* at Roger Reynolds's Crosstalk International Festival in Tokyo (1969) and participated in the Summer Courses in Chocorua, New Hampshire (1973), and the 1974 Darmstadt Summer Course for New Music and Berlin Metamusik Festival. Central to his touring repertoire during these years were the cybersonic works *Hornpipe* (1967) and *Ambivex* (1972).

By the late 1960s many of Mumma's musical friends had accepted university teaching positions. In the fall of 1969 he taught for a single semester at the University of Illinois in Champaign-Urbana, replacing Lejaren Hiller while he was on leave. There Mumma connected with William Brooks and Maggi Payne, who would become significant artists and colleagues. Following several short-term residencies at the University of California, Berkeley, and at Dartmouth College, Mumma accepted two single-year teaching contracts at the University of California, Santa Cruz, beginning in the fall of 1973. He had intended to return to New York afterwards but was offered a tenured professorship in 1975. Mumma's university career at Santa Cruz, with intervening appointments at the University of California, San Diego, and at Mills College, continued until his early retirement in 1994.

The demands of full-time teaching—what Mumma has called his "Faustian relationship with academia"[15]—necessarily rebalanced his creative work as composer, performer, and writer. The "circus-life" of a touring musician was substantially tempered in new collaborations closer to home, especially with Norman O. Brown, Lou Harrison and William Colvig, James Tenney, dancer-choreographers Tandy Beal and Mel Wong, and the Portland Dance Theatre, directed by Jann McCauley Dryer. The focus of his writing also changed, shifting from the documentation of lived creative experience on the road to more traditional academic research, much of which has been omitted from this book. The most significant of the latter is the major article "Sound Recording," commissioned by H. Wiley Hitchcock for the *New Grove Dictionary of American Music* (1986). Teaching provided a major outlet for his creative writing during these years. His celebrated course syllabi on electronic music technology and twentieth-century music opened these subjects to a younger generation of performing musicians, composers, studio technicians, and computer geeks.[16]

Among the significant experiences of these years were his residencies at the Cursos Latinoamericanos de Música Contemporánea (Latin American Courses of Contemporary Music), held in January. Though he was invited yearly to participate, Mumma's academic duties permitted him to attend only three, bringing him to Cerro del Toro, Uruguay (1975), Buenos Aires, Argentina (1977), and Santiago, Dominican Republic (1981). Many nourishing creative connections and friendships emerged from the Cursos (as discussed in part V of this book).

Composition remained central to his activity. Profiting from the availability of instrumentalists in university settings, he returned to more traditional acoustical ensembles in works such as *Equale: Zero Crossing* for seven instruments (1976), *Faisandage et galimafrée*, variable trios in eight movements (1984), *Aleutian Displacement* for chamber orchestra (1987), and *Orait* for vocal ensemble and body percussion (1987). The electronic instrument building of his earlier career was now augmented by his building of historically based keyboard instruments including a single-manual Flemish-style harpsichord. The latter instruments was featured with innovative results in the *Eleven Note Pieces and Decimal Passacaglia* (1978), the first five of the *Sixpac Sonatas* (begun in 1985), and as sound material—along with Buchla synthesizer and electronics—in *Echo-D* (1978). Electronic music, often for use in theatrical settings, continued to engage him. Notable were the studio electronic compositions *Pontpoint* (1966–80) and *Cirqualz* (1980), both of which were featured in choreographies by the Portland Dance Theatre. With the emergence of the digital home computer in the 1980s, Mumma employed it in *Than Particle* (1985), a live-electronic touring piece for himself and percussionist William Winant.

In the late 1980s Mumma's health began to falter with the onset of chronic hepatitis B, which he had probably contracted decades earlier as a hospital worker in Ann Arbor. He scaled back his activities, retiring from the university in 1994. For the next four years he profited from the relative peace of his life by returning to solo piano music. Revisions of unfinished earlier drafts augmented by new compositions resulted in a group of poetic miniatures, a sort of microcosm of sound explorations for the piano. Among these are the last of the *Sixpac Sonatas* (completed 1997), *Graftings* (1990–96), the *Songs without*

Words (the most notable of which are those for George Exon, David Tudor, and Christian Wolff), the suite *Jardin* (completed 1997), and the nineteen *Sushibox* pieces (assembled in 1996). The latter set is the source of the "construction-set" principle that emerged in Mumma's works of the next decade.

In 1998 Mumma nearly died from acute liver failure. An emergency organ transplant at the UCSF Hospital in San Francisco saved his life. Following a long convalescence, he resumed creative activity with his quadraphonic electronic *Ambulare* (1999). In 2000 he was honored by a major retrospective of his music at Mills College and the biennial John Cage Award from the Foundation for Contemporary Performance Arts. His engagement with live-electronic music has continued in *Yawawot—Spectral Portrait* for live solo violin and electro-acoustical soundscape (2003), *From the Rendition Series*, a "construction set" for solo piano with internal electronics (2006), and *Gambreled Tapestry* for piano and electronics (2007). His *Comitatus 2* for violin and piano (2009) and *Abrupted Edges, for Alvin Lucier "a diamond among . . ."* for string quartet and piano (2011) return to acoustical ensembles. In addition to ongoing compositional projects, Mumma is currently engaged in a major project to publish his music.

PART I

Unmarked Interchange:
Ann Arbor and the ONCE Years (1960–66)

Editor's Introduction

The essays in this part capture the diversity of new music in Ann Arbor, Michigan, during the years of the legendary ONCE Festival from the perspective of one of its central figures. Although Mumma's official studies at the University of Michigan were short-lived (1952–54), his creative activity within the Ann Arbor community remained vigorous until he moved to New York City in 1966 (see his biographical sketch for further details). The centerpiece of this period was the series of ONCE Festivals, beginning with the first festival of February-March 1961 and ending officially with the ONCE AGAIN Festival of September 1965, after which funding was withdrawn. The festival was extended, however, in the ONCE Recording Concerts of 1966 and in three events featuring members of the ONCE and Sonic Arts Groups in 1968.[1] The ONCE milieu also embraced several ancillary groups, including ONCE Friends, Mary Ashley's Truck, Milton Cohen's Space Theatre, the New York Theater Rally, the Judson Dance Theater, and Unmarked Interchange. Taken together, ONCE proved a major, multi-stage locus for international new music in the American Midwest for much of the 1960s.

Mumma's feature article "Music's Avant-Garde: What's New?" was written for the *Michigan Daily* in May 1960. Its purpose was to prime the Ann Arbor public for the performances later that month by John Cage and David Tudor, which Roger Reynolds, Robert Ashley, and Mumma had arranged with sponsorship of the University of Michigan Dramatic Arts Center and the School of Architecture and Design. The essay reveals his perspectives on emerging media, audience response, and the international politics of new music a year before the first ONCE Festival. Here as well we see the young composer assembling his community of like-minded artists such as Stockhausen, Pierre Boulez, and Luigi Nono, with pride of place granted to Cage in a gesture surely motivated by more than advertising hype.

The previously unpublished *"Manifestations: Light and Sound"* (1961) is the earliest first-hand account of Milton Cohen's Space Theatre in Ann Arbor. Its core was drafted on the cusp of Mumma and Ashley's earliest large-scale magnetic-tape concert pieces for Cohen's light-projection performances, including Mumma's *Vectors* (1959) and Ashley's *The Fourth of July* (1960), followed by Mumma's works for quadraphonic tape, including *Mirrors for Milton Cohen* (1960–61) and *Music from the Venezia Space Theatre* (1963–64).

"An Electronic Music Studio for the Independent Composer" (1964), commissioned by Robert Moog, provides a glimpse into the technological resources newly accessible to the independent electronic music composer working "off the grid" of commercial studios and institutional funding. A mainstay of the composer of today, the home studio was a novelty in the early 1960s, when the large institutional electronic studios were accessible only to an elite minority. Its detailed rationale for the selection of equipment and its practical configuration projects a low-cost home studio targeted to young composers and the contemporary high-fidelity industry. It provides insight into the compositional processes for tape music at that time, as well as specific data about the equipment used in Mumma's major electronic music of the ONCE era, including the iconic *Megaton for Wm. Burroughs* (1963–64) and *The Dresden Interleaf 13 February 1945* (1965).

"The ONCE Festival and How It Happened" (1967) has become a primary source for all later historical accounts of the festival. The current version incorporates revisions from the author's corrected 1970 typescript of the article. Ancillary is a short account of two productions by the ONCE Group, "*Unmarked Interchange* and *Night Train*" (1967), the first of which provides a poetic analogy for the open exploration and collaborative spirit of the ONCE years.

CHAPTER 1

Music's Avant-Garde
What's New?
(1960)

In April of this year [1960] the American musical public heard a broadcast of three recent musical compositions played by the New York Philharmonic conducted by Leonard Bernstein: *Antiphony One* by Henry Brant (from Canada), *Improvisation I sur Mallarmé* by Pierre Boulez (France), and *Concerted Piece for Tape Recorder and Orchestra* by Otto Luening and Vladimir Ussachevsky (United States). For a good part of the audience this was the most "advanced" music they had ever heard. The responses ranged from shock and bewilderment to fascination and excitement. Conservative critics assured their readers that the "avant-garde" was only having its field day; next week everything would return to normal and the Philharmonic might again play Brahms. For radical critics the program had not gone far enough. As the dust settles, it proves easier to appreciate Bernstein's program in the context of what's happening in the contemporary musical world and to determine what sort of menace the avant-garde really presents.

Brant's *Antiphony One* is an example of "music in space" scored for several orchestras located at different points in the concert hall.[1] Each orchestra requires its own conductor, and the audience sits in the middle of the sound. This is not a new idea. Giovanni Gabrieli wrote antiphonal music for Saint Mark's Cathedral in Venice in the sixteenth century, while Johann Sebastian Bach, Hector Berlioz, Gustav Mahler, and numerous others have exploited space in their music. Recently in Ann Arbor, Josef Blatt and the University Symphony performed Leoš

Source: *Michigan Daily Magazine* (Ann Arbor) 6, no. 9 (May 8, 1960): 5–11, abridged, with stylistic revisions.

Janáček's *Sinfonietta* with the orchestra on stage and a retinue of brass players in the balcony. Current sales of stereophonic apparatus indicate that the public is as excited about spatial music as are many composers.

Three further examples of spatial music deserve mention. The unfinished and undated *Universe Symphony* by the American visionary Charles Ives was conceived for several orchestras to be placed at various heights on the mountains surrounding a valley in which the audience is seated (to date there have been no performances). For *Ein irrender Sohn* (1959) by the Swede Bo Nilsson, the performers are spaced about ten seats apart throughout the audience. A more extreme case is *Poem for Chairs, Tables, Benches, etc.* (1960) by the American La Monte Young, performed this April at a concert at The Living Theatre in New York City. The performers included the pianist David Tudor, composers John Cage and Toshi Ichiyanagi, and dancer-choreographer Merce Cunningham. As the title suggests, the instruments were large wooden benches and bar stools that the performers dragged around the reverberant tile floor of the theater lobby, while the bewildered audience wandered among the incredible scraping sounds.

Improvisation I sur Mallarmé (1957) by Pierre Boulez, for soprano, harp, and six percussionists, is an example of avant-garde serial music for conventional instruments. The term "serial" denotes a predetermined order or sequence of sounds (or "series") within the structure of the music (much as the progression of tonal centers or keys determines structure in the music of Beethoven's time). The avant-garde serialists have expanded their applications of serialism beyond the series of pitches (or "tone row") used by Berg, Schoenberg, and Webern in the early twentieth century to include other musical properties: the length of sounds and their rhythmic patterns, the loudness of sounds, methods of attack and articulation, and instrumentation and timbre. The serialists who compose spatial music have also applied their techniques to the direction of sound.

Some composers employ elaborate mathematical procedures of group theory, set theory, Markov processes, and differential calculus for both analysis and composition. Journals such as *Die Reihe*, *Melos*, and *Gravesaner Blätter* are laced with mathematical formulae. Much of this may be bunk, but some of it has revealed exciting new musical relationships. These rigorous procedures have resulted in music that is often extremely difficult to perform. Many serious musicians may even consider it unplayable, and understandably, for music academies and conservatories are still teaching techniques that apply largely to music of the nineteenth century and before. Yet this music is being played with increasing frequency. A confirmation that even radical innovations are soon absorbed into general performance techniques is provided by Robert Craft's recent recording of the serial music of Anton Webern with the Twentieth Century Classics Ensemble.[2] Rehearsals of each of the earlier (and easier) works consumed several weeks, while increasing familiarity with Webern's musical language enabled them to record the very difficult *Concerto for Nine Instruments*, op. 24, with less than two hours of rehearsal. After hearing the American pianists Paul Jacobs or David Tudor perform, it is conceivable that anything can be played, and played well.

The broadcast of Luening and Ussachevsky's *Concerted Piece* was one of the first American network radio performances of music in an area now in its second decade of development. *Concerted Piece* is a recent American electronic—or "tape recorder"—composition,[3] and was written especially for this New York Philharmonic concert. It combines electronic music and conventional instruments. Significant early work in electronic music was produced between 1950 and 1956 in the studios of the Nordwestdeutscher Rundfunk in Cologne and Radiotelevisione italiana (RAI) in Milan. Although electronic music has been composed in many other centers, the German and Italian electronic music composed before 1956 by Karlheinz Stockhausen, Gottfried Michael Koenig, Luciano Berio, and Bruno Maderna has clarified the problems of the genre and has established musical precedents on which other composers of electronic music could depend or against which they could rebel. But electronic music is not the sole province of younger composers: Luigi Dallapiccola, Roberto Gerhard, Ernst Krenek, and the musical radical of the 1920s, Edgard Varèse, have also worked in the medium. Varèse's *Poème électronique* was heard in the Le Corbusier–Philips Pavilion at the 1958 Brussels World's Fair.

The patronage of two large European publishers, Universal Edition and Schott, has assisted avant-garde composers with financial support and with the publication of both conventional and electronic scores and related journals. A particularly effective proponent of the avant-garde is conductor Hermann Scherchen, who founded the publishing house Ars Viva Verlag in Mainz and established an electronic studio in Gravesano, Switzerland, to encourage advanced work in music.[4] In the United States, conductor Robert Craft has performed, recorded, and encouraged avant-garde music for conventional instruments.

The amount of electronic music composed since 1956 has steadily declined for several reasons. The first of these is the change in the character of major European contemporary music festivals that occurred around 1955, shifting emphasis from well-established to lesser-known composers. The outcome brought younger avant-garde composers international hearing while encouraging them to write for conventional instruments without recourse to the laborious processes of electronic music. Second, European electronic composers have recently been having trouble accessing certain state-supported electronic studios because of political problems. Finally, and most important, is the development by RCA of a radical new "synthesizer" that makes it possible to compose electronic music with a vast range of sounds and precise control, while eliminating most of the time and labor of tape splicing and mixing (Stockhausen spent nearly two years producing his thirteen-minute *Gesang der Jünglinge* in 1955–56). Numerous foundations, including the Rockefeller, have facilitated work with the new RCA Synthesizer. To date, however, there has been little progress with this huge machine due to the encumbrances of legal, patent, and security restrictions and professional jealousies.

In contrast to the ideas and music of the above composers is the phenomenon of John Cage. Cage has explored a wide range of musical ideas, from pianos prepared with stove bolts, furniture tacks, and pencil erasers to music using the electronic modification of sound and the exploitation of silences. Certainly the most radical of these ideas is the composition of music by chance techniques or random processes. Although it has historical precedents—Mozart composed some music by drawing cards[5]—and is justified by the aesthetics of certain Eastern philosophies, the concept of "random music" has created a greater storm of protest than even serial music. The most extreme critics are further annoyed because Cage—unlike the serialists—refuses to respond to their attacks; he is more likely to answer them by lecturing about mushroom hunting.

Surrounded with anecdote, legend, and enigma, Cage has gained many supporters. Although his following in America is predominantly of artists, writers, and dancers, with few musicians among his supporters, the young serial composers in Europe take him quite seriously (paradoxically, perhaps, as total serialization would seem to preclude random processes). Cage's popular success may be due more to his theatrical talents than to his musical ones, yet his serious musical influence is forcing composer, performer, and listener alike to re-evaluate the basic meanings of music.

Cage—the man, the music, the ideas, and the attitude—is an invigorating experience, a liberation from set and stagnant patterns of thought that appeals to the avant-garde. Under his influence some very innovative music has been conceived, such as Sylvano Bussotti's *Five Piano Pieces for David Tudor: Extraits de Pièces de chair II* (1959). The pianist performs these pieces on the keyboard and in the piano by plucking, scraping, and striking the strings by hand (gloved, on occasion) and with various metal and wooden objects. One piece requires the pianist to perform dexterous, rapid passages on the tops of the keys in such a way as to make as few notes audible as possible. Those that sound, then, are by chance. The distinguished musicologist Paul Henry Lang said he was "scared" when hearing these pieces.

The listener who wants to hear new and advanced music without traveling to the European festivals or New York City has recourse to recordings. The complete works of Webern and most of Schoenberg and Berg are available, and music of the younger composers Milton Babbitt, Boulez, Cage, Morton Feldman, Koenig, Luigi Nono, Gunther Schuller, and Stockhausen has been recorded. Ann Arbor audiences will remember lectures and concerts of Babbitt, Dallapiccola, Gerhard, and Stockhausen in recent years and will note that Berio, Cage, and Tudor are scheduled for appearances here this month.

The work of the musical avant-garde may be open to criticism for its over-abundance of mathematical pseudo-physics or theatrical outrages such as scraping bar stools, but its influence on younger and older composers alike is considerable. Even the conservative Samuel Barber is studying Boulez, and contemporary classic Igor Stravinsky has employed numerous serial techniques in his recent music. Among influential avant-garde music of the past fifteen years, I would mention Boulez's *Le Marteau sans maître*, Stockhausen's *Gesang der Jünglinge*, Stravinsky's *Canticum Sacrum* and *Movements for Piano*, Gerhard's Symphony no. 2, Dallapiccola's *Canti di Liberazione*, and perhaps the two string quartets of Elliott Carter.[6] It will be surprising if, in the next few decades, some of these works do not achieve the stature held today by Bartók's Violin Sonata and six string quartets, Stravinsky's *L'Histoire du soldat*, Schoenberg's *Pierrot lunaire*, Webern's *Variations for Orchestra*, and Berg's *Wozzeck* and Violin Concerto. Our complex and often confusing contemporary musical world has borne some healthy children.

CHAPTER 2

Manifestations: Light and Sound
Milton Cohen's Space Theatre
(1961)

Manifestations: Light and Sound made its official debut at the Alumni Memorial Hall of the University of Michigan Museum of Art on January 11, 1961.[1] *Manifestations* brings together elements of painting, cinema, theater, and concert in an artistic experience of music and imagery wholly its own. Its materials include projectors for specially created films and slides, prisms and mirrors, and electronic music equipment, all assembled under a large translucent dome where the audience enters a new experience of light and sound. At times the shifting colors and myriad images—realistic, surrealistic, or abstract—move over the entire span of the dome, extending beyond the observer's visual periphery. Suddenly the imagery dissolves into sparse, brilliant points of light that shimmer elusively from a seemingly infinite distance. The electronic music, composed on magnetic tape, moves through the space of the dome in a similar manner, sometimes reinforcing the visual drama, at other times playing against it in counterpoint. Most of the electronic music for *Manifestations* is by Robert Ashley and myself, although we have on occasion used music by Luciano Berio, Karlheinz Stockhausen, and several other younger composers.[2]

Source: In January 1961 the New York–based *Music Journal* asked Mumma to write an article on the upcoming exhibition *Manifestations: Light and Sound* in Ann Arbor. Despite extensive notes and drafts made throughout the year, he never completed the essay. The current text is based primarily on these 1961 drafts (typescript, GMC), complemented by Mumma's unpublished notes from the mid-1960s regarding the Space Theatre and an unpublished prose biographical sketch (ca. 1970). Supplementary details were verified in interviews with Mumma in July 2011.

Fig. I-1. Milton Cohen in his Space Theatre studio, 617 East Liberty Street, Ann Arbor, August 1959. He sits amid early construction of the new dome for the coordination of light and sound. (Photo by Harold Borkin, with his permission.)

The originator and guiding spirit of the Space Theatre is artist Milton Cohen, faculty member of the University of Michigan School of Architecture and Design since 1957. Architects Harold Borkin and Joseph Wehrer designed and engineered the dome-theater areas as they evolved from the initial spheroid canopy in Cohen's East Liberty Street studio, installed in August 1959 [fig. I-1] to the portable geodesic dome now erected in the University of Michigan Museum of Art [see fig. I-3 below]. Borkin and Wehrer have also applied their ingenuity to the design and construction of the projection and lighting apparatus on a small budget. Cohen's intention for this project is to explore the mobile relationships of projected light and color in space and their dramatic integration with music. It differs from conventional theater in that it is serial and cyclic in form, dispensing with traditional introduction, climax, and conclusion. Each two-hour evening performance is open-ended, inviting the audience, in Cohen's words, "to remain as long as the experience proves invigorating."

I connected with Milton Cohen in 1957, shortly after his arrival in Ann Arbor. The previous year he had begun developing a theater based on projected

Fig. I-2. Gordon Mumma with early electronic music equipment in Milton Cohen's Space Theatre studio, ca. 1958. (Photographer unknown.)

images, and was seeking collaboration with composers working with innovative procedures in music. It was in Cohen's studio that year that I connected formally with Robert Ashley, who had already begun collaborations with filmmaker George Manupelli. Ashley and I soon began working together for the weekly Space Theatre performances in Cohen's studio.

Early in 1958, Ashley and I also established the Cooperative Studio for Electronic Music in Ann Arbor, at first largely to supply electronic music for the Space Theatre. The studio has evolved to supply original music for independent filmmakers and for commercial films, as well as to design unique "cybersonic" equipment for live-electronic concert music. It consists of three facilities: two home studios for our individual composition of electronic music, and a smaller one in Cohen's studio for his Space Theatre performances. Figure I-2 shows me in Cohen's studio at work on my *Vectors—Soundblock 5* (completed 1959) with a typical equipment configuration: a portable tape recorder, amplifier, turntable, sound generator, and assorted tape samples and loops.

The use of electronic music in *Manifestations* was a gradual process. Our earliest studio productions used an eclectic mix of recorded music, including solo violin partitas or concertos by J. S. Bach, Gesualdo madrigals, modern jazz, and music of the Balinese and Japanese classical theaters that Cohen had used prior to his collaboration with Ashley and myself. At this stage a true compositional integration of light and music was not possible, since the light projections had to be adapted to the dramatic structure of the music (at first, slides of realistic images of animals or natural landscapes were often used). An alternative plan to compose specially designed music for conventional instruments to be recorded on tape and played back during the performances also proved impracticable. Electronic music was the most feasible choice, permitting the integration of light and sound moving together in space without undue influence from traditional musical practice. The decision was, however, not without challenges. The ongoing design, construction, and modification of electronic music equipment can be tedious and disheartening, and is certainly expensive. Borkin often assists us in the design of efficient electronic music apparatus.

The most important characteristic of our music for the Space Theatre is that it is developed as a *live-performance* medium using tape only as a means of storage and retrieval of sound. The performances of 1957 and 1958 were often entirely "live," using electronically amplified and modified "small sounds" from conventional instruments and other natural sources or from electronic sound generators and other specially constructed apparatus. These sounds are stored on magnetic tape, from short loops of a few inches in length to long strips stored on reels [seen in fig. I-2]. The sounds are then played back in performance, using up to three or four tape recorders, with live modification by procedures of mixing, filtering, and reverberation that are fairly standard in all electronic music studios.

Because changes are often required during the integration of the light and sound and the crucial placement of the loudspeakers, we seldom make detailed scores. We prefer to work with general outlines or charts that include timings and abbreviated descriptions of types or volume of sounds to be used in particular sections. Our structural choices depend on the particular requirements of each piece and vary from strict serial organization to free improvisation and from performance to performance. The last few years have seen the first com-

Fig. I-3. Live performance in Milton Cohen's Space Theatre, August 1964. (Photo by Makepeace Tsao, © the family of Makepeace Tsao, with their permission.)

mercial feasibility of transistor circuitry in electronics, and since 1959 I have been designing and building electronic music equipment and using this emerging technology in the Space Theatre.

More recently, some of the electronic music composed for *Manifestations* has been successfully presented by itself in concert and broadcast performances, creating independent concert pieces of tape music. Ashley's *Issues I*, a large multi-movement tape work composed for the Museum exhibition, is a case in point. One of its movements, titled "The Fourth of July," was presented in the ONCE program of February 25, 1961. *Manifestations* recently moved to an abandoned firehouse in San Francisco for several months of experimentation and performances.[3] Its greatly expanded musical facilities have allowed us to present works recorded on four separate tracks of tape.[4] My 4-channel *Mirrors for Milton Cohen* (1960–61) was performed at the Monday Evenings at the Firehouse in November 1961. In this work each track is directed to a different loudspeaker encircling the dome, making the location and movement of the sound important dramatic elements.

My collaboration with Milton Cohen and Robert Ashley has become a major artistic influence in my own work and has provided me with intensive ensemble-performance experience in which improvisation has become increasingly important.[5] What is achieved through our creative interaction is a theater of space whose participants are the mobile images and colors of projected light; the dynamics of a music that is defined by its location as well as the loudness, duration, and pitch of its events; and the audience, who by virtue of their presence in the manifestations of this theater are active participants in an audiovisual drama of light and sound [fig. I-3]. At the present time I am convinced that electronic music will reveal its greatest potential in a spatial context.

CHAPTER 3

An Electronic Music Studio
for the Independent Composer
(1964)

Introduction

"Electronic music" generally refers to music that is composed directly on magnetic tape by electronic means. The interest of composers in producing electronic music is almost as old as the vacuum tube,[1] but was not widely practiced as an art until magnetic tape facilities became available after the Second World War. In less than two decades since then, electronic music has reached major importance as a radical force in the musical and artistic world. Most composers are seriously interested in the medium, and more than a few have worked with it.

The development of electronic music has produced many diverse compositional techniques and aesthetics. These include *musique concrète*, which derives its sound materials from purely acoustical sources;[2] electronic music, which is often rigorously serialized with techniques of additive waveform synthesis;[3] various combinations of these two approaches;[4] music that uses elaborate programming procedures and computer simulation;[5] and finally, music that is performed in concert with prepared sound-sources on tape by elaborate performance procedures on special playback equipment.[6]

Most electronic music has been composed in studios established by academic institutions, state-supported radio stations, and electronic equipment manufacturers. The major advantage of these institutional studios to the com-

Source: *Journal of the Audio Engineering Society* 12, no. 3 (1964): 240–44, © 1964 by the Audio Engineering Society. Reprinted with minor editing with their permission. Notes 1–7 are adapted from the original essay.

poser is the ready availability of specialized equipment and the technicians to maintain it. There are too few studios to accommodate all those interested in making electronic music, however, and those composers who are able to gain access to the busily scheduled institutional studios often have too little time to compose.

The composer has the alternative of building his own studio and assuming the engineering and financial responsibilities himself. This task is not as awesome as might at first be imagined, particularly in the United States, where a wide selection of high-fidelity components is available at reasonable cost. It should be understood, of course, that long-term stability and precise calibration are refinements that invariably mean higher cost and greater size. Where economy is a major consideration in the construction of an independent studio, compromises may be necessary.

Several independent studios have already been established.[7] This article describes one such studio, the Cooperative Studio for Electronic Music in Ann Arbor, Michigan, which was built by the composer Robert Ashley and myself. Construction of the studio began in 1958, largely to fill the need for electronic music for Milton Cohen's Space Theatre[8] and the films of George Manupelli. The studio is comprised of three separate working areas, two for the composition of electronic music and a third for the performance of the music in conjunction with Cohen's work [see fig. I-2]. This article is concerned with the two working areas, or composition studios, which serve as practical models of an electronic music studio for the independent composer.

The basic configuration of any electronic music studio can be divided conveniently into four parts: (1) general manipulation apparatus: tape transports, recording and playback amplifiers, and mixers; (2) sound sources: electronic oscillators and stored material of acoustical origin; (3) modification apparatus: filters and equalizers, transposition devices, gating and envelope control, and reverberation; and (4) accessories: power supplies, monitoring and analysis equipment such as meters, loudspeakers, the oscilloscope, splicers, and the bulk eraser.

Because of the practical goal of keeping the cost of an independent electronic studio within modest limits, the basic premise was that it would be possible to design it using generally available high-impedance, high-fidelity audio equipment. The cost, consideration, and planning were to correspond to the investment that any musician would direct toward choosing a conventional performing instrument.

An important consideration in the design philosophy for the Cooperative Studio for Electronic Music was to employ a maximum of "neutral" equipment.

Since a large part of the compositional work of electronic music is done with manipulation and modification equipment, considerable effort was spent to make these components effective regardless of the nature of the sound-source material that might be employed. Filters and modulation apparatus, for instance, were designed to operate as separate components that can be placed anywhere in the equipment configuration. Thus the composer has considerable freedom to pursue whatever compositional technique or aesthetic is desired. This neutral approach also extends to the human-engineering aspects of equipment configuration, which is no less important in the independent composer's low-cost studio than in a high-budget institutional laboratory.

The high-fidelity industry has produced an abundance of products well suited to the independent studio. Electronic and mechanical modifications of this equipment, where desirable, are basically simple. Only in the area of sound modification, which employs filtering, transposition, modulation, compression and expansion, and envelope control procedures, is it necessary to construct special devices.

The choice of equipment for a basic studio depends on the manipulation procedures the composer is likely to apply to his or her music. For instance, oscillators may not be necessary if the composer intends to work exclusively with sounds of acoustical origin and to forego those modulation procedures that require periodic waveforms as the modulating signal. Thus design considerations will be determined by the following factors:

Tape Transports

Since most tape transports are powered by synchronous AC motors, they can be operated as continuously variable-speed devices, with power supplied by a variable-frequency oscillator having suitable amplification and impedance matching. The oscillator and amplifier are likely to be part of the studio in any case, and impedance matching to the capstan-drive motor can be accomplished with a variable autotransformer. The desirable features for a tape transport are ease of modification for special head configurations and a mechanically simple drive mechanism.

The choice of basic speeds will be dictated by the probable application. Thus 7.5 ips [inches per second] is the best compromise between tape economy and frequency response, 3.75 ips is suitable for tape storage of source material of limited bandwidth, and 15 ips is desirable for detailed editing or extraordinary frequency requirements. The tape transport mechanism may but need not include pre-amplification and equalization.

Pre-amplification and Equalization

Separate pre-amplification and equalization equipment is available in a wide selection. Some units have provision for variable AC bias; this valuable feature can be added to those that do not. Ideally, both the record bias and erase current should be separately controllable from the audio-signal component of the record current.

Mixing

Mixing is the electronic process basic to most types of electronic music composition. The requirements for a mixer are usually met by any device that has wide, flat audio response, low distortion, and a high signal-to-noise ratio. Reverberation, when desired, is usually introduced at the mixing stage. The Hammond-type device, which is usually sufficient, is available in several inexpensive forms for this purpose. Passive mixers are often adequate.

Oscillators and Generators

Several inexpensive oscillators of the efficient and stable Wien bridge type are available. Most of these, however, do not extend their frequency range below 20 cps [cycles per second], and the sub-audio range from 20 cps down to around 5 seconds per cycle is often of use in special modulation procedures.

Low-frequency extension of most commercial Wien bridge oscillators is not difficult. It may be worthwhile to consider building one's own Wien bridge or phase-shift oscillator, which can achieve wide frequency range in a single band if necessary. If more than two or three oscillators are desired, it may ultimately be less expensive and space-consuming to build them separately as a bank that is powered from a single, regulated power supply.

The basic harmonic-containing waveforms (sawtooth, pulse, square, and half-sine) are obtainable either with passive diode shapers or simple, active wave-shaping circuits, or they can be generated directly with multi-vibrators.

Thyratron gas tube or reverse-biased diode devices with a stage of gain are sufficient as noise generators, since the product does not have to meet stringent statistical requirements. Noise-band products are obtainable with accessory diode modulators in series.

Modulation

The basic processes of amplitude modulation and frequency (or phase) modulation have numerous applications. The uses of amplitude modulation include gating (or keying) and envelope control; volume compression and expansion; frequency spectrum transposition, inversion, compression, and expansion; and complex spectrum production. Useful frequency modulation applications include swept frequency spectra and diverse vibrato products.

Modulation apparatus suited for use in electronic music composition is not commercially available, but is neither difficult nor expensive to build. Passive semiconductor modulators are useful for complex spectrum generation and are limited only by the quality and balance of their few simple components. With selective use, balanced diode bridge modulators or ring modulators can be applied to gating and frequency transposition as well.

Active modulators range from the simple twin-triode cathode modulator or transistor emitter modulator, for use in gating, compression, and expansion, to more elaborate devices such as the balanced push-pull output-type modulator with continuously variable control of the class of operation. This latter sophisticated device enables the composer to achieve sound-event sequencing without having to splice tape. The various types of passive and active balanced modulators, in conjunction with frequency filtering and wideband phase-shifting accessories, constitute an extremely important area of sound modification apparatus for electronic music composition.

Filters

Commercial bandpass filters might be considered beyond the budget of the independent composer, though they are no more expensive than some tape transports that might be seriously considered. The active R-C comb filter probably represents the best single solution for the independent studio, since it includes highpass, lowpass, bandpass, and band-attenuation characteristics in one unit. A relatively inexpensive nine-octave version of such a filter, with a 28 dB [decibel] slope per octave, is commercially available. High, low, and band-pass filters with slopes of 12–24 dB per octave are attainable with as little as a single stage of gain and proper feedback, and are adaptable for resistance tuning. Frequency selective amplifiers with variable bandwidth and frequency can be designed employing the Wien bridge, Twin-T, or similar phase-shift devices.

Since many timbre-shaping efforts, including most "coloring" of white noise, do not require sharp cutoff filter characteristics, passive R-C filter types are always useful. The composer interested primarily in shaping periodic waveforms and their modulation products with integration and differentiation procedures may find a few variable passive R-C filters entirely sufficient for studio needs.

Accessories

If several pieces of equipment such as active filters, modulators, or oscillators are to be specially built, a separate regulated power supply may be the accessory of prime importance. An inexpensive oscilloscope can be of the greatest assistance, both in the construction of equipment and as a monitor for various composition processes. It also supplies pulse and sawtooth waveforms over a wide range. The choice of further accessories depends on their foreseeable applications.

Configuration

The final issue is the choice of studio configuration and equipment placement. For the independent composer, who will likely be spending more time at the equipment than if he or she were sharing an institutional studio with many others, a flexible or at least easily accessible configuration is appropriate. Flexibility also allows the composer to pursue a specific working aesthetic in depth without ultimately being confined to that aesthetic because the equipment has been permanently bolted into place. This needs emphasis because the independent composer may have limited space for the studio, and this immediately tends to dictate a fixed equipment configuration.

In this respect, the composer who builds an independent studio with movable equipment will have an advantage over the composer who works with the rack-mounted or console-mounted laboratory apparatus found in most institutional studios. In sacrificing the precise calibration and long-term stability of large-size laboratory equipment for the more compact proportions of high-impedance, high-fidelity components, a configuration can be arranged that will put the entire studio within arm's reach of the comfortably seated composer. Consideration should thus be given to placement of the equipment allowing the most manipulation for the composer's chosen working procedure in a position that produces the least fatigue. Specific practical solutions can be illustrated in terms of the two working studios of the Cooperative Studio for Electronic Music.

The first of the two studios [fig. I-4], designed by Robert Ashley, employs three tape transports, associated playback and recording amplification, a five-channel mixer, an audio-frequency oscillator (sine, square, and pulse wave-

Fig. I-4. Robert Ashley (R) and Gordon Mumma in Ashley's compact electronic music studio in Ann Arbor, ca. 1960. (Photo by Mary Ashley, courtesy of Mimi Johnson.)

forms), a portable tape recorder for field work [not visible], and a monitor-amplifier with loudspeakers, all of which are commercially available. Specially constructed items include a reverberation device, passive R-C filters, and a ring-bridge modulator. The few simple modifications applied to the commercially available equipment include special head configurations for the tape transports and continuously variable controls for the erase and record currents from the recording amplifier. Three tape transports were chosen as the minimum, although with special head configurations and less practical convenience it is possible to achieve the same mixing and modification results with only two transports. The transports were chosen largely because their extremely simple mechanical design allowed modifications with relative ease.

The most important aspect of this first studio configuration is that the tape transports are mounted in a fixed location above the mixing and amplification equipment on the apparatus panel. Supplementary equipment, such as reverberation, filtering, and switching devices, can be located according to the immediate needs of the composer. Thus in a seated working position the composer has full access to the processes of electronic manipulation. The tape transports

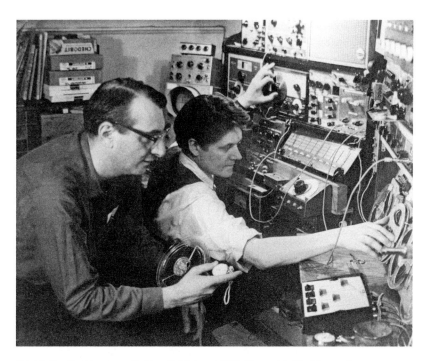

Fig. I-5. Gordon Mumma with George Cacioppo (L) in Mumma's Washtenaw Avenue electronic music studio in Ann Arbor, ca. 1964. The configuration is more elaborate than that depicted in fig. I-4. (Photo by Jacqueline Leuzinger, courtesy of Gordon Mumma.)

are mounted vertically in such a way that elaborate loops can be routed conveniently above the entire apparatus panel. By a special switching and monitoring procedure it is possible to record across two channels with a single recording amplifier. As a result, Ashley has developed facile techniques of magnetic tape composition that rely almost exclusively on switching and mixing procedures, with less use of splicing or cutting of the tape itself.

The second of the two studios [fig. I-5], designed by myself, employs three tape transports [of which two are visible in the figure], associated playback and recording amplification, two five-channel mixers, three audio-frequency sine and square wave oscillators, a nine-octave comb filter, a Hammond-type reverberation device, an electronic switch, a regulated power supply, and monitor amplifiers with loudspeakers. These components represent the commercially available equipment. Modifications made to this equipment are the same as those employed in the first studio, with the addition of a continuously variable speed control for the tape transports (over a two-octave range), low-frequency extensions for the oscillators and electronic switch (to 0.2 cps), and improvement of the shielding and power-supply filtering for increased signal-to-noise ratios.

Special equipment includes wave shapers for the oscillator outputs (half-sine, variable-width pulse, and sawtooth), passive diode-modulators, active cathode, emitter, and phase modulators, a variable-bias balanced-output modulator, a random noise generator, a frequency-selective amplifier with variable bandwidth, and assorted active and passive R-C filters. The remaining equipment, including an oscilloscope, R-C bridge, and meters, is used in monitoring or the design of special equipment. The basic configuration of tape transports, pre-amplifiers, and mixers is not mounted in a fixed manner but can be rearranged with a minimum of effort.

The most important aspect of the configuration of this second studio is that two tape transports are located below the mixing and amplification equipment within easy reach of my right hand [fig. I-5]. These transports are mounted on special brackets, tilted back at a slight angle from the vertical, and can be moved forward onto the worktable. Splicing is thereby facilitated when the two transports are placed in the panel, while the use of loops is facilitated when these transports are pulled forward on the worktable. The single upper tape transport [not visible in the figure] with associated electronics is used primarily for dubbing and portable playback and recording. This entire apparatus panel is mounted on wheels and can be moved for easy access to the plugboards at the rear. The remaining equipment [left-hand side of fig. I-5], including the oscillators, modulators, and filters, remains stationary, since all the plugs are on the front of the panels. This flexible configuration has facilitated complex and extensive tape-editing procedures in my music, acquired in my experiences with film editing and exploited in my tape music for Milton Cohen, such as *Soundblocks* and *Music from the Venezia Space Theatre*.

The total cost of the first studio was less than $700. It was in operation within six months of its inception. Much of that time was spent in researching and selecting from the diversity of available equipment. By exact duplication a similar studio could be put into operation in a few weeks.

The total cost of the second studio was less than $2,000, which compares favorably with the cost of a grand piano. Though design experimentation still continues, operation of the second studio was effective within two years of its inception. The electronic-music production component of the second studio could be duplicated in a few months, and since some of the equipment has proved sufficiently redundant, the cost of duplication could be held below $1,500.

CHAPTER 4

The ONCE Festival and How It Happened
(1967)

The primary sources of support for creative artists today are commerce and pedagogy. To put it bluntly, in commerce the artist must sell; in pedagogy, teach or research. Private support tends to be an investment in the future monetary value of an artist's present work. Foundation support is usually administered by universities, and as such tends to be an investment in future teaching potential. Today support usually comes on an individual basis, often to enable artists to travel and thus to escape the very community in which they work.

The "patronage" of the past, both public and private, had some sense of freewheeling benevolence about it. Such patronage often reached considerably beyond support of the individual artist to invest in a community of artistic and social endeavor—in a whole "scene." I would suggest that the creative artist might be better served if this older model were restored and financial support invested in the nourishment of the total artistic community. The outline of a specific example of community artistic endeavor that developed and flourished outside the established norms of support motivates this article on the ONCE Festival in Ann Arbor, Michigan, during the years 1961–65.

Source: *Arts in Society* 4, no. 2 (1967): 381–98, © The Regents of the University of Wisconsin. The current text is a substantial revision of the original publication that corrects errors and editorial issues, while incorporating additional material from Mumma's revised typescript of the article (August 1970; GMC).

Brief History of the ONCE Festival

The ONCE Festival happened because a community of artists took matters into their own hands.[1] They extended their responsibilities beyond the limits of merely producing their art to its organization and promotion. For the most part they worked outside the established institutions of commerce and pedagogy, and with minimum funding. The artists involved were from different disciplines: the initial group included composers Robert Ashley, George Cacioppo, Gordon Mumma, Roger Reynolds, Donald Scavarda, and Bruce Wise, architects Harold Borkin and Joseph Wehrer, filmmaker George Manupelli, and artists Mary Ashley and Milton Cohen. Their common ground was that they all lived in Ann Arbor. They had been working independently and together on various projects there from early 1957, including Cohen's Space Theatre, Ashley and Mumma's Cooperative Studio for Electronic Music, and the production of several films.

In 1960 at the suggestion of poet Keith Waldrop, the group decided to produce a festival of new music. Financial backing for publicity and the hiring of musicians was essential. Though a few members of the group taught at the University of Michigan, virtually all efforts to enlist support from that institution met with resistance and even animosity. Ashley and Reynolds approached a local organization, the Dramatic Arts Center, which had been providing modest support to repertory theater and experimental film programs in Ann Arbor for several years. They were immediately interested in the festival proposal and approved sponsorship of the concerts for February and March of their 1960–61 season.

The 1961 festival consisted of four concerts on two consecutive weekends. The opening concert featured members of the Domaine Musical Ensemble of Paris, with composer Luciano Berio and singer Cathy Berberian. The second included instrumental and electronic music by ONCE composers and film artists performed by the ONCE Chamber Ensemble. The third concert presented Paul Jacobs in a recital of classic piano music of the serial era, while the final program consisted of large ensemble pieces by ONCE composers. All four concerts were recorded for radio re-broadcast over the University of Michigan's WUOM-FM. The audiences were near capacity, a result we attributed as much to intensive pre-festival publicity as to the inherent glamour of the festival. The cost of the entire festival was $1,300; ticket sales amounted to $1,175.[2] The Dramatic Arts Center made up the difference.

Finances aside, the festival was an artistic success. Even before the end of the final concert, the audience was asking about the likelihood of another such festival, even of making it an annual event. Although its name implies that continuity had not been our original intention, before the summer of 1961, plans were under way for a second ONCE Festival.

Again the Dramatic Arts Center offered its support. The second ONCE Festival of February 1962 included six concerts and was again recorded in its entirety. The second festival both cost and lost more money than the first, but attendance was growing and the scope of programming widening. This time, however, there was some dispute about its artistic success. A fierce controversy that continued for several years followed the first evening program by La Monte Young and Terry Jennings.³ Yet the heat of this debate fueled the growing audience interest and the creative momentum that now gripped the ONCE artists, making a third ONCE Festival imperative.⁴ In February 1963 four concerts were presented. John Cage and David Tudor came from New York for the final concert; Tudor performed a brilliant version of Cage's *Variations II* with electronic processing.

The fourth ONCE Festival was the most ambitious. Eight concerts were presented on six days in February and March 1964. The guest ensembles were the Judson Dance Theater, the University of Illinois Contemporary Chamber Players, Alvin Lucier's Brandeis University Chamber Chorus, and the Bob James Trio with Eric Dolphy (in his last American performance). The ONCE Chamber Ensemble was expanded to thirty performers and presented three concerts of its own. The Ashley-Mumma "New Music for Pianos" series continued with a full recital of music since 1960. The entire budget for the 1964 ONCE Festival was less than $4,000, and the loss (this time of $2,400) was again assumed by the Dramatic Arts Center.

The publicity for the 1964 festival created as much controversy as the music. Mary Ashley designed an accordion-folded, purple-and-white flyer that featured on one side the detailed programs and on the other, George Manupelli's photograph of composers Ashley, Cacioppo, Scavarda, and Mumma costumed like Mafia henchmen, standing behind a voluptuous nude reclining on the lunch counter of a well-known local eatery called "Red's Rite Spot" [fig. I-6]. The flyer created a small uproar, and the Dramatic Arts Center called an emergency meeting. Appeals to withdraw the flyer were overcome, leaving us with the problem of finding funds for reprinting to meet the demand for souvenir copies. The extent of its notoriety was evident in New York City the following April when, at the seminar following one of Max Pollikoff's "Music in Our Time" concerts in which Ashley and I had just performed [April 12, 1964], the first question from the audience was a request for an autographed copy of the flyer.

The fifth ONCE Festival, in February 1965, consisted of four concerts and one lecture. The performers included Lukas Foss and an ensemble from the

Fig. I-6. The controversial flyer by Mary Ashley and George Manupelli for ONCE 1964. (Courtesy GMC.)

State University of New York at Buffalo; New York musicians David Behrman, Philip Corner, Malcolm Goldstein, and Max Neuhaus; Udo Kasemets from Toronto; the ONCE theater ensemble and festival orchestra; and an extra event, "A Composite Lecture" by Los Angeles critic Peter Yates.

The separate contemporary arts touring ensemble formed in 1963 as the "ONCE Group" was by now receiving numerous requests for booking during the spring season, making scheduling of future festivals at that time more difficult. The ONCE Group was also invited to appear as the U.S. cultural representative at the São Paulo Biennale in the summer of 1965, though without funding provided for travel to Brazil. We stayed home instead to produce a sixth ONCE Festival in September. Called ONCE AGAIN 1965, it was presented on the amphitheater-like roof of the Maynard Street parking garage in Ann Arbor. The festival included the ONCE Group performing *Unmarked Interchange*, an ensemble of Judson Dance Theater members (Trisha Brown, Lucinda Childs, Alex and Deborah Hay, Steve Paxton, and Robert Rauschenberg) in "A Concert for Ann Arbor," and a return concert by Cage and Tudor. They arrived several days early, allowing us to work out Cage's *Talk I* to include the participation of Ashley, Rauschenberg, and myself.

Because of the ample size of the parking-structure roof, with seating for five hundred and at least two hundred standing room spaces, we were able to accommodate more people. ONCE AGAIN 1965 drew enormous sell-out crowds. In fact, the turnout for a single concert was more than twice the size of all the performances of any previous festival. For the first time ONCE was able to return profits to the Dramatic Arts Center.

In summary, twenty-nine concerts of new music were presented during six ONCE Festivals, including sixty-seven premiere performances out of a total of 215 works by eighty-eight contemporary composers.[5] Music was the predominant focus of the ONCE Festivals, although modern dance and theater became increasingly prominent in each successive festival.

Hindsights 1

Waldrop's suggestion that we produce our own contemporary music concerts was perhaps motivated simply by his desire to hear the new music that his friends were writing. In the early days the composers' motives were not much more far-reaching. Over the next five years, however, our sense of possibility broadened considerably, as did the character and significance of the ONCE Festival as a developing institution.

Ann Arbor is primarily a university town and in some respects a cultural oasis. The ONCE Festival happened in spite of the University of Michigan. Despite considerable effort from within the university over the previous years, it had been impossible to establish modern music performances as a regular, ongoing activity in Ann Arbor. There was no lack of attention to the classics, but embarrassed silence generally followed the question: "Whose music did the classical composers perform?" In retrospect it is difficult for me to understand why it had not occurred to us earlier to produce our own concerts.

Foundation patronage was seemingly impracticable because we were not an institution but a diverse group of independent artists. Our applications for support to numerous foundations over the following years would prove unsuccessful. The Dramatic Arts Center stepped in. Its mission to "encourage important but little-known developments in the arts, including experimental creation in drama, music, films, and other media" is similar to the stated purposes of the foundations from which we had received polite rejections. The essential difference was that the Dramatic Arts Center was part of our immediate community and stood by its rhetoric. Its support permitted us to accomplish something of our own, independent of the depersonalization of the funding monoliths.

The problems of developing the programs for the ONCE Festivals were numerous, some unexpected. We assumed that if the scope of programming were broad enough we might reduce backlash from our detractors. We soon discovered that the more diversified the programming, the greater the controversy that ensued. A broad variety of repertory, however, allowed us to take greater risks with individual works and performers and to avoid trivial arguments about what repertoire was appropriate and pertinent. Everything became a risk worth taking.[6] Of course, when so much new music is presented within so short a time, audiences are not likely to attend every event. We still found it necessary at times to defend a concert of relatively conservative new music against the accusations that ONCE was "reactionary," or another concert of innovative music against the claims that it was too "radical." If, on the other hand, musical extremes were combined in a single concert, the complaint arose that ONCE was too "eclectic" or, worse, "disorganized."

Nevertheless audiences continued to grow in both size and diversity. Performance and rehearsal space became a problem, provoking a continual search for appropriate venues. For the first two ONCE Festivals we rented the small auditorium of the First Unitarian Church. When the rehearsals and concerts became an imposition on church activities, the third ONCE Festival was presented in the meeting hall of the Ann Arbor Community Center. When a still larger space was needed for the fourth and fifth festivals, the local VFW Hall was engaged. Except for the Community Center meeting room, Ann Arbor had no civic auditorium or larger performance space. Thus, for the sixth festival, ONCE AGAIN, the city council was petitioned for use of a municipal parking garage. Our series of untraditional concert venues proved curiously stimulating, contributing to the dynamism of the ONCE project. The composers had to consider the implications of unusual settings in the creation and presentation of their works.

Adaptation to these venues often required resourcefulness. The premiere of my *The Dresden Interleaf 13 February 1945* at the fifth festival on February 13, 1965 (the twentieth anniversary of the Dresden firestorm), for example, severely tested the VFW Hall. This four-channel studio electronic piece required a multiple-speaker system surrounding the audience. But because the audience was seated right up to the walls of the space, the loudspeakers had to be mounted considerably above their heads in order to achieve the optimal dispersion throughout the hall. Having abandoned the idea of suspending sixty-pound loudspeakers over their heads, I discovered that the Ann Arbor firm of Lahti manufactured lightweight, inexpensive mini U-2 speakers, sixteen of which could be hung throughout the hall by means of lightweight package twine. The dispersion for each channel of sound actually proved to be wider than that achieved with the four large speakers, while the undesired "point-source" effect was entirely absent. The U-2s competed successfully with the harrowing roar of live alcohol-burning model airplane engines in the central section of the work. Most of the audience had no idea of the physical source of the sound, and one audience member who inquired afterwards was skeptical when I simply pointed to the little boxes hung around the hall.[7]

The most challenging problem of the ONCE Festival was money. The budget of almost $4,000 for the 1964 ONCE had to cover eight concerts, including four guest ensembles that totaled more than fifty performers who traveled over five hundred miles to perform at ONCE. The two university guest ensembles subsidized a substantial portion of their own costs. The remaining guest performers agreed to participate for a reimbursement of their travel and accommodation expenses. Local union musicians were paid basic scale; nearly everyone else contributed their services. The remaining costs were publicity, rental of space and equipment, and publishers' fees.

All six festivals were run on this frugal basis. Although almost everyone who donated time and effort to ONCE considered it a worthy cause toward establishing a viable contemporary performance arts activity, after five years the ONCE Festival would have required a sounder financial basis to continue. It had become rather embarrassing to ask performers to choose between playing at ONCE at "cost" or elsewhere for adequate remuneration. Nevertheless, the ONCE Festival established a precedent of paying, however modestly, for the performance of new music in Ann Arbor.

Efforts were also applied to the propagation of the festival outside the immediate community. All concerts were recorded for FM radio broadcasting and international distribution. The tapes of even the earliest festivals still enjoy an active rebroadcast schedule. The concerts also received a fair measure of attention in the press.[8] To our surprise, more press attention was given to ONCE internationally than locally. For at least two of the festivals the local press had absented itself in an attempt to avoid the kind of disputes that extended beyond the music itself. Part of the problem arose from a combination of provincialism and the normal small-town jealousies, but the effects were sometimes demoralizing to the participants.

A distinct resistance developed among the community of the University of Michigan School of Music. Competition was a likely factor when, following the first ONCE Festival, a contemporary music series was finally organized under university auspices. But the real sore point was more likely the sense of alienation from the academic scene that developed among the university students who participated in or attended the ONCE Festival. Discussion and argument between students and teachers disrupted classroom schedules for weeks surrounding each festival. For some of the student performers ONCE became an extracurricular activity that almost completely usurped their attention. During the 1964 ONCE Festival there was a nearly unanimous boycott of the concerts by the School of Music faculty, with pressure applied to music students to do likewise on the grounds that such activities were academically, culturally, and morally disreputable. The rivalry reached a point of absurdity when two ensembles from other major universities participated in this very ONCE Festival, at their own expense.

Two further achievements of the ONCE Festival were not among our initial goals, but we quickly recognized and promoted them. The festival served as a model for similar community-based contemporary arts organizations in Seattle (New Dimensions in Music), Toronto (Isaacs Gallery series), and Tucson (New Arts Workshop), to name just a few. The festival also assisted in decentralizing the focus of contemporary performance activities from New York City. On the whole, ONCE had shown that a successful contemporary arts project can break free of the combined stranglehold of commerce, pedagogy, and geographical centralization with modest community support.

Environment

The ONCE Festival did not develop in isolation from its environment. It was but one of numerous related cultural activities in Ann Arbor, extending from the purely graphic arts to the performance realm and including several thriving collaborations.

1. The light-sculpture theater ensemble formed in 1957 and was called, at various times, "Manifestations: Light and Sound" and "Space Theatre." Included in this collaborative project were artist Milton Cohen, architect Harold Borkin, filmmaker George Manupelli, and the composers Ashley and myself.[9] Its performances gradually developed into the elaborate *Teatro dello spazio* productions by the group during the September 1964 Biennale in Venice, Italy.

2. The Cooperative Studio for Electronic Music, which was developed by Ashley and myself in 1958 to provide music for the films of Manupelli.[10] The studio also supplied music for other independent filmmakers and for commercial films, and designed unique "cybersonic" equipment for electronic music in live performance.

3. The Ann Arbor Film Festival, co-sponsored by the Dramatic Arts Center and the Student Cinema Guild, under the direction of Manupelli. This yearly festival of experimental films, a direct outgrowth of the ONCE Festival, has been presented on an annual basis since 1963. From this time onward, film was presented at ONCE only in the context of intermedia productions.

Fig. I-7. ONCE Chamber Ensemble in rehearsal at the WUOM radio studio in Ann Arbor, December 1963. L to R: Donald Scavarda (piano), Robert Ashley (conducting), George Cacioppo (drum), Gordon Mumma and Kay Maves (horns), Anne Speer Aitchison (flute, standing), Emily Hewitt (flute). (Photographer unknown.)

4. Chamber music at the ONCE Festival was performed by the ONCE Chamber Ensemble, a flexible group made up of ONCE regulars, University of Michigan students and faculty, and community musicians, formed as the program required. For larger scores, such as my *Sinfonia* (ONCE 1961) or Scavarda's *Sounds for Eleven* (ONCE 1962), the expanded ensemble became the ONCE Chamber Orchestra. In preparation for the major role of the Chamber Ensemble in ONCE 1964, a series of posed publicity photos were taken at the WUOM radio studios in Ann Arbor in December 1963 [fig. I-7].

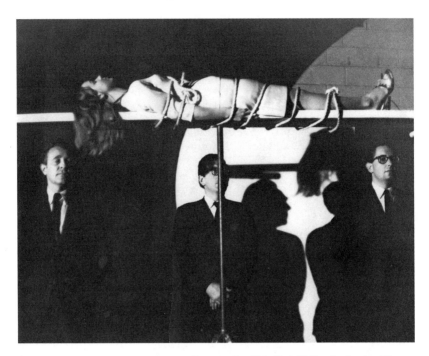

Fig. I-8. Robert Ashley, *Kittyhawk*, scene 5, at the Here² Festival, Walker Art Center, Minneapolis, June 1965. Ashley's score states: "A girl appears carrying a rope, goes directly to a plank resting on two stools (prepared), and ties herself prone to the plank. Two men appear with a six-foot (one-inch) pipe fixed to a tripod. The men life the plank above their heads and balance it on the end of the pipe. The girl balanced on the plank is left unattended." Girl: Jacqueline Leuzinger; Men (L to R): Joseph Wehrer, George Manupelli, and Harold Borkin. (Photo by Makepeace Tsao, © the family of Makepeace Tsao, with their permission.)

5. The large touring ensemble called the "ONCE Group" has presented large-scale theater works created and produced collaboratively by members of this diverse ensemble. By and large their predominant activity has involved the intermedia resources of new music, experimental film, sculpture, modern dance, electronically manipulated sound and light projection, and environment. In various productions certain technologies have tended to predominate: optics and electronic music in my *Music from the Venezia Space Theatre*; performed electronic and cybersonic processes in my *Megaton for Wm. Burroughs*; and manipulated sculpture and public-address/radio communication in Ashley's *Kittyhawk*.[11]

The ONCE Group has thrived since 1964, with more than two dozen performances on tour in the United States and a repertoire of ten original collaborative works. [Figure I-8 shows scene five of Ashley's *Kittyhawk* in performance by the ONCE Group at the Walker Art Center, Minneapolis, in 1965.] The ensemble has circumvented that difficult problem arising from collaboration: the designation of credit for individual work. Each of our artists has generally been content to acknowledge production "by the ONCE Group."

6. Contemporary music activity was extended throughout the year in the individual "ONCE Friends" concerts and recordings. Several ONCE Friends concert tours were also organized in response to requests from private groups and colleges outside Ann Arbor.

7. Mary Ashley's theater ensemble "Truck" was formed in 1961. In connection with the ONCE Group, Truck performed multimedia events, sometimes in the streets of Ann Arbor.

8. The "New Music for Pianos" series established in 1962 by Ashley and myself in connection with the ONCE Group was augmented by our series of traveling lecture-demonstrations in the performance arts.

9. Finally, performances by David Behrman and Alvin Lucier at ONCE Festivals led to the formation in 1966 of what would become the Sonic Arts Group along with Ashley and myself.

With the exception of three small research grants to the Space Theatre and support from the Dramatic Arts Center for the ONCE Festival and the Ann Arbor Film Festival, these activities have been self-supporting.

Hindsights 2: Impact on Individual Creative Artists

The impact of the ONCE Festival and related activities on its individual artists has been considerable. Music composition seldom enables an artist of today to make a decent living. Particularly in the United States, the number of isolated composers filing away their unperformed manuscripts is pathetic. Largely to blame are the performance institutions—the orchestras and instrumental ensembles, musical societies, the few existent opera companies, and academic institutions, which are generally unwilling to take the financial risks involved in performing innovative music by young composers of our time. Part of the blame falls on the lack of public interest in new music. But the composers themselves share the responsibility. Too many of them succumb to the compromising lure of academic teaching, while too few look beyond the established performance venues to establish new institutions pertinent to their work and their time.

The festival provided composers with opportunities for sustained involvement in an active and challenging cultural community. Its influence on the stylistic, technical, and artistic growth of composers such as Cacioppo, Ashley, and Scavarda was profound, amounting to something of a renaissance. I would suggest that the individuality and maturity of their recent works owe much to the opportunities for performance and access to the broader public afforded by the ONCE Festival and related activities. Further, the confrontation with performance arts other than music encouraged them to explore new practical applications and to extend their musical creativity into untried media. Ashley now spends a major portion of his energies in experimental theatrical production; Scavarda has also developed special means of film composition with visual materials; and my own work has extended to include live-electronic performance.

In the ONCE Festivals, inspiration was rapidly put to the test of public opinion, occasionally drawing criticism about the propriety of confronting paying audiences with "crackpot" experiments. I can only answer that this close blending of innovation and pragmatism produced valid and dynamic artistic results. The creative momentum that increased from festival to festival was sometimes truly invigorating. It supercharged the progress of a composer such as Cacioppo, whose works of the ONCE years followed a path from ever-increasing risk to ever-greater success. One of his prime achievements was the progressive exploitation of radical sound-producing procedures in an ensemble context. The faithful performers of the ONCE Festival shared in his ideas from the start, integrating his expanding musical vocabulary into their own.

It is tempting to cite what were, for me, the most exciting moments of the ONCE Festivals. I would have to mention the sequence of concerts in the fourth ONCE Festival of 1964, which premiered Ashley's symphony *in memoriam … Crazy Horse*, Cacioppo's orchestral-choral *Advance of the Fungi*, my own electronic-performance work *Megaton for Wm. Burroughs*, and Scavarda's chamber music–cinema integration *Landscape Journey*. I would also mention the fifth festival (February 1965), which included Cacioppo's *Time on Time in Miracles* for chamber ensemble, Mary Ashley's theater spectacle *The Jelloman*, and Cage's melodrama *Variations IV*.[12]

The demands of the festival format, with its tight scheduling of diverse activities, sparked this creative momentum in ways that once-a-year events would not have. It is healthy to be prodded by a sequence of relentless deadlines that the artist must struggle to meet. With at times only a few weeks' notice, we scheduled works that were not yet completed or in a few instances not even fully conceived. On several occasions the barest indication that a composer was thinking of a new work was enough for us to take action. In the latter case, the person responsible for the programming, publicity, and production of a concert would fabricate a title for a composer's still-unfinished work. Some of the most successful compositions resulted from this breakneck schedule.

The creative momentum that developed in the ONCE environment would have been unlikely without community support. As modest as the artistic and financial support of the Dramatic Arts Center was, it was always direct and immediate. Nor was it wasted on the overhead of institutional administration. Our financial precariousness had its advantages, too, in independence and flexibility.

It is a rare creative artist who survives in isolation from an audience or a community of other artists. Artists have little function or incentive for growth without the opportunity to communicate with others. Their greatest nourishment comes from the cultural community in which they live, not only because that community is the consumer of their art, but also because it reflects back to them much of the energy for their artistic insights. Likewise, the greatest nourishment for the community comes from its artists, who, living within it, have immediate access to the means of shaping its cultural potential. There are times in a community when the situation is ripe for action, when you find the right people in the right place at the right time. Such was Ann Arbor during the ONCE years.

CHAPTER 5

The ONCE Group's *Unmarked Interchange* and *Night Train*
(1967)

Unmarked Interchange is a ONCE Group theater work for a found cultural ritual. The cultural ritual may be found anywhere (symphony concert, vaudeville theater, circumcision rite, hockey game, honorary banquet, etc.), though it should be part of the cultural experience of the place where *Unmarked Interchange* is to be performed. The work superimposes upon the found cultural ritual, without changing it structurally, a number of cyclical episodes, each of which has a relationship tangent to the ritual as the cycle unfolds.

The first performance of *Unmarked Interchange* took place at the September 1965 ONCE AGAIN Festival in Ann Arbor on the amphitheater-like roof of a municipal parking structure. The found cultural ritual was that of an outdoor drive-in movie. A special vertical screen was erected (measuring 24 × 36 feet), which contained sliding panels, louvers, and mobile drawers. A projected film (*Top Hat* with Fred Astaire and Ginger Rogers) was superimposed by means of the cyclical manipulation of the screen segments by live performers involved in activities tangential to the film [fig. I-9]. The soundtrack accompanying the film was superimposed according to the same concept. The entire production was coordinated by wireless radio communication.[1]

The first performance of *Night Train* by the ONCE Group took place at Spingold Theater, Brandeis University, in January 1967. In terms of technology, *Night Train* was the development of an ensemble based on a special synthesis of the sensual aspects of the performance experience. In it we are not dealing with the

---

Source: Excerpted from Mumma, "Technology in the Modern Arts: Music and Theatre," *Chelsea* 20/21 (May 1967): 103–5, © Chelsea Editions, with their permission.

Fig. I-9. *Unmarked Interchange*, ONCE AGAIN, September 17, 1965: Caroline Player Cohen and Gordon Mumma (cornet), seen against Fred Astaire in *Top Hat*. (Photo by Peter Moore, © Barbara Moore/Licensed by VAGA, New York, NY; black and white photo, original size 227 mm × 161 mm, GMC.)

ordinary modes of synthesis (for example, direct relationships of sound to light or of performer actions to social structure). Our artistic responsibility is not to specific events or to the ordinary perspectives of subjectivity and objectivity but to the basic aspects of our media.

The structure of *Night Train* is free of constructivist framework. There are no plots of increase or decrease, no fabricated points of arrival. Rather, *Night Train* is a generated structure that produces conjunctions between the media aspects. On some occasions these conjunctions are the direct result of actions on the part of the individual responsible for that aspect, while others are the result of the dynamic sum of its parts. *Night Train* exploits the process of removing ourselves from ordinary perspectives, of defining "they" in the perceptual dimensions of the performance space and ritual. "They" is what we (who have assumed responsibility for the basic aspects of our media) perceive as the evidence of "they," what we might encounter of, say, some alien culture.

The basic aspects of *Night Train* can be delineated in terms of responsibilities or performance roles:

- the way they do the things they do (Joseph Wehrer)
- the way they see the things they see (Harold Borkin)
- the things they smell the things they taste (Carolyn Player)
- the way they hear the things they hear (Gordon Mumma)
- the way they feel the things they touch (George Manupelli)
- the stories they tell (Mary Ashley) and
- coordination (Robert Ashley).

Only extremes of lighting situations are operative. The brightest locality of light intensity possible with the available resources confronts the dimmest conditions of de-localized performance activity (you may consider, for instance, the analogy of a lighthouse). The sound realm is that of the variously conditioned responses to the origins and localities of the sounds of individual human experience and collective memory. Because everyone accepts the convention of sound being treated abstractly, we can quickly appreciate the possibility of abstracting the aspect of light. *Night Train* postulates an extension of the possibility of treating tactile events abstractly within the compositional and performance purpose.

PART II

Cybersonics and the
Sonic Arts (1966–75)

Editor's Introduction

In December 1966 Gordon Mumma left Ann Arbor and rented an apartment in Manhattan close to the Merce Cunningham dance studio. In August he had joined the dance company as musician and technical assistant, sharing the pit with John Cage and David Tudor on tours ranging from Brooklyn's Academy of Music to Rio de Janeiro and Paris, Persepolis and Belgrade. The Cunningham years, to be explored independently in the next part of this book, also witnessed Mumma's most intense activity in live-electronic composition, performance, and instrument building. The social fabric of the sonic arts was for him fundamentally collaborative and interactive, either within the Cunningham community or in the developing fields of the Sonic Arts Group (with Ashley, Behrman, and Lucier)—with roots in the social dynamics of Ann Arbor and the ONCE years. Under its new name, Sonic Arts Union, this artistic collective toured nationally and internationally, providing both the community for much of Mumma's cybersonic live-electronic music and the impetus for his writing about the subject until the mid-1970s.

"Cybersonics" was Mumma's own designation for the live-electronic processing of primarily acoustical sounds facilitated by the developing electronic transistor technologies. For Mumma this was an essentially interactive process of sound in space, as he described it:

> Beyond working with people, the concept of "collaboration" may also be extended to technological levels. In my creative work with electronic-music resources, I have explored a direction that I call "cybersonics." Simply, cybersonics is a situation in which the electronic processing of sound activities is determined (or

influenced) by the interactions of the sounds with themselves—that interaction itself being "collaborative."[1]

The late 1960s witnessed rapid technological change, which by its experimental nature produced one-of-a-kind instruments designed and executed for a unique creative purpose and incompatible with others. The handcrafted live-electronic units that Mumma built for his *Mesa* (1966), *Hornpipe* (1967), and *Cybersonic Cantilevers* (1973) rapidly became technologically obsolete. When manufactured commercial components started to be the norm by the mid-1970s, the field of electronic music changed fundamentally.

The essays in this section trace the evolution of Mumma's creative work in the sonic arts across these volatile years. The first, "Creative Aspects of Live-Performance Electronic Music Technology," was presented at the National Convention of the Audio Engineering Society in October 1967. It summarizes the philosophy, aesthetics, social context, and basic equipment terminology of Mumma's live-electronic music of the previous years, culminating in a detailed study of the technology of *Mesa*. It provides a state-of-the-art account of electronic-music technology at the outset of Mumma's most prolific decade of work in this genre. This is followed by a first-hand account of the technology and performance practices of Lucier's *Music for Solo Performer 1965*. Mumma was present at its premiere and performed the work several times with David Tudor, exchanging with him the roles of soloist and assistant. "Two Cybersonic Works: *Horn* and *Hornpipe*" brings together contemporary and recent perspectives on two works featuring Mumma's signature instrument, the horn, with emphasis on *Hornpipe*. His detailed analysis of its interactive techniques, instrumentation, and structure provides fresh insight into this iconic live-electronic work.

Three pieces with an international perspective from the early 1970s follow. It was from within the social ferment of France that Mumma, usually reticent about his political views, expressed many of the concerns shared by his friends and associates in the Vietnam War years in "Music in America 1970: Points of View." Compared to the traditional academic rhetoric of his taking-stock of a decade earlier, "Music's Avant-Garde: What's New?" (no. 1 in this book), the later piece demonstrates the impact of recent decoupage techniques of Cage, William Burroughs, Robert Rauschenberg, and Jackson Mac Low. "A Brief Introduction to the Sound-Modifier Console," with its ancillary prospectus for *Sun(flower) Burst*, introduces the saga and technology of the massive sound console that Mumma custom-built for the Pepsi Pavilion at the 1970 Osaka World's Fair. Finally comes a glimpse of the happening scene in London in "What We Did Last Summer: A Commentary on ICES 1972."

Part II closes with two pieces about the sonic arts from the first years of Mumma's appointment at the University of California, Santa Cruz, in 1973. "Two Decades of Live-Electronic Music, 1950–70" is excerpted from a larger study published in 1975 in the standard textbook *The Development and Practice of Electronic Music*, edited by Jon H. Appleton and Ronald C. Perera. Its personal take on two decades of sound innovation elucidates the context for Mumma's own development as composer and performer during these years. It also includes a new segment on Mumma's *Conspiracy 8* (1970) that illustrates emerging technologies of long-distance real-time collaboration by digital computer and high-speed telephone line. In closing, "Witchcraft, Cybersonics, and Folkloric Virtuosity," which elicited a mixture of enthusiasm, amusement, and bemused controversy at the Darmstadt Ferienkurse in July 1974, views recent innovations in North American music from a Californian perspective alien to many members of its European audience.

CHAPTER 6

Creative Aspects of Live-Performance Electronic Music Technology

(1967)

I am a composer and performing musician with considerable experience in acoustics and electronics, particularly solid-state technology. My professional work in electronic music began in 1954 with the making of film soundtracks and electronic music for theater. By 1957 I had established an electronic music studio. By the late 1950s I was exploring the resonant complexities of live-electronic music performance with Robert Ashley in Milton Cohen's Space Theatre productions. In that context I was developing and working with both acoustical and electronic sound modification procedures. Since that time my work with electronic music has evolved from its primacy as a magnetic tape medium to an almost complete preoccupation with the processing of acoustical sounds by live-performance electronic means.

My electronic music equipment is designed to be part of my process of composing music. I am like any composer who builds his own instruments, though most of my "instruments" are inseparable from the compositions themselves. My "end-product" is more than a package of electronic hardware: it is a musical performance for a live audience. On occasion my technical concerns may be differently oriented from those of the usual electronic engineer. Nonetheless, we are concerned with common ground: the applications of electronic technology, in my case to music.

Source: Mumma's presentation to the Thirty-Third National Convention of the Audio Engineering Society (New York, NY, October 16–19, 1967), A.E.S. Preprint no. 550, © 1967 by the Audio Engineering Society. Reprinted in the program for *Cross Talk Intermedia* (Tokyo, February 5–7, 1969). Minor revisions include Mumma's clarification of details regarding *Hornpipes* and the *Mesa* circuitry, with permission of the Audio Engineering Society.

There are some differences of process and design between the equipment for studio and live-performance use. In the studio the composer does not really work in real time. Work is done directly on magnetic tape, without an audience, allowing time for reworking. In live performance an audience is waiting to be entertained, astonished, amused, abused, or whatever, and there is no occasion for reworking. Live-performance equipment also differs from studio equipment in the requirement of portability.

I am concerned primarily with "system concepts"—configurations that include sound sources, electronic modification circuitry, control or logic circuitry, playback apparatus (power amplifiers, loudspeakers, and the auditorium), and even social conditions beyond the confines of technology. I suggest that the most important creative aspect of live-performance electronic music technology is not this or that circuit innovation but rather the total configuration itself.

My engineering decisions concerning electronic procedures, circuitry, and configurations are strongly influenced by the requirements of music making. Thus my designing and building of circuits is "composing" that employs electronic technology in the achievement of my musical art. Though I may describe my use of certain electronic procedures because they result in certain sounds, these procedures were not always chosen on a cause-and-effect basis. Sometimes I am looking for a certain kind of sound modification, and I work on various circuits until I have achieved that result. Other times in casually experimenting with different configurations of circuits I may chance upon some novel sound effect that becomes the germinating idea for a piece of music.

The four of my musical compositions that I will discuss have at least the following in common: all are live-performance works that use conventional musical instruments as sound sources for electro-acoustic sound processing. The first three indicate the diversity of configuration possible with very few basic electronic functions: amplitude and frequency modulation, and frequency filtering. The fourth composition is described in more detail because of its greater complexity.

The first of these works is the most elementary in conception and technical means. *Medium Size Mograph 1963* is an eight-minute composition for one piano with two performers. The piano sound is amplified by way of vibration pickups attached near the soundboard and connected to "cybersonic" circuitry in a small portable sound box.[1] The inherent characteristic of piano sound—an initial attack followed by a resonant decay—is modified by the electronic circuitry. As a result the attack transient of the piano is compressed (made quieter), its energy spread over into the later portion of the sound envelope, while the duration of the final part of the envelope is extended.

In concert performances of *Medium Size Mograph 1963* the performers play the notated score with the piano lid closed and muffled with a heavy blanket. The electronics "respond" to their performance, projecting the results to the large loudspeaker under the piano. What the audience hears is predominantly the sound from the loudspeaker: it obviously comes from the piano, but is at best a distant acoustical cousin. The major innovative feature of this otherwise fairly simple electronic configuration is that a small portable box can, by relatively simple means, effectively make a "new" instrument from a conventional one.[2]

The second piece, titled *Hornpipes*,[3] is currently under development. It is scored for a solo horn that has been modified and contains a microphone. A series of large metal pipes retrieved from junkyards is placed a few feet behind the performer (the bell of the classic horn faces behind the performer). The pipes contain their own microphones that resonate at different frequencies and are applied to the sound-modifying circuitry. Further behind is the loudspeaker from which the music is heard. The acoustical loop connecting the horn, the resonant pipes, and the loudspeaker creates an electronic feedback system.

In concept the performance will begin with the system in "balance." Electronic sound is produced only when something in the acoustic-electronic feed-back-loop is unbalanced. The initial sounds produced by the hornist unbalance parts of the system, some of which rebalance, thereby unbalancing other parts of the system. The performer's task is to choose the timing and materials within the acoustical space in order to influence the electronic balancing and unbalancing. *Hornpipes* has not yet been performed publicly.

The third work is *Diastasis, as in Beer* (1967), for two electric guitars. As the title implies, the two guitars are interdependent in performance, with the pitch (or frequency) of each guitar determined by the amplitude envelope of the other guitar. The frequency spectrum shifts continuously rather than discretely (as would ordinarily occur on a fretted instrument). Two special frequency modulators accomplish this task, while the process is complicated because the amplitude-envelope sensor circuitry is purposely frequency sensitive. The effect poses a musical challenge for the guitarists: they must strive to execute their separate parts with accuracy, but their individual efforts seldom produce a one-to-one correspondence with the results. Their attempted pitches do not remain constant, though the conditions of the music require the achievement of specific relationships of pitch and rhythm.

In 1966 I was commissioned to compose music to accompany a new modern dance for the Merce Cunningham Dance Company to be titled *Place*.[4] I had already been at work on a piece for David Tudor, and decided to modify and finish this project more quickly than anticipated to fulfill the commission for

Cunningham. The title of the piece is *Mesa*. The predominant character of the music involves sustained sounds at one dynamic level interrupted by sounds of greatly contrasting loudness. I had already given up the idea of a composition on magnetic tape, which would have proved incapable of producing the kind of dynamic range I wanted.

In order to achieve the frequency spectrum and sound density of *Mesa*, as well as to control aspects of the spatial perception of the audience and still maintain clarity in the musical continuity, I deploy related portions of the sound through different loudspeakers in the auditorium. The final "processing" of the sound is the mixing of these sounds in the listener's ears.

In contrast to *Diastasis, as in Beer*, the pitch changes of *Mesa* are discrete rather than continuous, a function of the instrument used. The bandoneon is a polyphonic metal reed instrument with a cube-shaped bellows and button keyboards; a member of the concertina family, it survives now in Argentine tango bands. *Mesa* exploits the capacity of the bandoneon to produce extremely long, sustained sounds over a wide frequency and dynamic range. The technical problems of this work included extension of the dynamic range, frequency-translation and equalization to obtain the desired timbres, and configuration of logic circuitry to control the continuity of the music. Extending the dynamic range proved the most complicated challenge, because a wide range of sound-envelope controls had to be included in the circuitry. In *Mesa* these functions are completely automatic and are achieved with four *voltage-controlled attenuators* (VCA) developed in collaboration with William Ribbens in Ann Arbor.

The general configuration of *Mesa* is indicated in figure II-1. Six microphones were used. The four central microphones are attached to the bandoneon, two to each side of the instrument (left and right). These microphones are each sensitive to different frequency bands. An additional two microphones (adder) pick up ambient sound as well as sound from the other side of the bandoneon. Thus, from the very beginning of this scheme six different channels of sound are being processed.

The two inner channels are of primary importance to the music, while the other four channels are outriggers. By means of logic circuitry the control signals (indicated by dashed lines) and program signals (solid lines) are routed from one channel to another during performance. The processed program outputs from the VCA modules are applied directly to power amplifiers and thence to loud-speakers at different points in the auditorium. The outrigger channels are usually heard from behind the audience. Though not indicated in this diagram, voltage amplification at various levels is included in the circuitry wherever necessary.

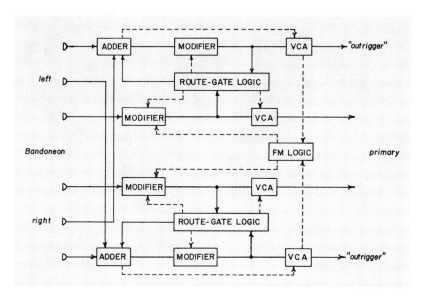

Fig. II-1. Gordon Mumma's general electronic configuration for *Mesa*. (Diagram © Audio Engineering Society, with their permission.)

A closer view of the interrelated sound modification functions can be seen within one of the system blocks, as outlined in figure II-2 and described as follows.

The *spectrum transfer* is a frequency shifter with equalization. The amount of frequency shift is determined either by variable internal control signals or by an external signal derived from the bandoneon itself. The source and nature of the control signal are determined by the *FM logic*, which controls the operation of the spectrum transfers, determining the amount of program-signal frequency shift by control signals derived from the outrigger VCAs.

The *multiplier* translates portions of the program spectrum by whole integers and equalizes the product.

The *product valve* is a combination amplitude and phase modulator, the product of which contains the output of the spectrum transfer plus a new spectrum derived by amplitude gating the spectrum transfer output with part of the multiplier output.

The *modifier route-gate logic* is an adder with three inputs, two outputs, and a control signal. This control signal comes from an external *route-gate logic* module; it determines the proportions of the three inputs (from the spectrum transfer,

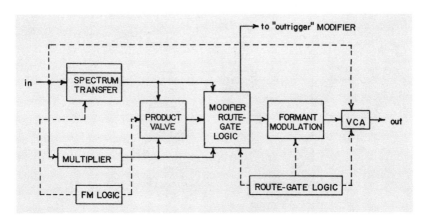

Fig. II-2. One of the system blocks from *Mesa*. (Diagram © Audio Engineering Society, with their permission.)

multiplier, and product valve) and the balance of the two outputs (to the *formant modulation* and the "outrigger" *modifier*).

The *formant modulation* is a class of voltage-controlled comb filter. The bandwidths and center frequencies of the several passbands are continuously variable by control signals from the external route-gate logic. The passband outputs are added and sent to the VCA.

The *VCA*, besides accomplishing what its name implies, includes time delay circuitry that shapes the envelope of the program signal. The control voltage is derived from both the original bandoneon signal and the external *route-gate logic* module, which determines aspects of the sound modification and, in conjunction with the actions of the bandoneon player, establishes the musical continuity.

The various sound delays at the controlled, variable speeds required for *Mesa* would be out of the question by direct electronic manipulation of the program signal or by mechanical means. The solution to these problems is inherent in the concept of *Mesa* itself, since at this point in the system it is the envelope of the otherwise sustained sounds that is to be shaped. This is achieved by subjecting the VCA control signals to frequency-sensitive thermal-delay circuitry.

All of the control signals for these sound modification functions are derived from the sounds of the bandoneon. Some are frequency (or phase) modulated, others are amplitude modulated, and some of the bias in the VCA module is derived from integration of control and program signal sums. Because the control signals are automatically derived from the sound materials themselves, I call the process and the music "cybersonic."

The most extreme performance situation for *Mesa* is possible when these logic modules are operated in their fully automatic modes, creating a duo between the bandoneonist and the electronic circuitry. More often they are operated semi-automatically, with a human performer making decisions and overriding parts of the internal logic. Usually this second performer is myself [as seen in fig. III-4].

During the past decade a substantial repertoire of live-performance electronic music has been produced by other composers in the United States, in Europe, and in Japan, including Robert Ashley, David Behrman, John Cage, Alvin Lucier, and Toshi Ichiyanagi. The diversity of this repertoire is already sufficient to support several performing ensembles. Some of their works extend beyond music into the realm of "intermedia," integrating theater, film, and dance with configurations of electronic manipulation. It is difficult not to be excited about the future of these arts.

CHAPTER 7

Alvin Lucier's *Music for Solo Performer 1965*
(1967)

Alvin Lucier's *Music for Solo Performer 1965* is a live-performance work employing electronic equipment.[1] An assisting technician attaches three small Grass Instrument silver electrodes to the scalp of the solo performer to obtain the alpha current. The alpha current is a low-voltage brainwave signal of approximately 10 Hz that appears at the scalp surface during the non-visualizing stages of human mental activity. These alpha currents, on the order of 25 microvolts of signal strength, are increased by means of a Cybersonics differential amplifier that contains a 14 Hz low-pass filter to remove extraneous signals, and are transferred by standard high-fidelity power amplification to several wide-range loudspeakers. The loudspeakers are deployed throughout the performance area in order to activate the sympathetic resonance of nearby percussion instruments.

The musical continuity of Lucier's *Music for Solo Performer 1965* is determined by both the solo performer and the assistant. The alpha current is triggered on and off by non-visualizing mental activity when the soloist's eyes are closed and opened, and is selectively directed by the technical assistant to the various loudspeakers with their corresponding resonant percussion instruments.

Only two types of sound occur in the performance of *Music for Solo Performer 1965:* the 10 Hz alpha wave and the various sympathetically resonant percussion instruments. The 10 Hz alpha is essentially a sine wave, and any harmonics of

Source: *Source* 1, no. 2 (July 1967): 68–69; reprinted in *Source: Music of the Avant-Garde,* ed. Larry Austin, Douglas Kahn, and Nilendra Gurusinghe, 79–81, © 2011 by the Regents of the University of California and published by the University of California Press. Reprinted here with minor stylistic and structural revisions with permission of the University of California Press.

its signal are suppressed by the 14 Hz low-pass filter. The subsequent amplification is nearly linear. The only sound modifications that occur are the harmonics in the waveforms produced by the loudspeakers, which Lucier likes to operate to maximum cone excursion at 10 Hz. He prefers large acoustic-suspension-type speakers, which, when operated in this manner, produce a very clean and rebound-free 10 Hz pulse waveform. As a result the loudspeakers, normally the ultimate sound producer in an electronic-music system, are used as intermediary transducers or triggers for the natural, resonant sounds of the percussion instruments. This is perhaps the most significant electronic-music aspect of this composition.

The great diversity of equipment configuration possible with recent electronic-music procedures seems to have made "system-concept" analysis fundamental to the creative process of many recent composers. For instance, in a special version of *Music for Solo Performer 1965* Lucier uses magnetic tape storage as an accessory to the alpha-articulated percussion instruments. The tape-stored material consists of continuous pre-recorded alpha signals that have been multiplied in frequency. In this version the performer releases his 10 Hz alpha signal in bursts or periodic wave-trains. Following the required differential amplifier and low-pass filter stages, the live soloist's alpha signal is divided and a portion applied to a special circuit that gates the tape-stored material. In performance of this version of *Music for Solo Performer 1965,* the gated bursts of frequency-multiplied alpha signals emerge, like a ghostly tessitura, from a loudspeaker at some remote part of the auditorium. The system-concept of this special version treats the original 10 Hz alpha signal with two different functions. On one hand, directly amplified alpha signals from the loudspeakers produce sound from the sympathetically resonant percussion instruments. On the other hand, a sub-system derives electronic triggering signals from the 10 Hz alpha signal to activate the tape-stored materials. The typical configuration of equipment and speakers in this special tape-storage version is illustrated in figure II-3.

The theatrical aspects of the work are simple and dramatic. The printed program simply lists the composer and title of the work, with enumeration of the soloist and assistant, and acknowledgment of Dr. Edmond Dewan (of the Air Force Cambridge Research Laboratories) as technical consultant. Performance of the piece begins with the appearance of the soloist and his assistant. The soloist seats himself comfortably near the differential amplifier, while the assistant begins the procedure of applying the electrodes to the soloist's head. This operation involves cleaning the scalp with alcohol, applying special conducting electrode paste and gauze pads to secure the electrodes, measuring

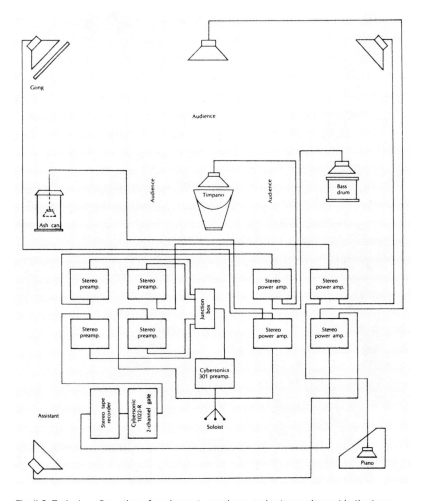

Fig. II-3. Typical configuration of equipment, speakers, and extra equipment in the tape-storage version of Alvin Lucier's *Music for Solo Performer 1965. (Diagram* © 2011 by the Regents of the University of California, with permission of the University of California Press.)

the electrical resistance between the electrodes (which should be rated below 10,000 ohms), and adjusting the gain and DC balance of the differential amplifier. The procedure takes several minutes to complete and generally has a remarkable effect on the audience, for whom the situation is both ambiguous and dynamic. Indeed, many may not immediately comprehend that electrodes are being positioned on the soloist's head.

The period of time before the first tapped brain waves are directed to their resonant instruments is really quite mysterious. After the sounds have begun, one comes to recognize the coincidence of the soloist opening his eyes with the stopping of the alpha-articulated sounds. Closing of the eyes will not necessarily start the alpha again. The process of non-visualizing must occur, a specially developed skill that the soloist learns with practice. And no matter how experienced, the soloist must accommodate the various conditions of performance that intrude on that skill. A successful performance of *Music for Solo Performer 1965* is a matter of exercising great control over conditions that are hardly ever completely predictable. The soloist who can achieve sustained sequences of rapid alpha bursts that are distributed from the resonating instruments throughout the audience creates a tour de force performance. Lucier's use of a performer's brain waves as sound material may be a musical innovation, but it is no longer an isolated example (for example, Alex Hay's *Grass Field,* premiered in October 1966 in New York at 9 Evenings: Theatre and Engineering).

To date, three people have served as soloists in performances of *Music for Solo Performer 1965:* Alvin Lucier, David Tudor, and myself. Tudor and I learned the work directly from the composer. At various times Larry Austin, David Behrman, Robert Bernat, John Cage, and Joel Chadabe have acted as the assistant. I am impressed with the paradox that, as the musical use of elaborate and sophisticated electronic technology increases, their transmission to succeeding generations requires reverting to a kind of oral tradition. The spectacular evolution of new musical notation procedures during the past two decades indicates that this problem extends beyond the electronic-music realm. But it is in the area of live-performance electronic music that the problem of notation as communication from composer to performer is most acute. The efficiency of Lucier's recently prepared score for *Music for Solo Performer 1965*—a kit of parts including three electrodes, paste, lead-in wires, a differential amplifier and low-pass filter, and an instruction manual—awaits verification in the hands of future performers.

CHAPTER 8

Two Cybersonic Works
Horn *and* Hornpipe
(1970–71/2012)

For several years Robert Ashley and I performed a remarkable work for horn and piano, *Duet II* (1961) by Christian Wolff. This and several of Wolff's other works inspired me to compose for the horn. In 1961 I began a series of compositions for horn with various accompanying resources, including live cybersonic processing. Two of these, *Horn* (1965) and *Hornpipe* (1967), were widely performed and have been recorded. Of these, *Hornpipe* would prove a major touring vehicle for me until 1976, with at least thirty-two performances across the United States, in Europe, and in Japan.

Horn

Horn requires a hornist, two voices, and a technician to operate the cybersonic console. The sounds of all three players were modified in live performance with cybersonic circuits, by which the sounds of one performer automatically and drastically modify the sounds of another. Technically, the process was an ensemble of ring-modulators in which the carrier frequency -input was derived from the other performers' complex sounds.

Source: New material was written in 2012 that draws liberally on earlier writings, including Mumma's program notes for the Mainstream and Tzadik recordings, his unpublished "Notes on Cybersonics" (1971; typescript, GMC), and his contributions to an unpublished essay co-written with Stephen Smoliar, "The Computer as a Performing Instrument (20 February 1970)," *Artificial Intelligence Memo* 213 (MIT Artificial Intelligence Laboratory, February 1971): 1–11 (typescript, GMC).

Horn employed two or three cybersonic units interconnected by audio cables, with the outputs directed to a stereo sound system. There were three audio inputs for live processing, two for the voices and one for the horn. A minimum of output control was left to the technician, who operated the control units, primarily to balance the spatial placement of the processed sounds and levels of output to the loudspeakers in the audience.

Except for the sounds of the horn near the end of the performances, the performers generally avoided producing loud sounds in order to facilitate balance in the cybersonic processing. The result was a gritty, spectral sound that obliterated the sonic identities of horn and voices. The process of variable interconnected circuitry in *Horn* became the basis for further design and development of the later *Mesa* (1966), *Beam* (1969), and *Cybersonic Cantilevers* (1973).

Horn was premiered and recorded at St. Andrew's Episcopal Church in Ann Arbor in March 1965, with an ensemble of ONCE regulars (Gordon Mumma, Robert Ashley, George Cacioppo, and William Ribbens). One of its notable performances took place on November 26, 1966, as a last-minute request for London's Saville Theatre during a Cunningham Dance Company residency. John Cage and David Tudor supplied the voice parts to my performance of the horn and cybersonics.

Hornpipe

Hornpipe is for solo hornist (playing Waldhorn and valve horn) and cybersonic console. Its origins extend back to the early 1960s with a related conceptual piece then titled *Hornpipes,* an acoustical experiment using an assortment of vertical metal pipes placed at varying distances behind the bell of my horn.[1] The vertical pipes, of different lengths and mass, resonated with my horn practice as I moved about the performance space. The invitation from Luigi Nono for Milton Cohen's Space Theatre project to perform at the 1964 Venice Biennale inspired me to rethink the cumbersome, fixed apparatus of my *Hornpipes* experiment. I put aside the collection of metal pipes, transferring their previous function to the smaller "pipes" created by the tube-like valve slides of the horn and my developing electronic processing.

This shift from acoustical to electronic resources was a significant factor in my development of the interactive acoustical ecology of *Hornpipe* over its multi-year gestation. I developed a single control unit: the cybersonic console, housed in a small metal box to be attached to my belt in live performance. This arrangement allowed me to move about freely in the performance space, as seen in figure II-4.

Fig. II-4. Gordon Mumma performing *Hornpipe* at the Metropolitan Museum of Art, New York, February 19, 1972. (Photo by Jumay R. Chu, with her permission.)

The cybersonic console for *Hornpipe* was a small analog-type computer and signal processor of my own design. The signal inputs to the console were two small lavalier-type microphones to be attached to opposite sides of my belt. The line-level outputs of the console traveled by an umbilical cable to the stereophonic amplifier and loudspeakers elsewhere in the performance venue. Figure II-5 shows a close-up of the cybersonic belt-box with its accessory cables

Fig. II-5. View of Mumma's cybersonic belt-box for *Hornpipe* in 1974, facing the jack panel on the top of the unit. It shows the belt clip control-switch cable (L), two microphones (input) to be attached to the belt, and (top) the output umbilical cable to be attached to the stereo sound system (amplifier to loudspeakers). The black knobs on the front side of the unit include volume and sound system controls. (Photo © Gordon Mumma.)

in 1974. Though I continued developing the internal cybersonic circuitry, the external configuration of this box remained largely unchanged from its construction in 1966 to the final performances of *Hornpipe* in 1976.

The inside of the cybersonic belt-box contained four parallel voltage control amplifiers (VCA) per channel (the left channel is illustrated in the functional diagram shown in figure II-6). The microphone preamp delivered the acoustical information supplied by the horn player and the acoustical resonances of those sounds in the venue on a straight-line audio path to the VCA amplifiers. Each

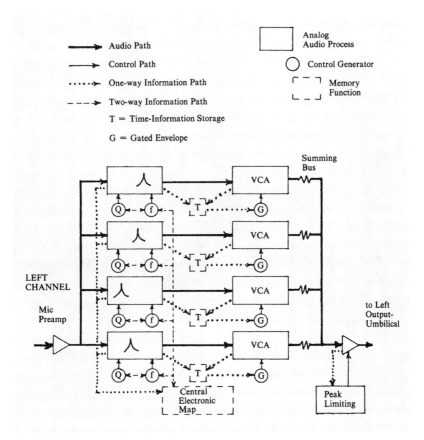

Fig. II-6. Mumma's functional diagram of the left channel of the cybersonic belt-box for *Hornpipe* (adapted from Cope, *New Directions*, 238).

amplifier connected via resonant circuits to a feedback loop (see dotted lines), which converted the acoustical sounds to electronic signals and held them in time-information storage (T) until the cybersonic unit determined that it had collected sufficient acoustical information. At that point the gate control (G) opened, passing the stored sound signals via the output umbilical to the external amplifier and loudspeakers. The "open" time of the gates was determined by the complex interactions of the sounds obtained from the microphones. Overload was controlled by a peak-limiting function.

An important aspect of *Hornpipe* was its instrumentation for horn, performed both traditionally and with extended techniques, including multiphonics. Two different horns were used: a Waldhorn or "natural" horn (without valves), the heroic hunting horn of the past, and a modern valve horn (a double horn or so-called French horn), to which a secondary control cable was attached. The valve horn used for *Hornpipe* was a 1949 Conn 6D horn modified by Carl Geyer to make the bell easily removable (as depicted in fig. II-4). Its sounds could be directed either from the traditional conical bell or from the cylindrical valve tubes when the curved slide-inserts (or "crooks") were removed. Finally, the horn sounds were generated not only with a traditional embouchure-based cone-shaped horn mouthpiece but also with special double reeds (as used with the Sarrusophone, which was still played in U.S. military bands into the mid-twentieth century). The rapid switching between horns and embouchure procedures was part of the theater of *Hornpipe* as I moved through the performance space, exploring the diversity of its resonances.

The basic structural premise of *Hornpipe* was preconceived, and was determined by a combination of the technical capacities of the equipment, the acoustical properties of the venue, and the musical input of the hornist. Because the microphones "heard" both the original sounds of the horn and the resonances of those sounds from within the venue, interactive cross-influences occurred, somewhat as in an ecological—or "echo-logical"—situation. During the performance the hornist learns the constellation of resonances of the particular space.

Hornpipe begins as a solo for horn, during which the cybersonic console is silently "listening," monitoring the resonances of the horn in the acoustical space and adjusting its electronic circuits to complement these resonances. When it has stored sufficient information, a gate opens and the electronic "response" of the console is heard from the loudspeakers. The hornist responds in duo, assessing the resonances of the performance space and choosing sonorities that will support, rebalance, or subvert the activities of the cybersonic console. The hornist is also able to deactivate the cybersonic circuitry by playing sounds that are outside the resonant constellation. The performance ends when the hornist provides new sound information that purposely contradicts the accumulated resonances and effectively shuts down the response activity of the console. In performance this basic game plan influenced both performance decisions and theatrical movement throughout the space.

The horn part of *Hornpipe* is without notated score. It was improvised in response to the acoustical properties of each distinctive performance space from diverse instrumental idioms and materials that I collected and prepared over the course of several years. Thus the substructures and internal details of *Hornpipe* could vary widely from one venue and one performance to another. Nor was the process foolproof. There were occasions when it would not work, as for example in a recording studio for the Italian radio network (RAI) in Rome. The space was practically anechoic, leaving nothing to resonate.

By late 1967 *Hornpipe* was ready to travel. Its premiere was at Pomona College in Claremont, California, on December 5, 1967, followed by a performance the next day on the First Festival of Live-Electronic Music at the University of California, Davis. The original recording of *Hornpipe* at the Rose Art Museum at Brandeis University, released on compact disc by Tzadik (TZ 7074), provides ready access to this work in a particularly lush sonic environment.[2] With its ample glass and marble multi-level space, reflecting pool, and direct access to the outdoors, the venue provided rich acoustical resources.

This fifteen-minute version of *Hornpipe* begins outdoors with the Waldhorn playing traditional hunting calls, followed by multiple interchanges with the valve horn. The sounds are sustained, articulated, or staccato. While the hornist is moving into the gallery, a loud chorus of birds makes an unscheduled musical entry (at 2:04). Following the shift indoors (at 2:26), the hornist moves continuously through the space, exploring its acoustics with increasingly diversified sound materials (beginning at 4:50), including multiphonics, double reeds, valve clicks, breathing and water sounds, and "open-pipe" sonorities (with one or more horn crooks removed). Many listeners are surprised to learn that the wide range of these sounds and timbres, some of which are barely recognizable as emanating from a horn, are purely acoustical in origin. The complexity of sound resources is partly responsible for the silence of the cybersonic console, occupied with processing the sound data until its dramatic entry at the halfway point (7:47).

In the second half of *Hornpipe* three kinds of ensemble interactions occur: horn in ensemble dialogue with electronic sounds (8:46–9:23), long solo sequences from the cybersonic console (9:23–10:36), and electronic sounds directly articulated by the horn (10:36–11:46). Following a dramatic duo for reed horn and electronics (11:46–12:38), their trio with the acoustical space reaches a highpoint (12:38–14:03). The performer then devotes major efforts to subverting the responses of the cybersonic console with various complex horn techniques. Following a closing section for console with reed horn (beginning at 14:04), the work ends when the horn produces the previously unheard sustained pitch of B-flat (14:58), which deceives the console into switching into dormant mode. The general time proportions of the structure varied from one performance to another but usually achieved a similar or newly appropriate balance for the situation.

The *Hornpipe* circuitry box has an elementary computer-like function. It receives and stores information in an analog rather than digital form, making "decisions" essential to the composition. By its responses the console informs the hornist which sounds are more likely to unbalance and rebalance the system. Thus the cybersonic console could well be considered independently "intelligent," although its range of capacity is limited to the highly specialized purpose designed by the composer. The "intelligent" decisions of the human horn player involve a history of vastly complex habits, performance virtuosity skills, and interactively responsive experiences.

Fig. II-7. Gordon Mumma self-portrait, Paris, February 1971. (Photo © Gordon Mumma.)

CHAPTER 9

Music in America 1970
Points of View

American composers are increasingly different from one another.
—Robert Ashley: Epic music-theater

Empires are dissolving. Universities are no longer the central focus of new music activity.
—David Behrman: Modulated frequency

America presently has more electronic music studios than the rest of the world combined. Becoming as common as pianos, the electronic music studio is declining as an obsession.
—Alvin Lucier: An explorer of sound and theatrical situation

Modern jazz is damn near dead in America. Swamped by the pressures of commerce and recording, the jazz musician has been driven into exile. The American audience is still isolated from the staggering resources of black talent. A miracle of the past two hundred years: black musicians continue to survive the undernourishment of neglect. Perhaps they flourish because of it.
—The lyrical cinema of Phill Niblock:
   Massive sound without musical gesture

Source: This aphoristic piece was written in June 1970 in Paris and Amiens at the request of Francis Miroglio for Nuits de la Fondation Maegt, Saint-Paul de Vence, France. It was printed privately in French as "Point de vue . . ." in the catalog of their Fifth International Festival of Contemporary Music and Art, devoted to les États-Unis (1970).

Music criticism is the least useful social function in America. The press, still centralized in New York City, is overbearing and oppressive.
—Pauline Oliveros: The concise image

The specter of the American war in Indo-China and the suppression of dissent in the United States have recently created something new. A coalition of artists from the performing and visual arts is organizing social action against certain institutions. The American composer now encounters coercion from below as well as above.
—From Terry Riley through Steve Reich to Philip Glass:
   A world of monody that,
   particularly in the elegant work of Philip Glass,
   is achieved—as in Webern—by eliminating the unnecessary

The cultural institutions of America are becoming politically unstable. Some are overthrown in social revolution, others are simply abandoned. The American composer is compelled to independence from institutions.
—David Rosenboom: System synthesis

At the same time, computers have become a musical obsession. Because of their great cost, computers are already institutions. Some composers build their own computers for music; others obtain theirs illegally.
—In Osaka for nine weeks: Ten pieces by David Tudor

Like Black America, Latin America is not yet part of the American conscience. Increasingly its own world, Latin America is drawing its cultural resources from its own ground or from North America rather than from Europe. Ignorant of the rape of Latin American human and mineral resources, a recent musical seminar in a North American university informed us that Gabriel Brnčić was from Santiago, making him "a Cuban composer."
—Christian Wolff: A theater of available resources
—La Monte Young: Exquisite intonation,
   a music expanding into days of length

Musical heroes are less common, and no longer belong to academic establishments. If you must have heroes, you must choose from the nation that includes Otis Redding, James Brown, and Jimi Hendrix. But no one really chooses heroes any more.

CHAPTER 10

A Brief Introduction to the Sound-Modifier Console and *Sun(flower) Burst*

(1972)

Author's Introduction (2013)

Constructed for Expo '70 in Osaka, Japan, the Pepsi Pavilion was coordinated by Experiments in Art and Technology [E.A.T.] and a collaborative team of over seventy-five industries, engineers, and artists in Japan and the United States. The massive faceted dome structure, surrounded by a constantly changing water vapor fog sculpture, contained a large state-of-the-art sound system situated in a lofty mirror room. In the words of one of the chief designers of the room, Billy Klüver, it was a technologically advanced theater environment, a "total instrument, using every available technology in which the accumulated experience of all the programmers [leading composers, dancers, visual artists, and scientists] expanded and enriched the possibilities of the space."[1]

David Tudor was invited to design the sound system. Tudor served as the coordinator for the sound functions and was primarily responsible for the loudspeaker design and the sound library. He brought me in to design and build the sound-modifier console.[2] Larry Owens designed the analog and digital interfaces and installed the system in Osaka. Tudor wanted twenty channels in the sound-modifier console but was compelled by circumstances to settle

Source: *Pavilion: Experiments in Art and Technology*, ed. Billy Klüver, Julie Martin, and Barbara Rose, 238–42, 303–4 (New York: Dutton, 1972), © Experiments in Art and Technology. Reprinted here with several minor stylistic revisions, with permission of Julie Martin, Director, E.A.T. The introduction was added in 2013 to provide context for the essay and the Sun(flower) project prospectus. It is based on material in Klüver, *Pavilion*, additional typescript materials (1982) in GMC, and interviews with Mumma.

Fig. II-8. Gordon Mumma in the final stages of constructing the sound-modifier console for the Osaka Expo '70 Pavilion, New York, February 1970. (Photo by Barbara Dilley Lloyd, with her permission.)

for an eight-channel system with twelve controls for each channel (for a total of ninety-six possible configurations). It would provide the performer with flexibility of pitch, loudness, and timbre within each channel. The sounds were to be projected to thirty-seven loudspeakers positioned in a rhombic grid surrounding the apex of the dome. I began designs for the console in New York

City and Champaign, Illinois, in the summer and fall of 1969. My system was completed at the E.A.T. loft on East 16th Street in New York by February 1970, resulting in the electronic console seen in figure II-8.

The console used the newest transistor technology of the time, so new that it required U.S. security clearance. Fred Waldhauer of Bell Labs called me one day to invite me on a kind of shopping excursion. "You won't remember any of this," he advised. Every part of the unit was soldered to survive the flight to Japan and was accompanied by my scrupulous installation instructions. In their sleep-deprived condition, the technical staff in Osaka overlooked my specifications and blew out most of the transistors. With only days to opening they were in crisis mode. Waldhauer managed to find more transistors in New York to be flown to Japan, I sent additional instructions, and the unit was successfully repaired barely in time.

Twenty-four original projects were accepted in competition for presentation at the Pepsi Pavilion. In its few weeks of operation before the artistic program was terminated by a sudden change of corporate leadership at PepsiCo, Tudor completed and recorded three major projects on the sound system, his *Pepscillator*, *Pepsibird*, and *Anima Pepsi*.[3] My *Sun(flower) Burst* suffered the fate of numerous other projects by artists such as Toshi Ichiyanagi, Allan Kaprow, Alvin Lucier, Terry Riley, and La Monte Young, scheduled for later in the exposition and cancelled when the magnificent artistic resources of the Pavilion were re-routed to soft-drink commercials. I never got to Expo '70 and never experienced at first hand the spectacular light and sound environment of the E.A.T. Pavilion in its short creative history. But the project witnessed some of the most innovative and creatively reckless work I ever did.[4]

The Sound-Modifier Console

1. INPUT-OUTPUT PROGRAMMING

The sound-modifier console contains eight separate channels. The inputs and outputs of the console are programmable by cards and tape. The eight inputs (one to each modifier channel) are controlled by the input program. Each of these eight inputs is the sum of up to four sound sources. Each of the thirty-two sound sources has a separate volume control.

2. BASIC MODIFIER FUNCTIONS

On the console itself the sound-modifier functions for each of the eight channels are operated manually. Each channel has three basic modifiers: FM (frequency modulation), AM (amplitude modulation), and filter (a high-pass filter). This

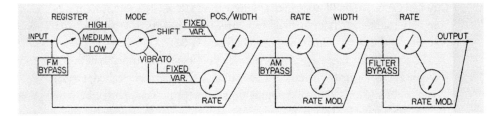

Fig. II-9. Schematic diagram of one channel of the sound-modifier console for the Osaka EXPO '70 Pavilion. (Diagram © Experiments in Art and Technology, with permission of Julie Martin.)

configuration is indicated in figure II-9, and detailed descriptions are given in section 4 below.

The three basic modifiers are in series, so that a sound source can be modified first by FM, the result modified by AM, and that result modified by the filter. This is the most complicated arrangement possible within a single channel. Any or all of these three basic modifiers can be bypassed by operation of an illuminated push button. Thus, it is easy to use the sound system with any amount of sound modification, or with no sound modification whatsoever.

3. EXAMPLES OF PROGRAMMING EXTREMES

Since the sound sources are applied to the eight modifier channels by the input program, it is possible to program the type of modification to which the sources are subjected. For example, if only a single sound source is to be used (such as a solo musician or monaural tape), the input program can be arranged to route that source to any four of the eight modifier channels in any sequence. If each modifier channel is preset to a different modification, then a sequence of up to four modifications can be determined by the input program.

By two further procedures it is possible to extend the number of modifications for a single sound source. First, the input program can be arranged to apply the sound source to two or more modifier channels at a time, allowing combinations of modifier functions. By this procedure alone a vast spectrum of modifications can be sequenced for a single sound source. Second, the manual controls of the sound-modifier console can be operated independent of the input or output programs, allowing rearrangement of functions within any modifier channel.

At the other extreme, if all thirty-two sound sources are used (summed in groups of four sources to eight console inputs), a programmed change of modification for any one input must be accomplished by exchanging modifier channels with another four of the eight modifier inputs.

4. SOUND-MODIFIER CONSOLE DESCRIPTION

There are three sound-modifier functions: the FM function, the AM function, and the filter function.

A. The *FM function* shifts the sound source upward or downward in pitch (or frequency) depending on the original pitch of the source. The FM function has five controls:

1. *register*: a switch with three positions (high, medium, low)
2. *mode*: a switch with four positions (fixed shift, variable shift, fixed vibrato, variable vibrato)
3. *pos./width*: a continuously variable control that determines the pitch shift position in the two shift modes, and the vibrato width in the two vibrato modes
4. *rate*: a continuously variable control that determines the basic vibrato rate for the two vibrato modes
5. *bypass*: an illuminated push button that bypasses the entire FM function.

Note: The "variable" designation is a condition wherein the pitch shift (or *vibrato*, when in that mode) follows the amplitude envelope of the sound source. This "envelope-variable" effect is direct. In the variable *shift* mode the pitch shift of the sound source increases with an increase in the loudness of the source. In the variable *vibrato* mode the rate of vibrato increases with an increase in the loudness of the sound source. In all three basic modifiers (FM, AM, and filter) the envelope-variable circuitry always follows the amplitude envelope of the original (unmodified) sound source, regardless of the modifications that may be applied after the console input.

B. The *AM function* imparts a periodically varying amplitude envelope to the sound source. The AM function has four controls:

1. *rate*: a continuously variable control that determines the basic period of the amplitude envelope
2. *width*: a continuously variable control that determines the on-to-off ratio of the AM. The "on" part of the AM period is always as loud as the sound source itself. The "off" part of the AM period can be adjusted from completely inaudible to the same audibility as the "on" part.
3. *rate mod*: a continuously variable control to enable the AM rate to follow the amplitude envelope of the original sound source. The maximum rate of change occurs at the maximum clockwise position of the *rate mod* control.

4. *bypass*: an illuminated push button that bypasses the entire AM function.

C. The *filter function* imparts a periodically varying high-pass formant to the sound source. The filter has three controls:

1. *rate*: a continuously variable control that determines the basic period of filtering
2. *rate mod*: a continuously variable control to enable the *filter rate* to follow the amplitude envelope of the original sound source. The maximum rate change occurs at the maximum clockwise position of the *rate mod* control.
3. *bypass*: an illuminated push button that bypasses the entire filter function.

5. FURTHER NOTES ON THE BASIC MODIFIER FUNCTIONS

Of the three basic modifier functions, the FM function enables the most extreme modifications of a sound source. Under some conditions a sound source can be modified beyond recognition. With some sources certain FM control positions not only shift the pitch but also compress or expand the harmonic spectrum of that source.

The *shift* and *vibrato* positions that are "envelope variable" will be of particular interest to musicians who are performing live. By varying their dynamics they can have considerable remote control over the type and extreme of modification of their sounds.

Though of interest in itself, the AM function has special applications in conjunction with the FM and filter functions of the same modifier channel. For instance, when the AM *rate* is set to a different period than the FM *vibrato* or filter *rate*, long-period changes of timbre or articulation are possible. Further, the AM *width* control can be set in long-period conjunction with the FM *vibrato* control in such a way as to produce secondary articulation or modification of a single sound source. One of these many effects is an inverted frequency-spectrum echo of the basic FM modification, a result that sounds as if two sources at different distances are being applied to the same modifier channel.

The filter function, which has the simplicity of only two controls (plus *bypass*), has particular relevance to the pavilion. A considerable part of the sonic action of the pavilion involves the rhombic grid of thirty-seven loudspeakers that, in conjunction with the sound output programming (switch matrix and sequence programs), enables great diversity of sound movement in the pavilion. Thus, of the various kinds of filters possible, a high-pass filter was designed in order to enhance the directionality of the sounds. The higher frequencies of sound are inherently more directional than the lower frequencies.

This high-pass filter has a fixed cut-off rate (approximately 12 dB per octave) and a periodically varying cut-off frequency. For reasons of increased diversity, when all eight sound-modifier channels are used simultaneously, the filter cut-off frequency range is slightly different for each sound-modifier channel.

Proposal for Live Programming: *Sun(flower) Burst*

1. *Program concept*: visual and sound patterns analogous to and derived from the Fibonacci "spiral" sequences of sunflowers and the "sunburst" motion of cathode-ray tube displays

2. *Elements*: sound activities: tape-stored sound (continuous), live sound (intermittent); visual activities: light sequencing (continuous), dance movement (intermittent)

3. *Cycle time*: approximately fifteen minutes

4. *Cycle continuity*: two basic procedures applied to the sound and visual activities, in four combinations:

   a. sound and visual activities both begin with high rates of information and gradually decrease to low rates of information;
   b. sound and visual activities both begin with low rates of information and gradually increase to high rates of information;
   c. sound activity begins with high rates of information, visual activity begins with low rates of information; sound activity decreases while visual activity increases;
   d. sound activity begins with low rates of information, visual activity begins with high rates of information; sound activity increases while visual activity decreases.

5. *Visual activity requirements*: lighting facilities of the pavilion, augmented by special miniature light devices operated by two or three dancers. The dance activity is integrated with and responds to the programmed light and sound sequences.

6. *Sound activity requirements*: stored material on magnetic tape, heard through the sound facilities of the pavilion, augmented by live miniature sounds within the pavilion. The sound materials will be subjected to modification (a) by the sound-modifier console and (b) by certain unique resonant characteristics of the pavilion dome and its associated microphone system and rhombic loud-speaker grid.

7. *General operating procedure*: the cycle continuity will be established in a relevant pattern that alternates among the four combinations of cycle continuity described in section 4.

Any cycle or sequence of cycles can operate with a minimum of two of the elements described in section 2. One element will always be a sound activity, and the other will always be a visual activity. This minimal procedure will allow effective operation of the program when no live performers are present.

The live performers are a fundamental diversification of the *Sun(flower) Burst* program. A performance area will be required for the dancers. The nature of this area is not critical and can be established within the realistically usable facilities of the pavilion. The dancers are professional performers who will be in Osaka at the time of the program.

CHAPTER 11

What We Did Last Summer
A Commentary on ICES 1972
(1973)

The First Festival of Live-Electronic Music was presented jointly at the University of California, Davis, and Mills College in 1967. It established, with a kind of formality required by many, the validity of live-electronic music. Now five years later, with the more inclusive name ICES [International Carnival of Experimental Sound], several generations of live-electronic musicians in a medium hardly old enough to have reached puberty were accessible in (almost) one place and time for two weeks of "Myth, Magic, Madness and Mysticism." If ICES 1972 didn't always live up to its promotion, it was a remarkable occasion.[1]

Its context was London, with its long tradition of patriotic obsession with the arts. Youth culture aside, the sociology of its performance arts remains rather conservative. Its contemporary composers and performers include a leading edge of experimenters, but I would hesitate to use the term "avant-garde" to describe that edge. The "now" heroes of the London music scene tend to be between ages 30 and 50 and include several people associated with the film and entertainment world such as Richard Rodney Bennett, André Previn, and the young "exotic" Stomu Yamash'ta. The underground "leading edge" is by no means ignored by the London arts community, but the activities of its participants are decidedly uncomfortable, if not disreputable, for the polite majority.

Cornelius Cardew is perhaps the best-known international "underground" personality in London, a status achieved through the diversity of his work, his

Source: Written on the road in London, Warsaw, and New York from September 1972 to February 1973, this previously unpublished review was prepared for the cancelled *Source* 12, projected for 1974.

relative longevity on the scene, and his association with Stockhausen. Cardew's recent political evolution into an openly proselytizing Marxist-Maoist spokesman has made him the sensational bad boy of a good many events, from cocktail parties of the intelligentsia to establishment concerts. Hugh Davies also carries an international reputation, though presently more for his editing of a monumental electronic music catalog than for his own intriguing work.[2] Besides his membership in two performance groups, Gentle Fire (which also includes Richard Bernas, Graham Hearn, Stuart Jones, and Michael Robinson) and Naked Software (with John Lifton, Anna Lockwood, Harvey Matusow, and Howard Rees), Davies is also an inventor of electro-acoustical instruments and an innovative composer. Both Gentle Fire and Naked Software are electro-acoustical ensembles involved with experimental and improvisational performance procedures. They seem to be the exceptions. Most of the other underground groups (such as Roger Smalley and Tim Souster's ensemble Intermodulation, and Eddie Prévost's improvisation group AMM) are fundamentally acoustical or are dominated by more traditional structural idioms such as jazz and notated scores.

Access to the new-music scene in London is fairly easy, partly because of the large quantity of writing about it in magazines and at least a dozen newspapers with serious arts critics. Despite the press attention, new music and dance in London suffer from lack of funds. Years of serious inflation have left much of London's population on the edge of survival, and official (British Arts Council) subsidies have been slow to respond to the needs of innovative artists.

Though ICES 1972 happened in London, it did not seem very British. It was the brainchild of the New York–born Harvey Matusow, apparently as a gift to the New Zealand composer Anna Lockwood.[3] Harvey did it in London just like it's done in New York, hustling in all directions at once. As a result almost impossible things happened with ease, simple details became impossible, an enormous financial deficit accumulated, and a staggering number of performances took place.

The basic premise and the key to the artistic success of ICES 1972 was that everyone was invited. This may also help explain why the London press did not respond with more serious attention. The style of promotion, a decidedly non-British mixture of New York "schlock" and California "happening," created a difficult-to-focus response in both the London public and the international participants. Many people simply did not believe it was going to happen.

Happen it did, for two relentless weeks (August 13–26) simultaneously in several parts of London and along the welded-rail roadbed of the Flying Scotsman on a chartered Music Train all the way to Edinburgh. Most of the performances occurred in the Roundhouse (a British Arts Council project near the Chalk Farm tube stop), at The Place (a busy modern dance center established a few years ago by Robin Howard), and in a recent experimental space called Global Village. There was no possible way to attend even half of ICES 1972.

Two results of the "everyone is invited" premise were gratifying. First, no one seemed to worry much about categories: rock bands, straight academia, electric folk, video art, tribal improvisation, dance environments, experimental film and video, one-man bands, a philharmonic choir, bio-electronics, conceptual events, and a good bit for which I'm hard pressed to find words. Second, deterred by conflicts with paying engagements elsewhere or by the lack of personal attention to which they were accustomed, some of the well-known "heavies" declined invitations to participate. More room was thus available for groups from all over the world (excepting only Africa, Antarctica, and Greenland). As a result, ICES 1972 provided a closer approach to a realistic cross-section of the new-music culture than usually happens at festivals. I meet many new-music people during the thirty or more weeks each year that I perform on tour. For the past fifteen years these contacts have been supplemented by exchanges of correspondence and tapes and more recently by sieving the commerce that flows through New York City. I had not heard live or met about half of the participants.

It has been difficult for me to evaluate the experience of ICES 1972 and its complex cross-section of new music because I was equally focused on how the participants and audience saw it. Here was a situation I should have foreseen: the strong representation from the United States made some participants from the British Commonwealth and many from Europe uncomfortable, if not downright hostile. The recent American reputation for militarism, racism, and economic exploitation are a part of the problem, but there is also the shock that occurs when innovative cultural manifestations from the United States are experienced directly by many Europeans, both young and old. It was a difficult task to reconcile my delight at the gentle, sometimes bizarre wit of a performance by Jerry Hunt and Houston Higgins with a Belgian's response that it reminded her of "two U.S. Marines messing up an Indo-Chinese jungle." My enthusiasm for Stanley Lunetta's electronic-percussion group Valhalla ARMA/AMRA was countered by a Dutch participant who found it "oppressively militaristic, like the U.S. Army Band." Cardew, for example, has come to reject the American achievements as "elitist." The reasons, influenced by the somewhat dilettantish interest of younger British intellectuals in Chairman Mao, are too involved to consider here.

While on the subject of my favorites, I should mention the Michel Waisvisz–Willem Breuker Show from the Netherlands and the Portsmouth Sinfonia from

England. Waisvisz and Breuker have built their own electronic music apparatus, one collection of which is worn like the barrel organ of an Amsterdam street musician. And how to describe the Portsmouth Sinfonia? They do something that could only happen (and flourish, perhaps) in England. They play the classical "chestnuts" (Beethoven, Rossini, Tchaikovsky) specially scored for performers who can barely play their instruments at the level of fourth-graders. But they rehearse to the extent that they achieve a unique quality of ensemble, and the result is so beautiful that I must beg the inability to describe it. I was also interested in Teletopa (David Ahern, Roger Frampton, and Peter Evans) partly because they came from Australia and have done original work in that country. They did not fare particularly well in the international context of ICES 1972, but that is an irrelevant comment to make about people who risk being pioneers in faraway places.

The above-mentioned activities were all at the Roundhouse. The Place presented many of the dance events. The Place is dominated by the technique and spirit of Martha Graham. In the British and European context The Place seems at present to be the best hope for the development of modern dance as something other than an American achievement. Marilyn Wood, formerly of the Merce Cunningham Dance Company, brought her Celebrations Group for a dance and music event in busy King's Cross train station [fig. II-10]. A happy discovery for me was the dance group called Strider, the nucleus of which includes Richard Alston, Christopher Banner, Jacqueline Lansley, and Wendy Levett. They work mostly collaboratively, enlisting other musicians and artists for their particular skills. Artistically and socially, Strider is at a place in history similar to that of the Judson Dance Theater in New York a decade ago. Their chances of survival may not be the same because the cultural milieu of London now is quite different from that of New York then. But they were a special inspiration to me as pioneers in the midst of a kind of plenty in the cultural energy of London. By the end of ICES 1972, many of my best wishes were reserved for Strider.

In the spirit of ICES 1972 it is not really fair to speak of only a few of the participants. But my alternatives are complicated by distractions such as the invigorating trip to Edinburgh, leaning out of the window toward the afternoon-sun-brilliant seacoast on the Music Train speeding between Tweedmouth and Eyemouth, Scotland.

The festival confirmed my conviction that the greatest diversity and highest technical and artistic achievements in live-electronic music and experimental sound are presently to be found in the United States. The reasons for this include a more culturally diverse population and less intimidation by the cultural establishments. Perhaps more important, electronic technology is more advanced and diverse in the United States, and access to that technology is easier.

Fig. II-10. Marilyn Wood and the Celebrations Group at King's Cross Station, London, during the August 1972 ICES Festival. (Photo © Gordon Mumma.)

Britain seems to hold second place in this respect, and it is difficult to say if some European country or Japan follows. There was perhaps not enough representation from Europe at ICES 1972. Yet my experience indicates that, aside from the activities of the Italian-American group Musica Elettronica Viva or Stockhausen and the "avant-garde pop" movement in Germany, live-electronic music is relatively few years under way in Europe. Britain is better under way for several reasons. First, they have two manufacturers of live-performance electronic music synthesizers, one of which, the EMS Synthi, is widely used. They also have London itself, which in recent years has become more culturally vital than any city in Europe. Finally, the social consciousness in contemporary Britain is reflected in the concerns of many younger artists about what they should be doing with their art. The Portsmouth Sinfonia, Cornelius Cardew, and the Scratch Orchestra are good examples. Though they avoid the use of electronic technology (in one instance because "it is too elitist to be of immediate use to the masses"), they have demonstrated with considerable success that new music can be innovative and useful, both socially and musically.

Is there a possibility of more ICES? The cultural interchange of ICES 1972 has refreshed the London arts scene with what looks to be a lasting effect. Yet its impact is overshadowed by a demoralizing sense of finite resources in London, nurtured by the coexistence of abundant cultural activity within widespread poverty and a rapidly rising cost of living. I encountered these concerns in constant complaints such as "ICES might be a good idea, but it's taking all the money and attention" or "If Harvey succeeds it's going to be difficult to do anything in the future." I do not generally share these concerns. In my experience an innovative use of resources usually develops new resources, though during ICES 1972 I found it difficult to comfort many of the British and European participants with this opinion.

If ICES is really international, perhaps it should move around, for the stimulating discomfort that ICES 1972 created for London could be just as beneficial somewhere else. If this is an idea whose time has come, it might achieve international performance standards akin to the ways in which composers of new music are already working and audiences are beginning to expect.

CHAPTER 12

Two Decades of Live-Electronic Music, 1950–70

(1975)

During the 1950s and '60s three forms of electronic media were used for the creation of live-electronic music. The first form involved the emerging technology of the magnetic tape recorder, which was generally available a few years after the Second World War and stimulated a rapid increase in electronic-music activity from 1950 on. Magnetic tape was the first storage medium for sound that was reasonably editable: it could be accurately cut and spliced. During the 1950s most composers treated magnetic tape in a "hands-on" manner analogous to that of filmmakers. As with film, tape music was composed largely through editing. Until 1960 there were few exceptions to the use of magnetic tape as a studio medium. These exceptions began to appear in the late 1950s and increased rapidly throughout the 1960s. Some composers used taped sound in live concert with instruments or voices. Others explored the use of tape in innovative performance situations without referring to traditional music; or they developed real-time studio techniques that were in a sense live performances, using tape only to record the results for distribution.

More significant, some composers discarded the tape medium as a musical premise and explored the use of electronic devices, separately and in conjunction with acoustic instruments, as a component for live performance.

Source: Excerpted from Mumma, "Live-Electronic Music," in *The Development and Practice of Electronic Music,* ed. Jon H. Appleton and Ronald C. Perera, 286–335 (Englewood Cliffs, N.J.: Prentice-Hall, 1975), © 1975 Prentice-Hall, Inc. Reprinted with revision by permission of Pearson Education, Inc., Upper Saddle River, N.J. The excerpt reissued here (pp. 292–300, 318–19) includes cuts of redundant material and other editorial revisions, and a new section on Mumma's *Conspiracy 8* (see note 5).

Finally, analog and digital computers became increasingly valuable tools for musical composition and sound synthesis, and by 1970 they were variously applied as live-performance instruments.[1]

Live Performance of Instruments with Tape

Composers who use magnetic tape continuously experimented with ways to present their work to audiences. Broadcast and recording are successful media because they allow the audience to determine for themselves how they listen. Playing tapes for audiences in the concert hall is another matter. Audiences expect to see as well as hear a performance, and loudspeakers aren't much to look at.

Furthermore, many composers who work with tape still compose for conventional instruments and have specific ideas on how to combine the media. Edgard Varèse's classic *Déserts* (1949–52) alternates conventional instruments and taped sounds, producing the effect of a monumental sound sculpture. Two additional examples are the collaborative compositions by Otto Luening and Vladimir Ussachevsky, *Rhapsodic Variations* (1953–54) and *A Poem in Cycles and Bells* (1954), both for tape recorder and orchestra, which by the mid-1950s had reached the American public through broadcast and recording.

Parts of Varèse's *Déserts* were completed in Paris, where before 1955 other works for acoustical instruments and tape had been composed by Paul Boisselet, Pierre Henry, André Hodier, Darius Milhaud, and Pierre Schaeffer. From 1955 to 1960 the repertory for instruments and tape was expanded by works from Belgium (Louis de Meester, Henri Pousseur), England (Roberto Gerhard), Germany (Mauricio Kagel, Karlheinz Stockhausen), Italy (Luciano Berio, Luigi Nono), the Netherlands (Henk Badings), Japan (Kuniharu Akiyama, Shin'ichi Matsushita, Makato Moroi, Joji Yuasa), and the United States (John Cage, Richard Maxfield, John Herbert McDowell, Gordon Mumma, Robert Sheff, Morton Subotnick). In the 1960s works for this medium also came from Canada, Latin America, Israel, and other European countries.

The sounds assembled on tape had many acoustic and electronic sources. A few composers, however, were more interested in electronic synthesis than in tape composition. For Milton Babbitt magnetic tape was primarily a way of storing the music that he had composed with the RCA Mark II Synthesizer. Babbitt also synthesized music that was stored on tape but was intended for live performance, such as his *Vision and Prayer* (1961) and *Philomel* (1964), both for soprano and recorded synthesized sounds.

The ways of combining instruments with tape and the methods of coordination are diverse. In Berio's *Differences* (1958–60) and Kagel's *Transición II*

(1958–59), the tape and instrumental sounds occur in ensemble. The tape at times sounds like a natural extension of the live instruments from which it derives. Mario Davidovsky's *Synchronisms I-III* (1963–65) and Gerhard's orchestral *Collages* (1960) use taped sounds of electronic origin with acoustical instrumental ensembles.

Live musicians must in most cases follow the tempo established on the tape. Some composers have invented special notation for the tape-stored sound and have added it to the musical notation of the instrumental parts. Over reasonably short durations, even with complex tape sounds, instrumentalists have found it practical to learn the tape "by ear," so that in Davidovsky's *Synchronisms*, for example, very strict timing is achieved. Another synchronizing procedure uses a special track of multi-channel tape for cues that the instrumentalist hears through headphones. An early example is Ramon Sender's *Desert Ambulance* (1964) for amplified accordion, stereo tape, and light projection. Sender used a special three-channel tape: two channels contained the stereo sounds heard by the audience, and the third, heard only by accordionist Pauline Oliveros, contained pitches, timing cues, and spoken instructions. In the *Lyric Variations for Violin and Computer* (1968), J. K. Randall synthesized the tape sounds with an IBM 7094 computer and also had the computer produce a metronome tape heard only by the violinist.

Many live instrument-with-tape compositions do not require precise synchronization. Indeed, some composers are interested in having the tape and live sounds occur quite independent of each other. A classic example is Cage's *Aria with Fontana Mix* (1958). Barney Childs's *Interbalances VI* (1964) requires the performers to prepare the tape from sounds and synchronization of their own making.

Performed Tape

In a collaborative tape-music project with Earle Brown, Morton Feldman, David Tudor, and Christian Wolff (with the technical assistance of Louis and Bebe Barron), Cage composed his *Williams Mix* (1952) for eight tracks of tape. The work has a score that constitutes a pattern for cutting and splicing the tapes, establishing an early premise for treating tape music as a non-fixed medium. Working at the Studio di Fonologia Musicale of Italian Radio (RAI) in Milan, Cage composed *Fontana Mix* (1958) for four tracks of tape. The score of *Fontana Mix* is used in live performance to modify and distribute the sounds in space. In Cage's *Rozart Mix* (1965) the performers, who may include members of the audience, supply tapes of sounds that are spliced into loops during performance for playing on a large ensemble of tape recorders. Other unusual applications of tape loops include Alvin Lucier's *The Only Talking Machine of Its Kind in the World* (1969) and Daniel Lentz's *Rice, Wax, and Narrative* (1970). Both use very long loops; in Lentz's piece the performers are encircled by the loops, while in Lucier's the entire audience is surrounded.

Robert Ashley's *The Fourth of July* (1960), a tape composition for theater as well as concert presentation, was made in a studio of the composer's design, which allowed for considerable real-time performance on the equipment. The multi-channel tape of Ashley's *Public Opinion Descends upon the Demonstrators* (1961) was performed live according to the interaction between a notated score and audience responses. The unusual works of Richard Maxfield, *Night Music* (1960), *Amazing Grace* (1960), and *Piano Concert for David Tudor* (1961), were composed on magnetic tape using his own live-performance studio techniques. Though belatedly recognized, his technical and musical procedures are now widely imitated.

Employing many innovative studio procedures, Pauline Oliveros composed a series of real-time stereophonic tape compositions in 1966, of which her *I of IV* is perhaps best known. At the same time, Terry Riley developed a live, polyphonic, solo-performance interaction among tape recorders, soprano saxophone, and electric organ used in compositions such as *A Rainbow in Curved Air* (1968) and *Poppy Nogood and the Phantom Band* (1966).

On commission from the Japan Broadcasting Corporation (NHK) in Tokyo in 1966, Karlheinz Stockhausen began his *Solo für Melodieinstrument mit Rückkopplung*. This open-structured work requires precisely fixed time delays achieved by means of a magnetic tape feedback loop. The precision necessary for these time delays was not efficiently achieved until a few years later with the construction of a special mechanism of adjustable playback heads.

Other composers explored tactics to overcome the theatrical weakness of the genre and infuse a live-performance component into tape music. Unusual examples are *MAP/1* and *MAP/2* (1969) by trumpeter Jon Hassell, who composed these works on large sheets of magnetic tape. The performers selected from the stored sounds by moving hand-held playback heads across the magnetized oxide surface of these sheets.

Live-Electronic Music without Tape (Amplified Small Sounds, Performed Electronic Equipment)

Electronic amplification had been used in music before the Second World War to make traditional instruments louder and to develop electronic instruments, as in Cage's *Imaginary Landscape No. 2* (1942). Cage's use of amplification was prophetic: instead of amplifying sounds that were simply not quite loud enough, he magnified micro-sounds that were practically inaudible without amplification, revealing a whole new world of sound resources. Following eight years of innovative work with the "prepared piano," Cage resumed composition for live-electronic means with *Imaginary Landscape No. 4* (1951) for twelve radios with twenty-four performers. This work, with *Radio Music* (1952), *Speech* (1955), and *Music Walk* (1958), explored the radio receiver as a live-performance instrument.

Following his use of contact microphones in *Imaginary Landscape No. 3* (1942), Cage did not return to their use until his *Winter Music* (1957) and *Variations II* (1961). David Tudor would further develop both as works for amplified piano. For *Winter Music* the piano part was performed from the keyboard and made ultra-loud; for *Variations II* contact microphones raised the micro-sounds from inside the piano to concert audibility. In 1960 Cage composed his *Music for Amplified Toy Pianos*, which used contact microphones, and the classic *Cartridge Music*, which used phonograph cartridges. These four Cage works were performed widely, particularly by Tudor and the composer, and were a considerable stimulus to experimentation in live-electronic music.

Only a few other composers worked with live-electronic music before 1960. In 1957 the members of the production group for *Manifestations: Light and Sound* in Ann Arbor began live performances of amplified small sounds, tape music, and light projection. In Ankara, Turkish composer Bülent Arel composed his *Music for String Quartet and Oscillator* in 1957. In New York, Dick Higgins composed *Graphis 24* for Theremin and feedback (1958) and Joe Jones created a menagerie of electrical, electronic, and mechanical instruments that on occasion could be heard performing by themselves in the lobbies of modern music concerts.

Live performance with amplified small sounds aided by the development of new live-performance electronic equipment became an important activity during the 1960s. It gradually attracted the attention of many who, philosophically committed to the tape medium, had previously dismissed live-performance electronics as an unworthy endeavor. Between 1960 and 1965 most live-electronic music activity occurred in the United States. It was nourished by both the spirited experimental music milieu and the solid-state electronic technology readily accessible there. The Americans who composed for live-electronic performance during these years included Robert Ashley, Philip Corner, Max Deutsch, John Eaton, Alvin Lucier, Gordon Mumma, Max Neuhaus, and David Tudor. Outside the United States, similar work was under way by Takehisa Kosugi in Japan, Gil Wolman in France, Karlheinz Stockhausen in Germany, and Giuseppe Chiari in Italy. From 1966 through 1970 live-electronic music multiplied rapidly, the majority of activity still in the United States. Live-electronic music compositions were occasionally issued on commercial recordings and were performed widely enough in concerts to establish a sense of repertory for the growing audiences interested in new music.

In the repertory of live-electronic music the continuing work of Cage in the 1960s assumes large proportions. His *Music for Carillon No. 4* (1961) with microphone feedback continues the series of works for electronic carillon begun in 1952. *Atlas Eclipticalis* (1961–62) is a work for large ensemble with variable electronic modification. Cage's series *Variations,* numbered from I to VIII, begun in 1958 and completed in 1968, holds far-reaching implications for ensemble performances of live-electronic music. By various elegant innovations in graphic notation, he specified the circumstances and outlined the procedures for each *Variation.* These works are plans for societies of activity, not necessarily limited to musical activity, and as good plans should, they allow for the updating of electronic and other means to achieve their ends.

Cage's *HPSCHD* (1969), completed in collaboration with composer Lejaren Hiller at the University of Illinois, combines up to fifty-one computer-synthesized tapes with live performance of seven amplified harpsichords, tuned microtonally. The first performance of *HPSCHD* took place in a very large round sports stadium with the seven harpsichords in a circle, leaving the audience free to remain in the bleacher-like area around the stadium or move into the center of the space itself, near the harpsichords. The speakers for the tape-recorded sounds were placed equidistantly around the perimeter of the stadium. The seven speakers from the amplified harpsichords were placed in an inner circle. There were eighty slide projectors, one hundred moving pictures, and eight thousand slides of travels through space and such things, so that visually one was seeing the world as if from a telescope in space. Some of the slide projectors flashed images on rectangular outdoor screens, so that from outdoors one got a visual impression of what was happening inside. When the five-hour performance was over the outdoor projectors were still working because it had been difficult to turn them all off.[2]

Closely associated with Cage, David Tudor was responsible for much of the technological and performance reification of these works. Tudor devoted much of his time in the 1960s to promoting and performing live-electronic music of other composers. He also emerged as a composer in his own right with *Fluorescent Sound* (1964), *Bandoneon ! (A Combine)* (1966), and *Rainforest* (1968).[3]

Max Neuhaus, a virtuoso percussionist and sound-installation artist, has not only applied complex electronic amplification to works of other composers—such as Earle Brown's *Four Systems* (1964), Sylvano Bussotti's *Coeur pour batteur* (1965), and Cage's *Fontana Mix-Feed* (1965) —but has also developed his own electronic works for public participation. In *Public Supply* (1966) the public is invited to telephone a radio or TV station to have their voices immediately modified and combined in the transmission. In *Drive-in Music* (1967) a series of weather-sensing, low-power radio transmitters was installed along a road in Buffalo, New York, so that the commuting public heard the effects of the changing climate on their automobile radios.

New York–based composer David Behrman also builds his own electronic music equipment. His live-electronic music has evolved to include the use of acoustic feedback with conventional instruments in his *Wave Train* (1966), the coordinated use of equalization and frequency shifting of instrumental sounds in his *Players with Circuits* (1967), and the construction of an elaborate ensemble of electronic instruments for *Runthrough* (1968).[4] *Runthrough* consists of oscillators, frequency shifters, voltage-controlled amplifiers, and a photo-electric sound distribution matrix; it is performed by three or more players with miniature flashlights. Behrman designed the interacting circuit configuration so that the various actions of the players with their flashlights do not necessarily produce one-to-one musical correspondences. His most recent work includes the construction of a purely electronic synthesizer with analog integrated circuits. It can be performed live by an ensemble of players or can be performed alone, making sliding chords of precisely tuned, complex intervals and spinning its gently shifting sonorities into a ballad-like continuity [fig. II-11].

By virtue of their wide performance and acclaim among audiences for new music, several live-electronic works have become staples of the repertory. Robert Ashley's *The Wolfman* (1964), for highly amplified human voice with tape accompaniment, and Salvatore Martirano's *L's GA* (1968) [Lincoln's Gettysburg Address], performed by a gas-masked actor in an atmosphere modulated by helium, stereo tape, and film projection, have theatrical, political, and musical impact. Pauline Oliveros has contributed a series of apparently self-sustaining works for amplified apple boxes, including *Applebox* (1964), *Applebox Double* (1965), *Applebox Orchestra* (1966), and *Applebox Orchestra with Bottle Chorus* (1970). Roger Reynolds's widely performed *Ping* (1968) is a multimedia work after a story by Samuel Beckett for ring-modulated and electronically distributed instruments (multiphonic flute, motorized piano, harmonium, bowed cymbal, and tam-tam), magnetic tape, and projected images with calligraphy. Reynolds's *Traces* (1969) and *Again* (1970) extend his integration of acoustic and live-electronic procedures.

A significant aspect of the work of Behrman, Neuhaus, Martirano, and others such as David Rosenboom, Serge Tcherepnin, and Stanley Lunetta is that they

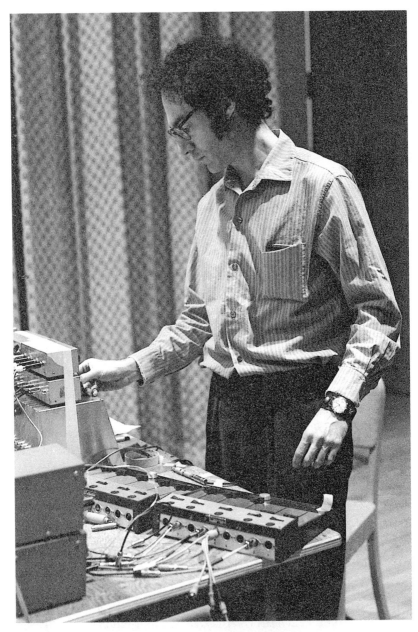

Fig. II-11. David Behrman setting up *sine rise* at the Metropolitan Museum of Art, New York, February 19, 1972. (Photo © Gordon Mumma.)

design and build their own electronic music instruments. A formal education in electronics is advantageous but not mandatory in order to create live-electronic music, particularly since commercial synthesizers have been developed for use in live performance. John Eaton, Max Deutsch, and David Borden were involved in the early use of synthesizers as live-performance instruments. In 1965 Eaton composed and performed works with the Syn-Ket, a portable synthesizer developed by Paul Ketoff in Rome. In the same year Deutsch composed in the United States two live-performance works that combined the Moog synthesizer with conventional instruments. A long-lived synthesizer ensemble was established by David Borden with the title Mother Mallard's Portable Masterpiece Company, seen in action with its fleet of Moog synthesizers in figure II-12.

Beyond the United States, live-electronic music activity emerged in Japan, where Takehisa Kosugi composed *Micro 1* (1961) for solo microphone. Beginning in 1967, Kosugi composed several poetic works titled *Mano Dharma* and *Eclipse*, which used radio-frequency and audio-frequency electronics. Toshi Ichiyanagi composed works for electronically modified Western and Japanese instruments, including *Space* (1966), *Situation* (1966), *Activities for Orchestra* (1962), and *Appearance* (1967). Ichiyanagi did not design his own equipment; instead he specified the electronic "instrumentation" and configuration of his pieces, much as a composer would enumerate the types and arrangement of conventional instruments, relying on the performers to supply the equipment and skill. In Italy, Domenico Guaccero introduced his *Improvvisazione 1962* in Rome; from 1964 through 1966, Giuseppe Chiari composed a series of live-electronics works using contact microphones, notably *Il silenzio (musica-verità)* (1965); and in 1966 Luigi Nono composed *A floresta é jovem e cheja de vida* for singers, instruments, and tape with electronic filters.

Of the German composers working with live-electronic media, Stockhausen has attracted attention, particularly in Europe, where most of his compositions are available on recordings and repeatedly broadcast. His large body of composition is diverse in style and idea, due to his expansive imagination as well as to his considerable facility in absorbing the procedures of other composers' work into his own. Following *Kontakte* (1960) for percussion and magnetic tape, Stockhausen's next live-electronic works were *Mikrophonie I* (1964) for amplified and electronically filtered tam-tam; *Mixtur* (1964) for five instrumental ensembles with sine wave oscillators and ring modulators; and *Mikrophonie II* (1965) for chorus, Hammond organ, and ring modulators. *Prozession* (1967) for amplified and filtered chamber ensemble and *Stimmung* (1968) for amplified singers soon followed. His *Aus den sieben Tagen* (1968) for a variable ensemble with indeterminate electronic modification employs graphic and verbal notation, and has

Fig. II-12. Mother Mallard's Portable Masterpiece Company performing on its ensemble of Moog sythesizers live at the broadcast studio of WBAI, New York, January 22, 1972. L to R: David Borden, Linda Fisher, and Steve Drews. (Photo © Gordon Mumma.)

evolved through performance into an attractively lyrical work of many hours' duration, similar in scope to the earlier *Treatise* (1967) by Cornelius Cardew.

Composer and violist Johannes Fritsch, independent of the usual German state-radio resources, has composed several works for instruments and live-electronic apparatus, including *Partita* (1965–66) for viola, contact microphone, tape, and equalization. Fritsch is a member of the independent German group "Feedback," organized in 1970, whose members also include Peter Eötvös, Rolf Gehlhaar, David Johnson, Mesias Maiguashca, John McGuire, and Michael von Biel.

Live Performance with Digital Computers

The digital computer is a configuration of logic modules to which are added an enlarged memory and various access and control functions. Logic modules are most commonly designed for specific functions in live-electronic music equipment and are not externally programmable to any great extent. With integrated circuitry, logic modules can become relatively involved, as in the 16-bit digital computer/decoder used in Stanley Lunetta's *Moosack Machine* (1970). Logic modules can be designed with memory functions and can be externally pro-grammed. Digital computers have found limited use in live performance due to their massive size. Either the live performance must be taken to the computer, or it must be connected to a remote computer by a data link. A common data link is a telephone line, with the computer at one end and a teletype among the live performers at the other.

This procedure was used for my *Conspiracy 8* (1970), a collaborative work with MIT engineer-mathematician Stephen Smoliar that used MIT's large PDP-6 digital computer with teletype communication.[5] Smoliar designed the sophis-ticated computer programming and its interactivity with my sound making, while I contributed the general architecture, timings, and live sound materials.

Aside from its title, *Conspiracy 8* avoids overt polemical commentary on the Chicago Conspiracy Trial, which had recently ended, with its eight—then seven—defendants plus Judge Julius Hoffman and many others. It is a social rather than a political piece, a theater of communication under hazardous condi-tions. It can have up to eight or more performers who bring to it whatever they wish. In an interaction of diverse personalities, the forces of social regulation (overseen by the PDP-6 computer) are neither predictable nor necessarily just. The viability and survival of a democratic ensemble implies—and virtually requires—a condition of constantly changing allegiances, raising unsolvable questions of conspiracy and reactions of repression.

The first performance at the Artificial Intelligence Laboratory of MIT took place on February 20, 1970—as it turned out, the final day of the Chicago trial. It featured two live performers, myself on bowed musical saw processed with cybersonics, and Smoliar at the (audible) teletype console, communicating in real time with the large PDP-6 computer. Table 1 provides a structural overview of *Conspiracy 8* from the recording of the MIT premiere before an amused (or bemused) specialist audience of computer scientists and mathematicians (is-sued on NWR 80632-2). The performance includes random bits of conversation between the performers and several spontaneous bursts of audience laughter, which act as unforeseen structural markers for the four major sections in the interaction of the acoustical and cybersonic saw, teletype, and computer.

The difficulties of taking a digital-computer work on tour remain daunting because of its dependence on a technological behemoth. When *Conspiracy 8* was performed live at the Guggenheim Museum in New York by members of the Sonic Arts Group with Smoliar on March 25, 1970, the live link with the PDP-6 computer in Cambridge, Massachusetts, was effected by the emerging technol-ogy of high-speed telephone lines. Using this data link, the remote computer received information about the performance and made decisions according to its basic program. The computer thus participated as a decision-making mem-

Table 1. Gordon Mumma and Stephen Smoliar, *Conspiracy 8* (1970),
as performed at MIT, February 20, 1970 (NWR 80632-2)

0:02	*Introduction:* teletype with electronic and computer responses
2:13	Short bursts of talk between the performers, with intermittent audience sounds
3:58	[Laughter 1] Setup of musical saw
4:12	*Part 1:* Musical saw solo begins
4:43	Teletype returns, with saw
	Computer gathers processing data
5:52	[Laughter 2] Introduction of cybersonic saw
6:02	*Part 2:* Solo cybersonic saw, with teletype
7:08	[Laughter 3] Computer responds
8:14	*Part 3:* Computer and saw player respond interactively; audience talking and laughing intermittently
10:40	The interactive processing grows more complicated
11:01	Thick repetitions lasting almost a minute
12:14	Transition to spatial reverb
13:09	*Part 4:* Pitch of C# is sustained in the saw
14:33	Electronic sound is articulated by saw with quiet background of teletype
16:06	Repeated pitch of G; F# and G waver
16:52	High-frequency sustained saw serves as cue to end; teletype continues rhythmic articulation
17:51	Cadence provided when Smoliar audibly slides his chair away from the teletype
17:59	End

ber of the ensemble, and the ensemble accepted the sonic contributions of its electronic decision-making, which were relayed back to New York by a second data link.

With the advent around 1970 of portable mini-computers that include a memory capacity of several thousand words, cost only a few thousand dollars, and occupy only a few cubic feet of space, the digital computer is now a practical live-performance instrument. With a basic program and micro-routines stored in its memory, the mini-computer is performed live by choosing from among its micro-routines. The complexity of the interactions and the rates of speed with which they can be made surpass any non-computerized live-electronic musical instrument. In the future a machine pre-programmed for specific tasks may be able to ease the composer's burden of working with a large configuration of electronic equipment.

If we admit of musical performance as social intercourse, then we may include the varieties of artificial intelligence in our musical ensemble, not merely for their sophistication and speed but also for their "personalities." We may treat artificial intelligence not as a slave but as a collaborative equal in a democratic musical society.

CHAPTER 13

Witchcraft, Cybersonics, and Folkloric Virtuosity

(1975)

In the eighteenth century the Jaquet-Droz Grotto, a mechanical landscape-automaton, was exhibited throughout Europe. Approximately one meter square in size, it was an exceptional example of clockwork art. Its clockwork landscape contained grazing cattle and sheep, singing birds and barking dogs, flowing streams and fountains, and people in promenade, with the sun and moon following their daily paths. The Grotto was a celebrated entertainment as it traveled through Europe. When it reached Spain, however, it was confiscated by the Spanish authorities and destroyed as a demonic manifestation, a threat to the church, and a danger to the culture of Spain.

The Spanish of the time were also settling in the New World and establishing religious missions in California. The spiritual influence of early Spanish culture is still important in California. It is now mixed with the spiritual ways of the indigenous peoples and the immigrant Asians and European Protestants. Witchcraft and occultism are part of the spiritual legacy—and politics—of California.

I have been in northern California this past year, establishing contemporary performance arts activities at the new University of California campus at Santa Cruz. Santa Cruz is an incredibly beautiful part of California, situated among giant ancient redwood trees overlooking Monterey Bay on the Pacific Ocean. There I collaborated with composer-musicologist William Brooks, students at the university, and people from the surrounding community in indoor and

Source: An extended version of this essay was presented at the Ferienkurse, Darmstadt, on July 24, 1974, and published in *Darmstädter Beiträge zur neuen Musik* 14 (1975): 71–77, © Gordon Mumma; reprinted with revisions.

outdoor performances of new music, theater, and dance throughout the year. We presented as diverse aspects as possible of contemporary culture: music of Webern, Cage, and Alec Templeton; theater of Edward Albee and Walter Marchetti's *Zaj* collective; and original work of the people living in Santa Cruz.

On our first concert I performed my *Schoolwork* (1970) for musical saw. It was not controversial. One of our collaborators was a carpenter, cabinetmaker, and jazz clarinetist named Paul Stricklin. He made a composition for a later performance in April 1974 at the University Theater. Stricklin's sonorous *Cradle Song* was scored for a quartet of gasoline-powered chainsaws and conductor. In front of each chainsaw performer was a wooden cradle that held a large redwood log. The logs were cut in half on cues from the conductor. Though the audience was enthusiastic, a serious controversy ensued when a group of witches in the community protested the imposition of mechanical devices on the sacred redwoods.

Some of the cultural activities unique to this part of northern California push the boundaries of European-influenced concepts of art. Just north of Santa Cruz at Greyhound Rock a dozen people work with a mystical artist named Gary Aro Ruble. At night they transform large areas into performances. One performance occurred at a Pacific Ocean beach surrounded by mountain caves. With a red railroad flare one performer traced a long path along the barely visible beam of a helium-neon laser, which was directed outward from inside a cave. After this task was completed the laser was shifted a few degrees and the performer made another tracing, continuing this process until several traces were completed. Simultaneously a large sailboat was dragged from the ocean across the beach and up into the mountains. Every few meters the sailboat would stop and a red or blue strobe light would flash behind the triangular sail.

Throughout other parts of the night landscape, a small circle of dancers moved. At each new position a hand-held strobe light flashed, making the dancers momentarily visible. This performance ritual lasted throughout the night. The only spectator was a large sheet-film camera overlooking the scene from the ridge of a nearby mountain. The camera shutter was open for the entire night, capturing on a single sheet of color film a single, time-telescoped, Breughel-like image. Ruble calls the photographic memory of each performance a "PowerFlick."[1]

The United States has a long history of ruggedly individual creative artists such as Stricklin and Ruble. Some, like the composer Charles Ives, are well known. Technology is now one of the major fields of interest for many of these musical individualists, who reflect the general concern that technology be put to good use in the service of living creatures. Recent individualists of this inclination include the composers Salvatore Martirano, Alvin Lucier, Pauline Oliveros, Paul DeMarinis, and David Rosenboom.

Fig. II-13. Salvatore Martirano at the control panel of the Sal-Mar Construction, University of Illinois, December 1973. (Photo © Gordon Mumma.)

Martirano has a small but formidable list of compositions. Following his multi-media *L's G A* (1968), he began experimenting with digital computer technology in his studio at the University of Illinois. He went beyond standard programming procedures to create a unique live-performance electronic music instrument derived from digital computer procedures and known as the "Sal-Mar Construction" [fig. II-13]. Its sounds are initiated and controlled by the performer at a large keyboard panel that contains a complex matrix of touch-sensitive points arranged according to function. One group of twenty-four points corresponds to the twenty-four loudspeakers that project the sound to the audience. Other groups of points control entire sequences of musical continuity rather than individual pitches. The Sal-Mar Construction is a live-performance instrument of collaboration because its digital computer and memory functions share musical decisions at the process level with the human performer. One of Martirano's live performances with the Sal-Mar Construction has the bluntly descriptive title *Let's Look at the Back of My Head for a While* (1970).

In *The Queen of the South* (1972) by Connecticut composer Alvin Lucier, the visual environment is of equal importance to the sound materials. This environment has the character of an exotic ritual. The performers sing into microphones or produce sound with oscillators. By means of electromagnetic transducers,

Fig. II-14. Alvin Lucier examining the sand patterns created by sound vibrations in his
Queen of the South at The Kitchen, New York, March 1973. (Photo © Gordon Mumma.)

large steel plates suspended horizontally near the floor are made to vibrate with these sounds. The vibration patterns are made visible in the sand that the performers sprinkle onto these plates. As they change the pitches of their sounds the granular images on the plates shift from one pattern to another [fig. II-14]. The spectators move freely around these vibrating islands, choosing their own degree of involvement with the ritual.

Composer Pauline Oliveros, now working in California, is equally involved with both rational and non-rational aspects of music, including procedures of extra-sensory perception and telepathy. She is diversely skilled in instrumental and electronic music techniques. While working on her composition *In Memoriam: Nikola Tesla, Cosmic Engineer* (1968), commissioned for the Merce Cunningham Dance Company, she studied the many diverse scientific and industrial patents granted to Tesla, collected in a large book published by the Tesla Museum in Belgrade.[2] Oliveros found this book of Tesla patents at only one place in New York City: a bookstore specializing in occult literature. In recent tours Oliveros has presented *Sonic Meditations,* in which everyone participates. Her work has become an important influence on the way people think about music.

Also in California is Paul DeMarinis, a young composer who works with Robert Ashley. Like Martirano and Lucier, DeMarinis builds electronic instruments that perform alone or with human collaboration. DeMarinis builds his instruments with integrated circuits and uses digital shift-registers to determine musical continuity. He has named these instruments "Pygmy Gamelans," and their music uses the same "hocket" techniques practiced by various Southeast Asian and African peoples. No two of these Pygmy Gamelans are exactly alike. Though built of electronic components rather than acoustical materials, in many ways they are folkloric instruments.

David Rosenboom is one of several composers who integrate biophysical phenomena into their music. His New York Bio-Feedback Quartet is an ensemble in which four performers play commercial electronic music synthesizers. Some of the control signals for the music are obtained in the usual way, from the standard function-generator components of the synthesizers, while others are electro-encephalic currents obtained from electrodes attached directly to the heads of the performers.[3] These electro-encephalic alpha and theta signals control the amplitude and frequency of the synthesizer-generated sounds. For most people in the Western world these currents are involuntary manifestations of brain activity. Rosenboom and the members of the New York Bio-Feedback Quartet have developed skill in controlling these currents and consider them a reasonable extension of human activity into musical performance. For some it is as unsettling to see electrodes protruding from a person's head as it was for the California witches to see their trees violated by power saws. But many people now accept these procedures as normal after seeing electrodes covering the heads of our astronauts or the actors in Stanley Kubrick's film A *Clockwork Orange* or Michael Crichton's *Terminal Man*.

The work of the five composers I have mentioned is typical of the diverse new music activity in the United States, particularly outside New York City. Common among them is their attitude toward the use of electronic technology in their work. Rather than imposing the formalities of European concert traditions, they develop their art from their experiences with electronics and the diversity of the culture in which they live. My own live-electronic music explores similar principles. *Hornpipe* (1967) employs a cybersonic console by which the sounds are controlled by their own characteristics. For *Telepos* (1972), performed with Merce Cunningham's choreography *TV Rerun,* I made belts for the dancers containing small accelerometers, a voltage controlled oscillator, and a radio transmitter. Through a process called "telemetry" the dancers created the music by their movements in a process similar to that encountered in space travel, undersea, or biomedical research.

Much folkloric art is no less innovative in its virtuosity. Likewise, the innovative, virtuoso work I have mentioned is also in some sense folkloric. Although electronic technology is the manifestation of a highly literate society, it has many characteristics of non-literate art. None of it is mass produced, very little of it is notated, and it is mostly practiced by people who teach it directly to one another and distribute it by performance.

Though not everyone has equal access to electronic resources, one resource shared by all peoples is the human voice. There are many virtuoso examples of vocal innovation in folkloric traditions, such as the "sygyt" style of singing by the Tuvinians in Russian Central Asia, in which the oral cavity resonates the harmonics above a voiced fundamental pitch. An interesting variation of this procedure, practiced by the Nivkh peoples of Asia as well as by Central Africans, is the holding of a bowed string in the teeth so that the harmonics can be accentuated by the mouth resonances. To many European ears the Nivkh music sounds "electronic." Examples of hybrid instrumental-vocal procedures can be found in many non-literate parts of the world. The Australian aboriginals practice a skilled circular breathing technique while simultaneously blowing and singing into the didgeridoo, a wood stem instrument borrowed from the insects that have eaten a meandering tunnel through the marrow of the wood.

Recent innovations with the voice include works by Robert Ashley and Meredith Monk. For several years Ashley has been at work on his vocal-electronic hybrid *In Sara, Mencken, Christ and Beethoven There Were Men and Women.* The words from a poem by John Barton Wolgamot are spoken in a continuous, rapidly articulated phrase lasting forty minutes. The problem of breathing while speaking has been approached in several ways, including the obvious solution of alternating two performers. Its live-electronic sounds, developed in collaboration with Paul DeMarinis, occur automatically as a result of the inflections of the spoken text, which the performer adjusts according to the electronic responses.

People from non-literate societies often perform several activities simultaneously, such as the dancer who plays an instrument while singing. This kind of virtuosity is uncommon in Western literate arts. There are exceptions, such as Meredith Monk, a singer, dancer, and composer of poetic theater in the United States. She uses her voice in ways that exceed the accepted expressive gestures of Western art music.

I have suggested that all of this work, though of substantial virtuosity, is basically folkloric. This may seem an unorthodox perspective, but it makes possible several considerations. It is clear from our now relatively easy contact with the music and art of other cultures that everyone can be a virtuoso with the resources to which they have access. But those of us from Western technological cultures have access to more resources than do the peoples of the non-literate and "third-world" cultures. This inequitable distribution of resources has many causes and outcomes, the most complex being that of colonialist exploitation. Colonialism has been a part of history for so long that its origins are obscure, its victims weary with anger, and its solutions difficult. Performing artists can be a positive influence in redressing these inequalities by sharing their unique virtuosities on a person-to-person basis across cultures. The human and spiritual values manifested in the arts, particularly the folkloric arts, are universal resources that can help to overcome the uneasiness with cultural differences that pervades much of the world.

PART III

In the Cunningham Circle

Editor's Introduction

Gordon Mumma's entry into the creative circle of the Merce Cunningham Dance Company happened in stages.[1] Mumma met John Cage in 1953, drove overnight from Ann Arbor to attend piano recitals by David Tudor in New York, and provided technical assistance to Cage and Tudor for their May 1960 performances at Ann Arbor High School.[2] During the 1950s and early 1960s the Cunningham Dance Company toured the United States with Cage and Tudor—and sometimes Robert Rauschenberg—often appearing at colleges or universities. Mumma and Robert Ashley soon began canvassing to bring the Cunningham Dance Company to Ann Arbor: with the sponsorship of the Dramatic Arts Center, the company appeared at the Ann Arbor High School auditorium on December 4, 1961. The program included classic choreographies of the time: *Suite for Five* (with excerpts from Cage's *Music for Piano* performed in duo with Tudor), *Antic Meet* (with Cage's *Concert for Piano and Orchestra* with *Fontana Mix*), and *Crises* (with selected *Studies for Player Piano* by Conlon Nancarrow).[3]

In the wake of their monumental Lincoln Center *Variations V* of July 1965, it became clear that Cage and Tudor needed assistance with the expanding technology of their live-performance electronic collaborations. While they were performing together at the September 1965 ONCE AGAIN Festival in Ann Arbor, Cage and Tudor invited Mumma to join them for the upcoming European tour of the Cunningham Dance Company. In July 1966 Mumma and his wife Jackie [Jacqueline Leuzinger] left Ann Arbor to tour with the company; his first professional appearance with them was in Sitges, Spain, on July 29.[4] The connection was flexible from the start—no contracts needed—and as work progressed Mumma soon proved himself an indispensable member of the musical trio with Cage and Tudor.

During his seven full seasons with the Cunningham Dance Company, Mumma composed the music for two Cunningham choreographies, *Place* (1966) and *TV Rerun* (1972), and collaborated with Cunningham for *Loops* (1971) and with Cage and Tudor on the creation of the music for Cunningham's *Assemblage* (1968), *Signals* (1970), and *Landrover* (1972). He also performed with individual artists from the circle—such as Cage, Tudor, Rauschenberg, and dancers Barbara Lloyd, Steve Paxton, and Yvonne Rainer—in separate concerts and creative activities. Mumma observed dance classes and rehearsals of the company, often armed with camera or recording equipment, and witnessed at first hand the gestation of numerous Cunningham choreographies. As a result he became a skilled reader of the physical syntax of Cunningham's choreography and of its implications for musical composition. Mumma also appears in several early film documentaries of the Cunningham Dance Company, including the NDR-Hamburg filming of *Variations V* and German director Klaus Wildenhahn's *John Cage* (1966) and *498 Third Avenue* (1967).[5] He also participated in at least eighty Cunningham Events, one-time choreographic performances frequently combined with live-electronic music. His continuous connection with the company would end in the summer of 1973, when Mumma accepted a teaching position at the University of California, Santa Cruz. Officially listed in the company roster until 1975, he would retain to the present a vital connection with the Cunningham circle as guest musician, historian, advisor, and friend.

The "Mumma years" with the Merce Cunningham Dance Company correspond with a distinctive phase in its history. He joined the company at a time of rebuilding following the 1964 world tour that had brought it international attention but had left it on the brink of financial, physical, and emotional bankruptcy. The *Variations V* project (1965) indicated things to come in its unprecedented panoply of electronic equipment and its rigorously collaborative process. The later 1960s also witnessed the burgeoning of Cage's independent career as composer, literary figure, and visual artist, leaving the operation and maintenance of electronic sound increasingly to Tudor and Mumma, with the growing presence of David Behrman beginning in 1970. This period also witnessed Tudor's emergence as a notable composer of live-electronic music. During these years Mumma's work entered a new phase as well, shifting from discrete musical works (such as *Mesa* or *Hornpipe*) to "things that happen because of the circumstances" in which sound is generated by physical activity[6] (as in his *Ambivex* and *Telepos*).

The musicians of the Cunningham Dance Company had access to the standardized, mass-produced electronic music equipment developed after 1965, when the synthesizers of Robert Moog, Donald Buchla, and others became commercially available. But except for specifically practical devices such as tape recorders, mixers, and (from the 1980s) digital computers and sound-processing equipment, these musicians preferred the challenge, risk, and reward of electronic instrument building and system design. This resulted in nonstandard, often one-of-a-kind systems unique to each piece. The impetus of the inventor-explorer prevailed, in contrast to the rising tide of homogeneity in commercial electronic music of the time.

By 1973 the company was again in transition. New composers were widening the classic Cage-Mumma-Tudor trio. The shift away from the individual dancer that had characterized the choreographies of the 1950s and 1960s—the height of Cunningham's own career as a soloist of heroic brilliance—changed notably in the early 1970s to works increasingly featuring larger groups of dancers, mass effects, and unison choreography.[7] Film and video increasingly expanded electronic music as a partner to the dance, to be augmented by the glow of portable laptop computers in the orchestra pit of the 1990s.

Mumma's writings on the Cunningham milieu draw on his first-hand experience during these pivotal years. The previously unpublished "A Day on the Road with the Cunningham Dance Company" (1971) provides a glimpse of its day-to-day life on tour. "From Where the Circus Went" is a sweeping overview of Cunningham's choreographies until 1973 from the special perspective of a participating musician.[8] Written decades before David Vaughan's retrospective volume, Carolyn Brown's comprehensive memoir of her years in the company,[9] and the unprecedented access to documentary sources afforded by the Merce Cunningham Dance Capsules website,[10] Mumma's essay was the first account of its early history written from within the Cunningham circle. Originally published in 1975 as an extended excerpt of an unpublished larger study, the current version reinstates the missing material for the first time, including a major section on Cunningham's early Events and additional autograph materials from the author's drafts and diaries. Omitted from this volume, however, are Mumma's short "Four Sound Environments for Modern Dance" (1967) and the 1996 summary "Electronic Music for the Merce Cunningham Dance Company," both of which largely duplicate material appearing elsewhere in this volume. "Robert Rauschenberg in the Creative Fields of the Cunningham Dance Company" was one of Mumma's contributions to the 2012 John Cage centenary celebrations, presented at the Hirschhorn Museum in Washington, D.C. His decision to focus on another creative giant emphasizes the centrality of intermedia collaboration in the Cunningham milieu. The sequence closes with two essays on David Tudor completed in 2012–13 that sketch Tudor's evolution from organist to composer.

Mumma frequently speaks of the importance of Merce Cunningham to his own creative process as a composer. In some respects, the impact of Cunningham and

Rauschenberg was deeper than that of Cage. Cunningham's choreography for *Place* and Rauschenberg's light design for *Minutiae*, both analyzed in this part of the book, provide kinetic and visual analogues to the structural processes Mumma used in *Mesa* or *Conspiracy 8*. Especially relevant is the manner in which they interpolated discrete dramatic scenes or color modules within flexible units of time and space. As is the case with many Cunningham choreographies, the number and order of events in Mumma's music is often variable, determined for each performance. Especially significant to Mumma was Cunningham's model of artistic independence and respect for the individual in collaboration with others.

Fig. III-1. On the road with the Cunningham Dance Company, Schevenimgen, The Netherlands, July 1970. L to R: Charles Atlas, Gordon Mumma, Mimi Johnson, and Carolyn Brown.
(Photo © James Klosty, with his permission.)

CHAPTER 14

A Day on the Road with the Cunningham Dance Company

(1971)

The day begins the night before. It is generally a full sleep for the dancers and musicians, though not always sufficient for the stage and production personnel.

The heaviest day precedes an opening night, or every night of a series of one-night stands. We arrive the day before to settle accommodations, usually a hotel or motel. Merce, stage managers Richard Nelson and Beverly Emmons, production manager James Baird, assistant stage manager Charles Atlas, and one of the musicians (usually myself) visit the theater immediately after dropping our baggage to gather reality to sleep on.

Often the production and stage personnel cannot work in the theater until the day of performance. Lights must be hung and focused, decor assembled, electronic musical equipment set up, dressing rooms prepped, the stage cleaned, all before the dancers arrive for rehearsal. The load-in and setup rarely take less than four hours. The production crew is up by 6:30 A.M. and in the theater before 8:00. They will be there until midnight or 1:00 A.M., unless it is a final performance. In that case everything must be taken down and packed—"struck" is the term—and loaded out of the theater. Those days run to 4:00 A.M.

Off the truck comes our equipment, packed in a few dozen air-freight pallet-loading containers of about sixty cubic feet each and weighing anywhere from one hundred to six hundred pounds. Although designed for forklifts, manual labor is sometimes the only alternative. In each container are several black fiber cases. Years of trial and error, including experiments with reinforced aluminum, plywood, and various plastics, have reassured us that we have found the right

---

Source: Unpublished typescript draft (ca. 1971) in Mumma, "Decade 7, tour process" (GMC).

material. The only alternative is difficult to obtain—the prewar wicker baskets still used by some European opera companies.

The fiber cases contain costumes, lighting gels, electronic music equipment, rehearsal clothes, and parts of smaller decor. The largest sets, such as those for *Scramble*, *Tread*, and *Canfield*, require their own super-size containers. A theater usually has spacious wings and a backstage area to accommodate this equipment. Sometime, though, it is a precarious squeeze.

Unless the theater has its own, the lighting equipment is rented locally. After everything is unpacked, the lights are hung and wired to a lighting plot designed by Nelson. At the same time the decor is assembled, some of which is hung with lights. The decor for *RainForest* is inflated with helium and floated out of the way.

The musicians carry all of their own equipment: amplifiers, loudspeakers, musical instruments, and hundreds of pounds of electronic music apparatus. It is loaded into the pit, where the musicians begin work around 11:00 A.M. Cables are routed throughout the pit, into the auditorium, and under the stage. The musical apparatus covers most of seventy-five square feet of sturdy tables.

The dancers arrive around noon and do their private warm-up exercises in whatever space remains—theater aisles, corridors, lobby. Sometimes a vacant spot in the orchestra pit allows for some gentle yoga.

We often do not have the occasion to speak during intensive days of work. We maintain necessary formalities, missing humanities—or we nourish humanities, abusing formalities. The matter never rests. A small smile of the eyes is sometimes the only possible response of human resonance in the rigors of a tour. Short occasions—a Friday dinner in Paris with French friends and Merce, just arrived from Teheran in February 1971—are especially cherished. At once intense and calm, they are no different than visiting a nearby neighbor, in spite of the great distances.

Fig. III-2. Gordon Mumma touring with the Merce Cunningham Dance Company, Holland Festival, July 1970. (Photo © James Klosty, with his permission.)

CHAPTER 15

From Where the Circus Went

(1975)

How I joined the Cunningham Dance Company was never very clear. My previous relationship to John Cage and David Tudor had been as a musical collaborator and technical assistant in several concerts. I had built special electronic music equipment for them, and at Tudor's request I was at work on a composition for his bandoneon.[1] On several occasions Tudor had mentioned that they were considering someone to assist them with the increasingly complex sound equipment of the dance company repertory. It was through a mutual friend, Anne Wehrer,[2] that word first reached me of their interest in inviting me to join the company for their European tour in the summer of 1966.

It became official in June 1966, when I received a direct invitation from Cage by long-distance telephone. I accepted. A week later Cage called again to ask if I would compose the music for a new dance that was to be premiered on the European tour in August. A bit stunned, I again agreed.

Merce Cunningham phoned a few days later to discuss details of the new work.

"I'd like it if you could do something for David Tudor to play."

Source: *Merce Cunningham*, ed. James Klosty, 64–73 (New York: Dutton, 1975; rpt. New York: Limelight, 1987), both © James Klosty, with his permission. The original publication was an extended excerpt of a hitherto unpublished larger study projected by Mumma. The current version reinstates the missing sections, to which autograph materials from the author's diaries and drafts of the time (GMC) have been added. Integrated as well are short excerpts from Mumma's earlier "Four Sound Environments for Modern Dance," with its preliminary comments on *Variations V*; *How to Pass, Kick, Fall, and Run*; *Place*; and *Scramble*, the totality of which was deemed too repetitive of the current essay to warrant separate publication.

I agreed, and asked about the title of the new dance.

"I haven't decided yet."

"How long will it be?"

"Between twenty and thirty minutes."

"I wonder what else I should know, maybe how many dancers?"

"Eight dancers, and we perform it at Saint-Paul de Vence, in France, on the 6th of August. It's beautiful there."

That was all. I now attempted to accumulate enough information to compose a work for them in two months. To meet the deadline, I decided to recast the elaborate composition that I was already preparing for Tudor and his bandoneon [*Mesa*].

Though the information that Cunningham had given me was minimal (I didn't have the presence of mind to probe further), his matter-of-fact tone was reassuring. I doubted that he knew any of my music, but I had the feeling that he trusted me, or at least seemed comfortable taking the risk. In the ensuing years it became clear that this initial encounter was representative of much of the Cunningham Dance Company collaboration. The best and worst aspects of "grapevine" communications and telephone arrangements, the minimal specifications between choreographer and composer, the blended sense of freedom and responsibility, and a pervading ambiguity about details and commitments were nourished by Cunningham's immediate trust in his collaborators and his invitation to artistic risk.

Cunningham's choreography exists for its own reasons—for the theater of human movement in "space and time,"[3] and does not have to be driven by anything outside it. Those familiar with the tradition of dancing *to* music sometimes find it difficult to comprehend the possibility of dance that can be simultaneous with but independent of the music. Actually, the procedure has now become established practice in modern dance.[4] The surprise is often greatest for those of the audience who inquire about the co-ordinations and correspondences that they have noticed between the music and the dance, and learn that these happen by chance at each performance. Not everyone agrees about these correspondences: it is often a very different experience for each.

Further, this independence of music and dance is true for only a part of the Cunningham Dance Company repertory. In the 1940s Cunningham and Cage collaborated in a relatively traditional way. Cage composed fixed, notated music that was played in combination with a fixed Cunningham choreography (as, for example, *Root of an Unfocus* of 1944 and *Amores* of 1943, choreographed in 1949). Yet there was still innovation aplenty. Cage was preparing the piano with miscellaneous hardware, Cunningham was creating movement independent of literal references, and the critics were already unsettled.

In the 1940s, Cunningham had also used music by Erik Satie, Alan Hovhaness, Alexei Haieff, and the jazz musician Baby Dodds. In 1949 Cage had returned from a trip to France with *musique concrète* by Pierre Schaeffer and Pierre Henry, an early disc recording of excerpts from their in-progress *Symphonie pour un homme seul* (completed in 1950). The *Symphonie* was composed using sounds recorded and edited on discs. Schaeffer's original recording was then copied to a fresh disc at the New York studio of Louis and Bebe Barron. The Barron copy was used for performances of Cunningham's choreography *Collage* (1952) in the early years, but was later transferred to magnetic tape as the latter technology evolved to commercial use.

In the 1950s the collaborations were extended to more experimental and then considerably riskier composers: Earle Brown, Morton Feldman, and Christian Wolff. Cunningham's first use of electronic music with dance was his 1952 choreography *Suite by Chance*, danced with Wolff's *Music for Magnetic Tape I* of that year.[5] Because of the unavailability of commercial tape players at that time, it was played from a disc copy in the early years.[6]

David Tudor's introduction to Cunningham had been as the pianist for Ben Weber's music in *Pool of Darkness*, which premiered in January 1950. At first listed on programs as "pianist," Tudor would soon expand his relationship to the music of Cage and others in an increasingly reciprocal collaboration. Tudor often supplied fundamental ideas as well as innovative performance procedures. By 1958 they were at work on the bizarre, virtuoso *Antic Meet*, for which a tape recording of Cage's *Concert for Piano and Orchestra* was often used.[7] Shortly afterwards they began to amplify the pianos in Cage's *Winter Music*, which was performed with the dance *Aeon* (1961). The diverse Cunningham repertory now included a variety of piano performance techniques, including Cage's classic prepared piano works of the 1940s, traditional music (the conventional piano music of Satie's *Nocturnes* [1956]), mechanically innovative music (Conlon Nancarrow's *Studies for Player Piano,* used in *Crises* [1960]), and the simultaneous performance of two works (selections from Cage's *Music for Piano* series as performed on two pianos for *Suite for Five* [1956]).

With the development of chance procedures in the 1950s came the beginnings of shared creative responsibilities: the functional distinction between composer and performer was becoming blurred. For the Cunningham musicians this distinction became more obscure with the increasing use of electronic technology in the 1960s and had become irrelevant by the 1970s.

The increasingly heavy touring schedule that culminated in the 1964 world tour often left little time for creative innovation. I once asked the prolific Cage, who had always made several new compositions each year, why there were none dated 1964. Surprised that I had noticed, he replied: "I spent that year writing letters to raise money for the touring." It was an exciting but difficult year. The Cunningham Dance Company became world-famous and Robert Rauschenberg won the Venice Biennale visual arts prize, yet the human and financial toll was staggering. Heavy touring usually decimates performance ensembles, and the Cunningham Company was no exception. The classic Cunningham ensemble that had developed through the 1950s was to change. Rauschenberg and over half the dancers departed from the ensemble at the end of the world tour, to be replaced by new members.[8] Undaunted, the company furthered its explorations of chance procedures, theatrical innovations, and electronic technology.

The first large step was the Cage-Cunningham *Variations V*, which was commissioned by the French-American Festival for a premiere at Philharmonic Hall at Lincoln Center in July 1965. Cage's conceptual score of the same name is one of a series of works titled *Variations* (now seven in number).[9] The costumes were conceived by the seven dancers themselves and executed by Abigail Ewert. Billy Klüver, Robert Moog, and others from Bell Laboratories built the special electronic music apparatus used in performance. The elaborate lighting included film and slide projections designed by Stan VanDerBeek and additional images by Nam June Paik. With virtually no precedent, this work established at once a coexistence of technological interdependence and artistic independence.

Every production of the immensely complicated *Variations V* was logistically precarious, and no two people could then agree as to its artistic merits. For the audience *Variations V* was like a multi-ring circus. For the performers it was participation in a machine environment, chock full of images and gadgets: movies, TV images, slides, a bicycle and gym mat, plastic plants, pieces of furniture (all of them wired for direct sound by special microphones), and a garden of vertical antennas projecting upward from the floor.

What was unique about *Variations V* is that the choreographed movements of the dancers articulated the sound environment of the performance space. The sound materials were "selected" and activated by two sets of sensors: the vertical capacitive antennas built by Moog from designs originally conceived in the 1930s by Leon Theremin (his "Terpsitone"), which responded to the locations of the dancers on the stage, and a network of photoelectric cells installed at the base of these antennas, which responded to changes in light intensity as the dancers moved past them. Both systems of sensors sent electronic signals to the central electronic complex operated by the musicians. With their technical support, the signals determined which of the sound sources would occur throughout the performance.

The sound materials included Cage's recorded audio collections from past and current projects, including *Williams Mix* and *Fontana Mix* or other stored sound sources. These were assembled "live" during performance using an ensemble of magnetic tape recorders and occasionally stereo disc recordings. Other sounds were produced from amplified objects in the space (stage props used by the dancers, film projectors, or radio receivers). The resulting sounds were then selectively released to loudspeakers in the audience by the triggering action of the dancers' movements on the stage.[10]

The complex interaction of the systems with the performers contained a measure of technological unpredictability. The audience rarely perceived a one-to-one correspondence between the dancers' movements and the sounds. Further, differences of venue, lighting, and musical materials from one performance to another contributed to non-repeatability of results. Because of these multi-leveled complexities, *Variations V* had the unsettling effect of being both the same and different at each performance.

Following the Lincoln Center premiere, Cunningham bypassed Cage's misgivings and decided to take *Variations V* on a nine-month tour in a series of tightly scheduled venues across the northern and northwestern United States into British Columbia, Canada. Even with the elimination of Paik's visual image equipment, the unhappy duo of Cage and Tudor struggled with its bulky trunks of musical and sensor apparatus. Following the close of that tour they invited me to join the Cunningham Dance Company musicians, partly to assist them with the massive challenge of further touring with *Variations V*. The implications of *Variations V* have changed my life in many ways. Against the extended periphery of opulent projected images one was pulled to concentrate upon the simultaneously bundled and freewheeling erotic energy of an ensemble of couple-dancers. The thunder-space of sound became a remarkably unobtrusive atmosphere for the lyrical encounters of Cunningham in duos with Carolyn Brown or Barbara Lloyd. In its best conditions of performance *Variations V* directed the perceptions of the audience in such a way as to create an intimate and at the same time panoramic theater experience. It was also my first experience of a recurring dilemma: I loved the work yet dreaded the preparations for every performance.

Besides *Variations V*, several other repertory works from the 1960s indicate the workings of technological, artistic, and social collaboration in the Cunningham Dance Company. Three of these, *Story* (1963), the notorious *Winterbranch* (1964), and the smaller-scale *Field Dances* (1963), were made previous to the world tour. The fourth, the extremely popular *How to Pass, Kick, Fall, and Run* (1965), was made right after *Variations V*. The music for *Winterbranch*, *Variations V*, and *How to Pass, Kick, Fall, and Run* was the result of electronic technology. But whereas *Variations V* was a complicated spectacle, *Winterbranch* and *How to* were elemental simplicity.

Winterbranch used "canned" music: a tape recording of two sustained sounds by La Monte Young played from loudspeakers at a near-deafening level. The sensation of *Winterbranch* was in its theatrical impact, due largely to its lighting. Rauschenberg lit *Winterbranch* with strongly focused, non-colored lights such that the light rarely hit the performing dancers directly except by chance. He also distributed this light over the duration of the piece differently at each performance. Cumulatively, about half of *Winterbranch* was often in total darkness. The choreography was derived from the physical gestures of falling. The performance began in silence. After a few minutes, just as the audience members invariably grew restless with its theatrical ambiguity, they were pinned to their seats by the massive shock front of La Monte Young's *2 Sounds* (April 1960), which continued to the end. *Winterbranch* remained in the repertory for nearly a decade because of its theatrical impact, especially when programmed between two entirely contrasting works.

Beyond its choreography, *How to Pass, Kick, Fall, and Run* was a relatively simple production. The ebullient choreography for eight dancers in practice sweaters and tights was inspired by the movements of sports and games, and (as with *Winterbranch*) was specific and fixed. The dancers moved in parallels rather than unisons, at shifting tempos that constantly changed phase from one dancer to another. Over the longer sequences of the dance—from one merging section to another—the contrasts of tempo were extreme, ranging from the effect of slow motion to ensemble activity faster than the eye could follow. The sound environment consisted of John Cage as raconteur, reading from his one-minute-long *Indeterminacy* stories[11] and using that most common live-electronic instrument, the public-address system.

The first year of *How to* corresponded with Tudor's ascendancy as a live-electronic composer-performer. He used Cage's voice as a sound source for complicated electronic modification procedures, resulting in a montage of sonic fragmentation that increased in verbal unintelligibility with each performance. Complaints came from both audience and dancers, and Tudor's electronic modification of Cage's reading was eventually abandoned. On occasion, however, David Vaughan joined Cage in the simultaneous but independent reading of those stories. *How to* enjoyed a long life in the repertory, its success due as much to its infectious humor and splendidly engaging choreography as to the verbal distractions of its sound-score, which invited the spectator into an active participatory role.

The artistic and social collaboration of *Story* (1963) was more daring. Its music was Toshi Ichiyanagi's *Sapporo* (1962), a notated but open-ended ensemble composition that allowed for considerable interpretation on the part of the performers. In *Story* Cunningham gave the scenic designers and dancers a degree of creative freedom uncommon in earlier repertory works. Rauschenberg (collaborating on the world tour with artist Alex Hay) assembled the decor anew during each performance, using materials found on the spot. Thus they were themselves performers. During the performance the dancers also chose what they would wear from a great pile of clothing and other paraphernalia on the stage. *Story* took a social and artistic direction that was also being explored by the pioneers of "happenings" at that time, one that seemed particularly fertile in the context of the highly trained ensemble of the Cunningham Dance Company. For some of the performers who had already participated in the more extreme explorations of the "happening" era, the process came naturally. In one performance, dancer Barbara Lloyd attempted to robe herself with the entire pile of clothing; in another, she stripped bare. *Story* left the repertory immediately after the world tour,[12] but the implications of its social and artistic freedom were long discussed by the dancers and artists involved.

The collaborative prescriptions of *Field Dances* (1963) were more extensive, beginning with its indeterminate duration. Cunningham's choreography was a vocabulary of physical gestures, while the dancers were free during performance to include their own syntax for that vocabulary. Further, the dancers individually chose whether they would perform in it at all. On occasion non-company dancers were included, even myself in an outdoor performance at the University of California, Berkeley. The music, however, was a rare example of "canning": musical sequences from Cage's *Variations IV* were recorded and retrieved using an ensemble of tape recorders. The choreographic sequences appeared to share a similar process, learned and retrieved from memory by the dancers. The overall structure of *Field Dances* varied from one performance to the next: the dancers independently chose the choreographic sequences and the musicians chose the recorded sound sequences.

The departure of Rauschenberg at the end of the 1964 tour and the arrival of Jasper Johns as "artistic advisor" shortly afterwards brought about a significant change in the nature of the decor. There was an expansion of collaborative activity: many other artists were invited to participate. The decor for *Place* (1966) was by Beverly Emmons, for *Scramble* (1967) by Frank Stella, for *RainForest* (1968) by Andy Warhol, for *Walkaround Time* (1968) by Jasper Johns and Marcel Duchamp, for *Canfield* (1969) by Robert Morris, for *Tread* (1970) by Bruce Nauman, and for *Objects* (1970) by Neil Jenney. The decor for *Second Hand* (1970), *Landrover* (1972), and *TV Rerun* (1972) was by Jasper Johns.

On an elementary level the decor for *Scramble*, *RainForest*, *Walkaround Time*, and *Objects* involved collaboration with the dancers, who moved the scenery around the space in performance. The helium-filled silver-colored mylar pillows of *RainForest* sometimes moved by chance encounters with the dancers. But elegant as some of it was, this decor was still basically a collection of decorative props. The audience might gasp with appreciation when the curtain opened, but except for the mysterious, animal-like character of Warhol's pillows in *RainForest*, the dancers did not sense much interactive affinity with either the decor or its production. Lighting designer Richard Nelson introduced more integrated approaches. His special "light score," *Lightgames 1^R*, for *RainForest* changed from performance to performance, thus extending an aspect of Rauschenberg's *Winterbranch* lighting tradition. For *Signals* (1970) Nelson employed several unusual procedures, including laser projection. He treated each performance as a new challenge to his ingenuity, and produced scenic wonders.

Robert Morris's decor for *Canfield* included the lighting design. The dancers, wearing iridescent gray leotards and tights, were lit by a vertical beam that extended from the downstage floor to a connection above the proscenium arch. The beam moved slowly back and forth across the proscenium opening. The effect was a vertical plane of brilliant light that, slowly edging through the space, was interrupted by encounters with the dancers, who seemed like an intermittently fluorescing population of some lunar landscape [fig. III-3]. The stage-production manager, James Baird, was responsible for the design and construction of the mobile vertical light beam, which came from a series of aircraft landing lights mounted within that beam and focused on a gray drop at the back of the stage. It required a series of interdependent innovations, including a lightweight, multi-sectioned, horizontal aluminum I-beam, from which the vertical light beam was suspended, and a unique electric motor and reduction-gear mechanism that traveled back and forth along the I-beam and pulled the vertical light beam hanging below it. This elaborate mechanism had to be adaptable to the various sizes of proscenium stages that we would encounter over the next several years; it would also need to operate with wide variations in electrical power, voltage, and frequency, and be efficiently installed and dismantled on one-night stands by different (often foreign-language) stage crews at each theater.

As impressive as these various decors were, if any collaboration existed between Cunningham and the designers it was a private affair. Moreover, some people had the sense that the collaborative potential between musicians and dancers suggested by works such as *Story* and *Variations V* was held in suspension during these years. At the same time, however, the interactions among the musicians were becoming increasingly complex and fruitful.

The performance of my music for Cunningham's *Place* (1966) was a closely interactive process. I had secretly decided on the title of my composition for Tu-

Fig. III-3. Robert Morris's decor and lighting design for *Canfield* in performance at the Brooklyn Academy of Music, February 1972. Dancers (L to R): Valda Setterfield, Susana Hayman-Chaffey, Sandra Neels, Meg Harper (foreground), Merce Cunningham (seated). (Photo © Gordon Mumma.)

dor's bandoneon before the invitation to work with the Cunningham Company came. It was to be called *Mesa*, referring to that butte-like landscape unique to the southwestern United States and characteristic of its broad sound continuity. In *Mesa* Tudor's bandoneon performance was drastically altered by my elaborate system of electronic sound modulators, seen in a photograph from the recording of *Mesa* at the CBS studio in July 1967 [fig. III-4].[13]

Traveling in France to Nice on the Trans-Europe Express a week before the August 1966 premiere of *Place*, I discussed the lighting and decor for the new work with its designer, Beverly Emmons. She explained that it employed a special point-source lighting apparatus—a set of small geodesic light globes placed on the stage floor. They were to be moved around by Cunningham himself during performance in such a way as to project aspects of the geodesic light structure, the dance movement, and the decor into unpredictable places of the performance space. She continued: "No one knows what the dance is about, and here's something else no one knows: Merce's title for it is *Place*." The work was a simultaneous, intuitive coming together of an unpremeditated idea of "place"—places of the landscape, of the musical continuity, of the stage, of the mind. It would provide my first experience of the remarkable phenomenon of independent nonverbal communication in the Cunningham Dance Company.

Fig. III-4. Gordon Mumma, cybersonic console, and David Tudor, bandoneon, recording Mumma's *Mesa* at the CBS studio on East 30th Street, New York, July 1967. (Photo by Barbara Dilley Lloyd, with her permission.)

The premiere was held out-of-doors in the evening, on a mountain above the French medieval walled town of Saint-Paul de Vence. It was a premiere in a larger sense of the word than usual: the elements of *Place*—decor, lighting, music, and choreography—had been prepared and rehearsed independently, and came together for the first time at the performance itself. As Barbara Lloyd later told me, the dancers had already formed their initial impression of the work based on their dance movements alone, with minimal glimpses of Cunningham's solos, as a light-hearted romp of children at play. They were surprised by the dark power and aura of menace that the work assumed when Cunningham's part joined with the lighting and music.

Its mysterious chain of events, rigorously and invariably choreographed, has led many viewers to seek an implied narrative for *Place*. Some have even seen it as a clinical panorama of the schizophrenic experience, culminating in stark, outright withdrawal. In this work for eight dancers, Cunningham has a predominant solo role that suggests an individual who repeatedly attempts and fails to establish relationships with the people and events of his world. For me, *Place* is a drama of human anxiety.

Emmons's decor, constructed of modern urban materials—plastic costumes, newspaper-embellished grids, and the onstage geodesic lights—reinforces the sense of alienation. Her handwritten draft of the structure of the choreography, which she used as a cue sheet in performances of *Place*, provides a detailed account of its danced events (see sidebar). As a dancer herself, Emmons cued the sections by choreographic action rather than by time units (as had Rauschenberg for *Minutiae*).[14] The "BAG" scene at the close was terrifying for some: it consisted of Cunningham's frenzied thrashing on the stage floor in a plastic bag, which rustled loudly in duo with the cybersonically modified bandoneon sound.[15]

Disorientation of time and space is an essential condition of the sound environment of *Place*. The bandoneon produces sustained clusters of gradually changing sound-color over long periods of time. Its extremes of dynamics range from a quiet backdrop of sound to brief, transilient episodes of considerable volume. The music seems to float free of coordination with the articulation of the dancers and avoids establishing any sense of rhythmic propulsion for their movements. Moreover, the locus or "place" of the sound articulation is not simply the actual origin of the sound, but rather its *apparent* source as perceived by the listener. The location of sound origin is manipulated by deploying acoustically inharmonic portions of the processed bandoneon sound through different loudspeakers in the auditorium. These dispersed sounds mix in various spatially disorienting ways to produce the impression of continually changing size within the sound space.

Although *Place* was theatrically dramatic and achieved an immediate success, it had a repertory life of only three years, with nearly thirty performances in the United States, Europe, and Latin America (it was revived once in 1971).[16] For the dancers *Place* was exceedingly strenuous, literally a bone-bruiser. *Place* was designed and worked best for a proscenium stage and came toward the end of the predominantly proscenium stage performances. The Cunningham Company was expanding into more diverse dance venues.

Scramble was premiered at the Ravinia Festival in Chicago in July 1967 and was subsequently presented at the American Dance Festival in New London, Connecticut.[17] The decor by artist Frank Stella, horizontal bands of brightly colored fabric held taut at different altitudes by aluminum frames, emphasized the vertical as well as the horizontal perspectives of the stage. The dancers scrambled the positions of these bands in performance. Toshi Ichiyanagi's music for

Beverly Emmons: Cue sheet for *Place* (1966); transcription of pencil draft, 2 pp., GMC.

Cue 1	MC [Merce Cunningham] enters alone.
Cue 2	Stands and looks.
3	BL [Barbara Lloyd] enter[s] alone.
	She pulls group on.
4	Group moves off slowly *as*
5	MC + CB [Carolyn Brown] violent duet
6	MC + CB quiet duet [leading to] CB exit.
7	MC to special lights Globes
	Group for long hoppy diag. [dialogue?]
8	Group drops it + exits.
	MC solo leap-fall.
9	Boys enter for group couples.
	Energy dies
	Group filters off
10	MC Bird solo
	Quiet.
	Violence
11	CB enters into folk dance. Ends with cavs.
	Valda [Setterfield] + Al[bert Reid] left
	MC solo.
12	Al + Sandy [Sandra Neels]
	Sandy is picked
13	Group falling running
	MC
14	Released group.
	BL on face.
	classroom girls.
15	MC claps.
	Girls on floor.
16	"Sack of potatoes"
17	Al + Sandy exit
	MC enters
	BAG.

Scramble, adapted from his *Activities for Orchestra* (1962), was well suited to its flexible performance practice. Like Ichiyanagi's earlier music for *Story*, this was a notated but open-ended composition in which cued sequences are scrambled in performance. The musicians (a minimum of three) each performed multiple activities: several instruments simultaneously or a single instrument with complex electronic sound manipulation. At the premiere performance our ensemble was joined by members of the Chicago Symphony. Though scored for Western instruments (horn, bandoneon, piano and celesta, and percussion), the sound textures of *Scramble* are reminiscent of Japanese classical theater music. Quiet, transparent bands of sustained sound, some steady and some sliding, are punctuated with abrupt percussive timbres.[18]

The two new works of 1968 were *RainForest* and *Walkaround Time*, with music by Tudor and David Behrman, respectively. Both have taken on near-mythic status: *RainForest* for Tudor's music, then a collaborative duo between him and myself performing with a forest of electro-acoustic transducers of his own uncanny design, *Walkaround Time* for the beauty of Cunningham's choreography, situated in decor by Jasper Johns based on Duchamp's epic *Large Glass* of the 1920s.

The March 9, 1968, premiere of *RainForest* in Buffalo, New York, was a great success, an extraordinary combination of Cunningham's gently romantic choreography, Andy Warhol's enchanting decor of floating helium-filled pillows, and Tudor's lyrical music.[19] The *RainForest* performance in Rio de Janeiro was notable, part of the Cunningham Dance Company's Latin American tour in the summer of 1968.[20] That tour had started in the high altitudes of Boulder during a summer residency at the University of Colorado. This period of preparation was crucial: the first performance of the South American tour was to be in Mexico City (over 7,000 feet in elevation), where the Summer Olympics were also under way. As with the athletes, the dancers needed altitude adjustment in advance—as did Warhol's helium-filled pillows, which were resized in Boulder with analysis provided by NASA so as to float properly at such high altitude.

For the Rio de Janeiro performance of *RainForest*, obtaining helium for the floating pillows was impossible. The United States controlled the production of helium at that time, and it was prohibited for production in Brazil. Arriving at the Teatro Novo for the setup and first rehearsals, Tudor and I found the orchestra pit filled with pressure tanks of hydrogen and many large fire extinguishers. We rearranged this mélange as best we could so as to make room for our electronic performance equipment, and we assembled the basic instruments for *Rainforest* that had been used in the Buffalo dance premiere. Tudor was a bit nervous, not so much about the hydrogen causing a fire as that the water from the fire extinguishers might get his equipment wet. He took time off from that first rehearsal, returning with a collection of large rubber gloves, which he planned to pull over his small *Rainforest* devices in case of emergency.

The Brazilian audience was as open to innovation, intrigue, and danger as was much of Rio de Janeiro that summer. They were delighted when some of Warhol's hydrogen-filled pillows drifted over the audience during the performance, and were enchanted by the lyrical character of Tudor's music, Cunningham's choreography, and the superb dancers. Perhaps the added excitement of "explosive hydrogen" had contributed to their enthusiasm.

For *Walkaround Time*, Jasper Johns's reconstruction of *The Large Glass* separated the individual parts of Duchamp's "see-through" work. Working with Duchamp, Johns re-created the "subjects" of those parts onto individual transparency screens on rectangular structures movable by the dancers on the stage, thus integrating the decor into the choreography. The music by David Behrman, with the title ... *for nearly an hour* ... , often employed outdoor landscape sounds along with the voices of the dancers speaking Duchamp's words about *The Large Glass*.

The choreography of *Walkaround Time* was unusually theatrical. It began as the curtain opened, with the work of Duchamp and Johns placed in sections among the dancers around the stage. Nothing moved for several minutes, making them a part of the decor. At the 1968 premiere the only sound was the audience, repeatedly gasping at the stunning beauty of it all. Gradually the dancers and lighting began moving, and this extraordinary occasion was under way. Because of the length of *Walkaround Time*, an intermission was integrated into the choreography, with the dancers remaining on stage, as if on a picnic. Sometimes classic tango recordings of the 1930s were used for the interval music. Toward the end of the performance the dancers gradually moved the Duchamp-Johns sections of the decor toward center stage in a type of reassembly of Duchamp's original *Large Glass*.

Our proliferation of custom-built electronics even influenced the revival of an originally acoustical score such as that of *Night Wandering* of 1958, danced with Bo Nilsson's *Bewegungen*, *Quantitäten*, and *Schlagfiguren* for solo piano. Its 1968 revival was enhanced with electronics, which featured Tudor's legendary performance of Nilsson's *pieces* amplified to reveal quiet, pedal-sustained resonances and magnify the higher partials of the piano sonority. The result was a gentle and surreal timbral brilliance reflective of Tudor's virtuosity.[21]

In October and November 1968 we participated in a project that established stimulating artistic precedents. The Cunningham Company traveled to Ghirardelli Square in San Francisco to make *Assemblage*, a color-film television production for KQED-TV. This long-planned collaboration took a month on location and several months of processing and editing afterwards. It was visually stunning, with the dancers' multi-hued pastel leotards against the brilliant blue of the San Francisco sky. *Assemblage* was particularly interesting for Cage, Tudor, and myself, for whom the creation of the stereophonic soundtrack was our first formally structured compositional collaboration. We easily divided our labors, and clashes of ego were remarkably minimal. If the artistic results of the project fell significantly short of its ambition, this had largely to do with insufficient time and money and the tangled politics of public television production.[22]

More indicative of future directions, however, was *Canfield* (1969), notable in several ways beyond its innovative decor and lighting design. The choreographic structure included thirteen sections with interludes between each, analogous to the form of solitaire invented by Richard Canfield, a gambler at the casinos of Saratoga Springs, New York. The sections and interludes were arranged in a different order for each performance, usually on that day, and not all were necessary to constitute a full performance. Thus the continuity of the dance was different each time, varying in length from 20 to 105 minutes. The character of the choreography was one of extreme contrasts, with elements of the lyrical, preposterous, baroque, serene, and surreal juxtaposed in often jolting succession and displayed in all manner of solo and ensemble activities.

The music by Pauline Oliveros, titled *In Memoriam: Nikola Tesla, Cosmic Engineer*, is as much a theatrical as a musical composition. In performance it occurred simultaneously with, but independent of, the dance and lighting decor. Both Robert Morris and Oliveros had fulfilled their commissions independently by supplying the Cunningham Company only with ideas about what should be done, leaving the implementation and execution of those ideas to the stage-production manager and musicians. In the sleep-deprived tradition of Cunningham Company production schedules for new works, the music as well as the elaborate lighting and decor specifications arrived within only weeks of the scheduled first performance of *Canfield*.

The musicians were in a more comfortable position than Morris or Baird. Oliveros's score was three pages of typewritten instructions that indicated, often in general terms, the kinds of sounds and theatrical effects desired and the general nature of the equipment that the musicians had to obtain or to develop, yet remained open-ended in its implementation. The musicians were committed to specific kinds of sounds and theatrical effects, but not to specific hardware.

Our *Canfield* music performance was in three sections, beginning with an audible discussion among the musicians concerning the past, present, and future of the performance space and the life and work of the pioneering inventor Nikola Tesla (1856–1943). The second section involved acoustical analysis of the performance space, accomplished by the performers roaming around the audience space with buzzers, starter pistols, slide whistles, bugle tattoos, walkie-talkies, and electronic acoustical measuring devices. The activities of these two sections gained complexity as the performance continued and were tape recorded for later playback. The third section began in silence, from which an ambiance of low-frequency sound emerged, tuned to the predominant reso-

Fig. III-5. David Tudor preparing to shake the hall with modest equipment resources in rehearsal for the Cunningham-Oliveros *Canfield* at Zellerbach Auditorium, University of California, Berkeley, July 1971. (Photo © Gordon Mumma.)

nances of the space. They gradually swelled in volume to a sea of oscillating pressure, analogous to Tesla's famous experiment in which a building was made to vibrate at its own resonant frequencies. Although we used a lot of equipment for Oliveros's piece—by the end of a performance the orchestra pit was an awful mess—the *Canfield* sound equipment [fig. III-5] could be packed into a few suitcases. The light-beam apparatus [shown above in fig. III-3] had to be shipped in large crates.

The impact of performances of the complete *Canfield*, which sometimes filled an entire evening, became very significant. Cunningham won the BITEF award for *Canfield* at the Belgrade International Theatre Festival in September 1972, but only weeks later it provoked an ugly riot at the Cologne Opera House. The dancers valiantly pressed on through the roar of aggressive shouting and rude insults from the German audience, which had no idea we were recording it as part of the ambient sound collection of the piece. The *Polizei* arrived on the scene to restore order at the start of the final, earth-shaking section of *Canfield*, barking orders to Tudor and myself to shut off the sound. We pretended not to understand German. When they shut down the electricity main to the pit, they were horrified that the resonant sounds continued, spewing the audience's venom back onto themselves from the rear speakers. The police never could discover the secret energy source for that uncanny effect: a single extension cord that I had earlier run into the backstage men's restroom in my usual ploy of equipment redundancy—a tactic that saved the day in many a Cunningham performance.

More than any other work in the repertory at that time, *Canfield* was a continual production-in-progress. By the early 1970s we were rarely presenting the abbreviated version of this piece in combination with other repertory works, as we had previously. *Canfield* seemed to be metamorphosing into the genre of the Event, which had come to occupy more of our performances. In several non-proscenium Event performances the entire choreography of *Canfield* was danced, but with different, specially made lighting, decor, and music.

Increasingly preoccupied with the idea of interactive creative process and encouraged by the results of our Event collaborations, we musicians decided to share creative responsibilities for the next repertory work. We determined in advance that each performance would have different music, with each musician making an independent contribution of sound materials. Each contribution would also be sparing in its resources, with a specific character or idea. Further, we would title this collaborative music by the week and month of each specific performance, for example, "the second week of November." Finally, the participating musicians would be extended beyond the three regular Cunningham Company musicians, and all names would be listed on the program in rotating order.

Cunningham's new choreography to this collaborative music was called *Signals* (1970). I have already described Richard Nelson's contribution to its lighting and decor. Sensing the various implications of its title, Cage generally played sparse abbreviations of early music on the piano, which he derived during performance of *Signals* by chance operations with the *I Ching*. I often chose a sound ambience of signal-type sounds, such as bells ringing quietly outdoors at a great distance. Tudor commonly selected a continuous sound from a single source, such as insect activities, electro-encephalic signals, or a snippet of sentimental parlor music.

Objects (1970) turned out to be an interim production that, for various reasons, had a short life in the repertory. When a composer outside the Cunningham Company was commissioned to provide music for a new production, the choice was usually made by a consensus between Cunningham and the regular musicians. If Cunningham had a specific musician in mind from the outset, everyone else was likely to concur. Alvin Lucier had been in our minds for several years, but the Cunningham Company had procrastinated in making a commitment to him until a few weeks before its scheduled premiere. A solution was to ask Lucier for an already completed work. For several days I carried with me a portable tape of Lucier's *Vespers* as recorded by the Sonic Arts Union (myself with Lucier, Behrman, and Robert Ashley).[23] This live-electronic piece in which the musicians moved blind through the performance space, finding their way by echolocation with the use of sonar-like devices, was already familiar to Cage and Tudor, but not to Cunningham. Eventually my path crossed Cunningham's in a dressing room between rehearsals. He listened to *Vespers* and replied:

"I like it, don't you? Will you play this tape in performance?"

"No, we'll do it live, with the original instruments. Besides meeting the requirements of Lucier's score, it will allow us to adapt to various performance circumstances of the new dance. It can be any length, and the texture can be more transparent."

Merce asked, "What are the instruments called that make that clicking sound?"

"Sondols."[24]

"Well, if we all like it, let's give it a try. Thank you for letting me hear it."

Only seven days remained until the premiere.

In 1971 Cunningham and I worked together on a collaboration titled *Loops*. He performed solo, and my "music" was entirely from his breathing and heart sounds. He wore small medical sensors on his chest and back, from which his internal sounds were transmitted by FM telemetry to loudspeakers in the performing area. Charles Atlas provided the projected slides, and Richard Nelson, the lighting. The first performance was at the New York City Museum of Modern Art on December 3, 1971. It took advantage of the first display there of Jasper Johns's large painting *Map (Based on Buckminster Fuller's Dymaxion Airocean World)* (1967; rev. 1971),[25] which provided a stunning backdrop to the production. This can be seen in figure III-6, which shows Cunningham in rehearsal of *Loops* at MOMA several days before the performance. The work was also revived under the title *Loops and Additions* at the Whitney Museum of American Art in New York City on May 18, 1973—though without Johns's decor (which had since moved on to a European collection). Portions of *Loops* would also resurface in Events to follow.[26]

In 1972 Cunningham produced three new works, *TV Rerun*, *Landrover*, and *Borst Park*. The first of these, danced with my composition *Telepos*, extended the technology of FM telemetry already used in *Loops*. It also marked a modest return to the repertory collaboration between dancers and musicians that had been suspended following *Variations V*. For *TV Rerun* I designed lightweight elastic belts for the dancers such as that worn in rehearsal by Carolyn Brown [fig. III-7]. Each belt contained accelerometers, an integrated-circuit func-

Fig. III-6. Merce Cunningham in rehearsal for *Loops* with Jasper Johns's *Map (Based on Buckminster Fuller's Dymaxion Airocean World)*, Museum of Modern Art, New York, November 26, 1971. The body monitors wired to Mumma's FM telemetry device are visible. (Photo © Gordon Mumma.)

tion generator, and a miniature UHF radio transmitter. The accelerometers responded in three dimensions to the dancers' movements and modulated the frequency of the function generators. The output of the function generators, a triangular waveform, was then transmitted as audible pitches to an FM receiver in the orchestra pit. There I monitored the transmissions, which provided sound sources to be projected from loudspeakers around the audience to create a live-electronic performance. This process of telemetry was new technology

Fig. III-7. Carolyn Brown wearing Mumma's *Telepos* belt in rehearsal for *TV Rerun* at the Cunningham studios, New York, February 1972. (Photo © Gordon Mumma.)

related to that used in the space program. The cost of developing each belt and its electronic hardware in the orchestra pit was about $1,500, nearly half the yearly salary of each dancer who wore them. Thus only three *Telepos* belts could be developed, interchanged among the ensemble of ten dancers during the performance. With their assistance, the dancers collectively articulated the nature and continuity of the sounds, though the implications of this technological extension of human activity suggested more interactive potential than the dancers and I actually felt in performance. The belt transmitters were very fragile, and would not sustain contact with the floor; by happy circumstance, Cunningham's choreography avoided falling and rolling movements.

Like the earlier *Canfield* and *Scramble*, the choreography of *Landrover* existed in sections, the order of which could be arranged differently for each performance. Taking our lead from this procedure, Cage, Tudor, and I decided to do the same with the musical structure. The choreographic sections of *Landrover* were of unequal length and four in number, but did not all have to be performed. We established the musical sections to be equal in length and three in number, with the total length equal to that of the choreography. Each of us was completely responsible for a single section, and immediately preceding the performance straws were drawn to determine the order of the three musical sections.

For his earlier contributions to *Landrover*, Cage sometimes chose to read a short fragment from his *Mureau* (1970),[27] which he would place somewhere in the large, remaining silence of his section. For the entire length of his section Tudor sometimes presented seismological signals, which he sped up and scrambled to an audible range and modified gently with electronic equalization. I made a set of verbal instructions that specified "a phenomenon unarticulated insofar as possible and sustained at the threshold of perception." Although that phenomenon did not necessarily have to be sound, I created a kind of ultrasonic blanket with special electronic equipment. In accordance with the instructions I adjusted this phenomenon at the threshold of *my* perception. I could barely hear it, Cage said he never heard it, and Tudor found it "obnoxiously audible." Critics described it variously as "absolute silence," "intolerable roaring," and "something like crickets." The process of *Landrover* seemed almost too simple to deserve being called collaboration. Yet the combination of elements that were chosen by the participants, in that inexplicably independent yet parallel way, would have been inconceivable to me under any other circumstances. Indeed, the totality of *Landrover* assumed for me the qualities of an epic.

The music for *Borst Park* was a quick decision. Christian Wolff, Frederic Rzewski, Jon Appleton, and I had performed a small-ensemble version of Wolff's *Burdocks* at New York University on January 9, 1972, four weeks before the Cunningham premiere of *Borst Park*. *Burdocks* is an expandable, transcendental work of one to ten sections and for one to ten orchestras (an orchestra consisted of a minimum of five musicians).[28] Cunningham was in the audience, and immediately wanted *Burdocks* as the music for his new choreography. It was unique in nature, more of a theatrical entertainment than a dance. In a departure from custom, an onstage ensemble of five musicians with their music stands and acoustic instruments provided additional decor for the dancers. The audience loved this slightly irreverent "divertissement."

A sign of the times was *Changing Steps* (1973), in which everyone including the newest dancers had solos, along with duos, trios, quartets, and quintets. Made as though a repertory work, *Changing Steps* was performed only in Events. Coming at this time of change, its title had prophetic implications.

The first of a long series of Event performances had taken place in the signal year of 1964. Events were flexible performance situations crafted especially for each occasion, especially on tours. They were generally complete, uninterrupted performances in non-proscenium spaces, and held implications of greater collaborative endeavor than most of the repertory works.[29] In the ensuing decade— especially from 1970 onwards—Events became more frequent and increasingly important in the artistic development of the Cunningham Company.

Event no. 1 of June 24, 1964, was created during the world tour for the Museum des 20. Jahrhunderts in Vienna.[30] The Event was born of practical necessity when it was discovered that none of the Cunningham Company repertory for the world tour was suitable for the venue. The audience was seated on three sides around the dancers, while in the background was a huge window through which Viennese life unfolded as twilight fell. The choreography for this Event consisted of sections of dances from the repertory, arranged to function in the rectangular space, while the music consisted of the electronically modified percussion parts from Cage's *Atlas Eclipticalis* (1961–62).

The first outdoor Event—and the first Event in which I participated—was *Event no. 4* of August 7, 1966. It was presented both outdoors and through the inside galleries of the Fondation Maegt in Saint-Paul de Vence, on the French Riviera. The dancers and audience moved among the large collection of Giacometti sculptures for which the gallery is famous.[31] As with *Event no. 1* in Vienna, its music was from the electronic percussion parts of Cage's *Atlas Eclipticalis*.

One of the most taxing Event productions was *Event no. 5*, performed outdoors at the estate of architect Philip Johnson in New Canaan, Connecticut, on June 3, 1967. *Event no. 5* was a benefit for the Cunningham Company, to dispose of the considerable deficit that had resulted from the two European tours of the previous year. The company members contributed their energies, while food and drink for the audience (who paid a hefty admission charge to attend) were catered by fancy establishments. Andy Warhol's Velvet Underground rock band was obtained for "popular" dancing after the Cunningham Company performance. Our business manager, Lewis Lloyd, obtained a substantial rain-insurance policy.

The circumstances of *Event no. 5* proved especially difficult. A platform for the dancers was constructed on the side of a hill among the trees, overlooking

Fig. III-8. Merce Cunningham and Carolyn Brown in rehearsal for *Event no. 5*, with other members of the company looking on, at the Philip Johnson Estate, New Canaan, Connecticut, June 3, 1967. (Photo © Gordon Mumma.)

an artificial lake [fig. III-8]. Communications went awry. The specifications for the platform were forgotten: the musicians got separated from the dancers and were located up the hill with the audience in between, while the loudspeakers were mistakenly focused on the dancers instead of outward toward the audience. Elaborate plans for a fireworks display came to naught. In the midst of this chaos a German television company was filming the proceedings for a documentary on the Cunningham Company,[32] and glamour magazine photographers swarmed like gnats. We consoled ourselves with the thought that at least we might enjoy a catered picnic after our performance, but a demoralizing rumor descended upon us: the performers were expected to pack their own lunches.

Cage, Tudor, and I were joined in the musical production by Toshi Ichiyanagi, who was in New York at the time working with the company on *Scramble*. We took our way of working together for *Event no. 5* from the idea of a picnic, each bringing something of his own to share with the others. Cage amplified the sounds of cars along the adjoining country road, Tudor became an electronic disc jockey, from a pavilion by the artificial lake I performed romantic calls on a hunting horn and electronically modified violin, and Ichiyanagi amplified the sounds of his performance of a huge Chinese gong. Opinion concerning our musical picnic might have been quite favorable except for the loudspeaker placement. Caught in the crossfire of piercing sound, the dancers suffered at times near paralysis. Carolyn Brown was practically blown off the performance platform in a sea of her own tears.[33] But it did not rain, the rumor about bringing our own food proved untrue, and in many respects it was a beautiful evening.

Sometimes an interesting theater would inspire us to use the proscenium format in special ways. Such was the case at the College of St. Benedict in St. Joseph, Minnesota, site of *Event no. 12* (September 23, 1969). Its theater was a concert hall seating several thousand, built so that the rear wall of the stage was back-to-back with that of a smaller dramatic theater. This wall was actually a huge door that could be raised up out of sight into the flies. Since both spaces were free that evening, we arranged *Event no. 12* so that the dancers performed on this double stage, with the audience seated on opposite sides in both theaters. At one point the door was slowly lowered, dividing the dancers and musicians into isolated ensembles. We also had a two-sided situation for *Event no. 8* (May 3, 1968) in the Fieldhouse of Bradley University in Peoria, Illinois. It had basketball courts in the center and seating for thousands of people on two opposite sides. The space was so large that the dancers and large decor (Frank Stella's set for *Scramble*) were dwarfed. The lighting was such that from the audience on either side the view through the dancers was like a glimpse into infinity.

Besides repertory performances and the growing production of Events, in the late 1960s the Cunningham Company became more involved in university residencies. A residency lasted as little as three days or as long as a month and made use of all the resources of the ensemble. Besides lecture-demonstrations, repertory, and Event performances, the dancers taught classes in technique, repertory, and composition. The musicians presented seminars, workshops, and extra concerts, and the lighting designer taught stage design courses. The schedules sometimes allowed for the creation of new works as well.

The four-week residency at the University of California, Berkeley, during the summer of 1971 was memorable on several counts, including the production of the unusual *Events nos. 24–25*. The Cunningham Company had performed previously at Zellerbach Auditorium on the Berkeley campus and was looking forward to producing Events there. Although basically a proscenium stage, its physical structure was flexible and held promise for experimentation; moreover, it boasted a large orchestral pit and an unusually fine sound system. Because of the residency, the two Berkeley Events were blessed with more preparation time than usual.

Event no. 24 on August 1 was made in the traditional Cunningham Company manner: sequences from past and present choreography were arranged to make a continuous and unique work. Cage, Tudor, and I prepared an extravagant music for *Event no. 24*. It was also one of the few Events that I was able to record.[34] *Event no. 25* on the next evening was perhaps the most radical achievement of the Cunningham Company to date. The performers (dancers, musicians, and technicians) assumed responsibility for anything of their choosing (for example, a dancer could be responsible for music, decor, lighting, or choreography), established among themselves the degree of their collaboration, and had several weeks to plan. In preparation, the stage was enlarged by removing all the traditional proscenium accoutrements except for fly rigging and lighting mounts. The performance area was divided into geographic areas, the planned time span for the Event was divided into segments, and the performers selected the area and the time segments for their contributions.

The choreography was mostly original material. Sandra Neels made a solo for Valda Setterfield and performed a spectacular tap dance. Carolyn Brown performed from a swinging bar, suspended from the flies and dramatically isolated in focused side-lighting. Susana Hayman-Chaffey, Neels, and Chase Robinson made a hilarious trio derived from private party imitations of famous Cunningham choreography. Ed Henkel executed an extended convulsion harrowing in its conviction. Neels performed a Barbara Lloyd solo from *Variations V* that she had always admired, while Cunningham, Carolyn Brown, and Viola Farber re-created the classic trio from *Story*.

With the assistance of students from his lighting-design class, Richard Nelson made a monumental lighting of often-subtle means. Two effects deserve mention. One was achieved by projecting from a distance various colors of light onto a small, flat disk that hung over part of the stage in such a way as to spill an eerie corona effect onto the cyclorama at the rear of the stage. The other came at the end of the performance, when he used the cyclorama on a huge scale to create vertical bands of colored light in a spectrum, not unlike that of a test pattern displayed on a color television screen at the end of daily transmission.

From my perspective, *Event no. 25* was the riskiest and most impressive artistic and social achievement during my years with the company, a bold and unpredictable co-existence of the awful and the sublime. It featured performances astonishing even to those who took for granted the spectacular virtuosity of the Cunningham Company.

The production of Events increased considerably in 1972 (by mid-1973 they numbered at least eighty-two), and with them the musical collaborations became more diverse. On May 5, 1972, Christian Wolff and fourteen student musicians from Dartmouth College collaborated with the Cunningham Company for *Event no. 36* on the three basketball courts at the University of New Hampshire.

At the time, Cage, Tudor, Behrman, and I were performing independently at a new-music festival in Bremen, Germany [see fig. IV-1 in the next part]. The dancers were on the middle court, between the audience and the musicians. For Cunningham the "sound was superb, and the space was slightly like Versailles."

In the 1972 tour of western and eastern Europe and Iran, we presented nineteen Events (nos. 43–61). What we did created more controversy than confrontation: response was diverse rather than monolithic (except for the brutal audience demonstration in the Cologne Opera House during the performance of *Canfield*). *Event no. 44* was presented in the incredibly beautiful ruins of Persepolis in central Iran on September 8, 1972. We danced on a platform surrounded by the guards for the Shahbanu, Empress Farah. Warhol's helium-filled pillows lighted the stone columns. The continual body searches by the secret police and the overbearing presence of military troops armed with automatic weapons were offset by the most friendly and intelligent people, exquisite indigenous culture, stunning landscape, and the most delicious yogurt and rice to be found anywhere. I had the feeling that Iran was a much greater confrontation for us than we were for it.

As the tour continued, *Event no. 45* of September 14, 1972, established something of a precedent: with no artificial physical isolation we performed in the midst of the Piazza San Marco in Venice, competing with throngs of tourists and pigeons for a segment of the busy square.[35] We separated the crowd using chairs, and then swept the square with brooms, brushing the dirt and dust onto the feet of the spectators. *Events nos. 52–53* (October 13–14, 1972) were presented in the Théâtre Mobile of the Maison de la Culture in Grenoble, France, a space seemingly designed for us. Sections of the Théâtre Mobile, including part of the audience, rotated in coaxial circles at various speeds and in different directions. The last performance of the 1972 European tour was *Event no. 61*, presented on October 29 in the packed Théâtre de la Ville in Paris. It was a particularly emotionally charged performance for everyone—the end of a remarkable tour and the last performance with the Cunningham Company of two of our dancers. Carolyn Brown was leaving after twenty-one years to pursue her own work,[36] while the Australian dancer Nanette Hassall, who had performed with us for two years, was prevented from returning by United States immigration restrictions.

With the exception of *Changing Steps* and a single performance of *Canfield* at the Brooklyn Academy of Music, all the performances of 1973 were Events or lecture-demonstrations, for which our musical endeavors were expanded by the full-time addition of David Behrman as a company musician. One of these, the lyrical *Event no. 70* at Cornell University (April 1, 1973), included a collaboration of the four company musicians with the live-electronic music group Mother

Mallard's Portable Masterpiece Company. The three Mother Mallard musicians—David Borden, Steve Drews, and Linda Fisher—added their sprawling collection of synthesizers to the Cunningham Company sound menagerie in this dance performance. The year 1973 also brought my last full-time engagement with the company to a close. Following the tour, I left for a position at the University of California, Santa Cruz.

Changes in artistic and cultural traditions sometimes conflicted with politics in ways beyond our control. We performed *Event no. 23* in Los Angeles in a large ballroom at UCLA on February 4, 1971. The format of the evening and physical arrangement of the hall allowed the audience freedom to move about the space during the performance. A corps of nervous ushers, wary in this era of constant civil unrest, actively discouraged the audience from moving about and intimidated those who left the performance area. In other situations we were particularly conscious of our influence, which to some seemed politically motivated. Jean Tinguely once suggested to me that it was immoral to condone a repressive and elitist regime in the Middle East by accepting an invitation to perform in that country. This is a delicate argument, for what could be viewed as a condoning action from outside the country can in reality be a subversive action if seen from within. And in countries with heavily controlled communications, declining an invitation for political reasons has no effect when it goes unreported, bypassing an opportunity for cultural interaction and exchange of ideas. The decision to decline an invitation or refuse to perform requires astute consideration of all sides.

For me the South American tour of 1968 and the ten-week European tour of 1972 were our most important international accomplishments during my years with the company. With the exception of a few places, these were not glamorous or even comfortable occasions. We were pioneering—confronting one culture with others in circumstances where the risks were not always easy to accommodate. Many ideological reactionaries had trouble with the very *ideas* of freedom embodied in our work.

Yet one aspect of our work is uncomfortably clear: as much as we may aspire to collaborative equality, there is hierarchy in the social dynamics of the Cunningham Dance Company, an extremely complex hierarchy that is always changing. The inherent inequalities begin with the sheer danger of physical injury faced by the dancers.

By contrast, the social dynamics of the musical productions have had a relatively simple and inspiring course. The history began in the 1940s, with Cage as pianist and composer. In the 1950s Cage was music director, with Tudor as pianist. In the 1960s these categories became irrelevant as the functions became increasingly shared and diverse, and I joined the ensemble. When Cage became uncomfortable with the idea of being "music director," all categories disappeared. By the 1970s, with the addition of Behrman (and others on occasion) we had evolved into a remarkable collaboration. We were not equal: each had specializations and some of these were not interchangeable. No one could imagine me reading Cage's stories for *How to Pass, Kick, Fall, and Run*, Cage performing Bo Nilsson's music for *Night Wandering* (instead of Tudor), or Tudor (or anyone else except Cage) playing Satie's music for *Nocturnes*. Everyone worried if I wasn't around when some complicated electronic problem had to be solved quickly, and I lost sleep over the prospect of Tudor not being available to set up his own electronic menagerie for *RainForest*. But minor disagreements notwithstanding, with the Events of the 1970s the musicians had reached a remarkable coexistence of specialization and creative community.

There are few persistently innovative groups of performing artists that, like the Cunningham Dance Company, manage to survive their preposterous economic circumstances and thrive for a quarter century—and beyond. Even if their economic situation improves with rising fame, they must learn to survive the erosion of their private lives. The constantly widening generation gap between the oldest and youngest member of the ensemble also has its consequences. Yet the theatrical traditions, physical vocabulary, social dynamics, and lifestyles of our world are posited on a span of generations: elements of imperial ballet, decades of modern dance, centuries and poly-cultures of music, gas-jet, greasepaint, or lasers and quantum-electronic technologies, vaudeville, circus, review, proscenium formality and tennis court, costume-bag and warehouse. Under conditions at once lyrical and brutal, temperamental and magnanimous, serene and preposterous, formalities are abused, egos enlarged, temperaments battered, humanities nourished. We cope with confrontation, acceleration, exhilaration, exhaustion, sometimes attrition. Yet it does not seem an eclectic effort. It is a precious opportunity: to collaborate in a process with an ensemble of exceptionally high performance standards and of different people meeting perhaps at only a single point. The congruence of disparate ideas is based on the premise of rigorous discipline and risky experimentation, "a continual preparation for the shock of freedom," as Peter Brook spoke of Cunningham's work.[37]

Among the many reasons for the success of Merce Cunningham's work with modern composers, one is outstanding: his expansion of the concept and function of music for modern dance into a sound environment for choreography. Cunningham's aesthetic has not only given new dignity and possibility to the meanings of modern dance but has also created an invigorating atmosphere in which so many musicians and artists have fruitfully collaborated.

CHAPTER 16

Robert Rauschenberg in the Creative Fields of the Cunningham Dance Company

(2012)

John Cage has emerged as a central spokesman for the artistic community of the Merce Cunningham Dance Company largely because of the polemic energy with which he wrote and spoke about so much of it. But for almost sixty years the Cunningham Company proved a fertile creative field for *all* those associated with it. Here I am taking the broadest definition of the "Cunningham Company"—the dancers, musicians, directors, lighting and costume designers, poets, writers, technical engineers, and eventually computer software designers and video artists who worked together in its creative fields. One of the most distinctive features of working in the Cunningham Dance Company was the disciplined freedom that Cunningham and Cage inspired among its creative individuals. David Tudor, for example, developed from a virtuoso pianist into a significant composer of live-electronic music. And dancer Remy Charlip was also a choreographer, decor and costume designer, theater producer, and virtuoso knitter, and is still celebrated for his children's books, most of which remain in print.

One of the most energetic contributors to the shared creative field of the Cunningham Company during its first decade was visual artist extraordinaire, photographer, lighting director, stage and costume designer, and occasional dancer-choreographer Robert Rauschenberg (1925–2008). Rauschenberg's first collaboration with the Cunningham Dance Company and the beginning of his formal theater activities was Cunningham's choreography *Minutiae*, pre-

Source: This is an expanded excerpt from "Shared Fields of Creative Ideas in the Cunningham Dance Company Milieu," lecture presented at the Hirschhorn Museum, September 9, 2012, as part of the John Cage Centennial Festival held in Washington, D.C., September 4–10, 2012.

miered at the Brooklyn Academy of Music in December 1954. Its duration was about twenty minutes, typical of choreography to be included on a mixed program of three or more dances with different decor. The music was by Cage—selections from his ongoing compositional series *Music for Piano 1–20* (1952–53), which was often performed on two pianos by Cage and Tudor.[1] The decor and lighting were by Rauschenberg.

Rauschenberg had come to the company with a developing profile in the visual arts. From his Texas childhood onward he had always been a creator of images. During his early years in New York City he earned a minor income by designing window displays for Bonwit Teller and Tiffany's. He was also an innovative photographer, developing his skills in balancing lighting, shadow, and distance perspective and in defining frame edges. His unique procedure of blueprint photography was exhibited at the Museum of Modern Art in New York in 1951.[2]

Part of Rauschenberg's idea for the *Minutiae* decor came from Cunningham's suggestion that it be placed in the performance space itself so that the dancers could move in, out, and through it. Except for the proviso that the decor should allow efficient assembly and disassembly for transportation on tour, Rauschenberg was on his own. The result was his first freestanding "combine."[3]

The three artists who collaborated on *Minutiae* made their separate decisions about such issues as performance timings and placements individually and without consultation. Cunningham developed his own structural concepts and plans for the choreography. Nothing of the physical dance movements was improvised: for their own safety the dancers learned each individual choreographic section to be performed as rehearsed in both solos and fast-moving ensembles. The performance order of these sections, however, was determined and assigned by Cunningham with his use of chance operations. For each performance of *Minutiae* the music and lighting followed a similar process, pieced together in groups independent of each other. Cage and Tudor chose by their chance operations which of the compositions from the pre-composed *Music for Piano* series would be performed. Rauschenberg adapted his lighting by his own chance operations.

Rauschenberg's work with the lighting for *Minutiae* was a new experience in his creative and performing life. No longer painting and assembling combine materials alone in his studio in solo time, he was now a member of an ensemble. At the time he was only beginning to learn the techniques and possibilities of theater lighting, a high skill that requires constant adaptation to diverse venues, often with clumsy or unreliable equipment. Yet Cunningham trusted him. For *Minutiae* Rauschenberg developed detailed plans that involved specific timings

Table 2. Robert Rauschenberg, Lighting Map for Cunningham's *Minutiae* (adapted from Cunningham, *Changes*)

Time: 15 minutes, 20 seconds

Requirements: small set in stage area 5
3 strong spots stage area 5 from light bridge or 1st pipe
one dimmer each color—primary red, blue, green

CYC[LORAMA]	Time	Spots on set	Stage L	Stage R	Borders	Area spots
Bl ½ Gr ½	0'00"	R	Mag	Mag	R	4, 6, 7, 8, 9 up ½
	0'30"					1, 2, 3 up ½
Gr down Bl up	1'00"	Gr up	Yel up	Yel up	Gr up	
	3'30"	R down Bl up	Blgr up Mag & Yel down	Blgr up ½ Mag down Yel ½	R down Bl up	1, 2, 3 down 4, 6, 7, 8, 9 down
	4'00"					1, 2, 3 up ½ 4, 6, 7, 8, 9 up ½
	4'20"	R down Bl up				
Gr up ½	5'30"		Mag up Blgr down		R up ¼ Bl down	1, 2, 3 down 4, 6, 7, 8, 9 down
R up Bl down	6'00"			Blgr down Mag up ¼		1, 2, 3 up ½ 4, 6, 7, 8, 9 up ½
	7'05"	Gr down R up			Gr down Bl up	

Table 2. Continued

CYC[LORAMA]	Time	Spots on set	Stage L	Stage R	Borders	Area spots
R down Gr up	8'40"		Blgr up	Yel up		
	9'20"	Gr up ½		Mag up ½	Bl down Gr up ½	
Bl up, Gr down R up	10'30"		Mag down			
	11'00"	R down Gr up			R down ¼ Gr up	
	12'05"				R up	1, 2, 3 down
	13'05"					1, 2, 3 up ½
	13'30"	Bl up R up				
Bl down	14'00"		Mag up			
	14'30"	Gr down			Gr down	
	14'45"		Blgr down	Yel down		
	15'10"	Bl down				1, 2, 3 down 4, 6, 7, 8, 9 down
	15'20"	curtain				

Bl = blue
Blgr = blue-green
Gr = green
Mag = magenta
R = red
Yel = yellow

and placements for changes of lighting source, color and hue, intensity, and direction. Rauschenberg's original lighting map for *Minutiae* [see table 2 for a transcription] reveals his changing disposition of variables over time.[4] The process is analogous to Cunningham's charting of physical movement areas and actions in the choreographic sketches of the time. Rauschenberg modified these maps from performance to performance, adapting his decisions as required for touring venues. For me the wonder was that his stage and lighting designs for *Minutiae* gave the impression of structural coordination with the choreography and music, despite their independent creative processes within a community of shared ideas.

A notable aspect of Rauschenberg's work in the visual arts was his move from the single-color panels of the early 1950s, such as the famous "black" and "white" paintings, to the intense color complexities of the later 1950s. Working with Cunningham appears to have stimulated Rauschenberg to reverse this process. His *Minutiae* stage design was a complex montage of constantly shifting stage-lighting colors, with the use of shimmering fabrics and a mirror on the combine decor that gently rotated on its own by chance, activated by the air motions of the passing dancers.[5] As Rauschenberg's lighting procedures responded to the practicalities of on-the-road performances, however, he gradually moved away from complex color lighting. Some touring venues had primitive lighting at best. Within these crude resources he experimented with elemental target-projection and shadow effects. The results were often as innovative (read "controversial") as the choreography or music, notably his stark and dramatic lighting for Cunningham's 1964 choreography *Winterbranch*.

Besides his collaborations with Yvonne Rainer, Kenneth Koch, Jean Tinguely, the Judson Theater, and others in the 1960s, Rauschenberg made his own theater productions. His dance work *Pelican* premiered in 1963, with Carolyn Brown *en pointe* and Rauschenberg and another male dancer on roller skates with massive parachutes strapped to their backs.[6] Rauschenberg also supplied its choreography and sound collage. In Stockholm in September 1964 he directed a performance of his *Elgin Tie* in collaboration with David Tudor. It became Tudor's first listed musical composition under the title *Fluorescent Sound*. For *Elgin Tie* Rauschenberg not only designed the decor—it involved a live cow crossing the stage—but also participated in the performance in a slow descent from the very tall ceiling down an elaborate rope structure directly into a barrel of water. In *Elgin Tie* he brought together these commonplace objects in a theatrical context rather than in a fixed combine.

Rauschenberg's first prize in the visual arts at the 1964 Venice Biennale catapulted him to international fame and considerable fortune. He left the company at the end of the 1964 world tour and was replaced by Jasper Johns, who took over the decor and related functions in the Cunningham Dance Company. Rauschenberg's theater work continued in other venues in 1965. He toured that year, for example, with the ONCE Group and members of the Judson Dance Theater. Their *Joy Road Interchange*, which was premiered at Antioch College in April 1965, was conceived as a "total-performance interchange" that "can be performed in various arrangements separately, sequentially, or simultaneously (and often requiring improvisation during the course of performance)."[7] One of its performances was at the First New York Theater Rally in May 1965, which Rauschenberg co-organized and financed.[8]

He also mounted an extraordinary nighttime performance at the September 1965 ONCE AGAIN Festival in Ann Arbor. Titled *Spring Training*, Rauschenberg's work was performed outdoors on the roofless top floor of a large parking garage. It had already achieved status as a touring event of the Judson Interchange. Rauschenberg's involvement with animals was life-long and serious, perhaps most famously captured in the stuffed goat with tire in his late 1950s freestanding combine *Monogram*. For *Spring Training* he employed a large ensemble of live turtles to which he attached flashlights. The turtles moved freely throughout the performance and audience space, creating part of the lighting for the work. Not knowing how he obtained and trained dozens of live turtles for that occasion, I asked him about it several decades later. Remembering that 1965 event with delight, he answered simply: "The turtles were rented locally, and I just talked with them individually." Besides the turtle-controlled lighting, Rauschenberg also designed the choreography and decor for *Spring Training* and composed its music on magnetic tape.

Marcel Duchamp died in October 1968. That year both Cage and Rauschenberg created visual arts tributes to Duchamp. Each used movable translucent plexiglass, as was the premise of Duchamp's *Large Glass*. Rauschenberg's *Solstice*, a large construction of screen-printed sliding glass doors, is large enough for people to walk through. Cage's *Not Wanting to Say Anything about Marcel* is small enough to fit compactly on a table, and the order of its eight glass plates can be rearranged. The contrasting if complementary nature of these two works reflects the surprising congruence that was often shared by creative individuals in the Cunningham community.

Minutiae is a case study for the creative process of the Cunningham milieu from the early 1950s, to be refined over the following decade. Rauschenberg's decor and lighting were created separately from Cage's music and Cunningham's choreography. But when joined together to form a complete performance, these components were compatible because they had emerged from a shared creative field. One of the most notable instances of spontaneous integration was Cunningham's 1958 "Lyric Dance" *Summerspace* with music by Morton Feldman, to which Rauschenberg contributed the bewitching dappled scenery and coordinated camouflaging leotards for the dancers. *Summerspace* has enjoyed a long life in several re-creations of the choreography and original production over the past fifty years. Most recently Rauschenberg's copy of the set has been acquired by the Walker Art Center in Minneapolis. Those of us who toured with the Rauschenberg sets and costumes as working components of repertory works had little sense of the enormous value they would acquire.

During his decade with the Cunningham Dance Company, Rauschenberg lived what he recalled in October 1974 as the "rare experience of working with such exceptional people under always unique conditions and in totally unpredictable places (all acceptable because of a mutual compulsive desire to make and share). . . . All of us worked totally committed, shared every intense emotion and, I think, performed miracles, for love only."[9]

CHAPTER 17

With Tudor the Organist
(2013)

David Tudor's activities as an organist in the 1940s have been well documented by John Holzaepfel: his early fascination with his father's church performances on the reed organ; his studies with organist H. William Hawke; and his appointments as assistant organist at Philadelphia's St. Mark's Episcopal Church and, at the age of eighteen, as organ instructor at Swarthmore College. As Holzaepfel rightly observes, "his career as an organist seemed well under way."[1] But Tudor's evolution from organ to piano—to become one of the prime piano virtuosos of new music of the 1950s—has obscured the continuing importance of the organ in Tudor's creative development as a composer of live-electronic music in the 1960s and beyond.

Tudor's mastery of the broad organ repertoire included works spanning several hundred years. Hearing him segue smoothly or dramatically between sections of toccatas by Buxtehude, Widor, and Reger revealed imaginative combinations of seemingly disparate sound sources similar to those found in his later live-electronic music. His encounter with the organ music of Olivier Messiaen in the late 1940s had profoundly changed his thinking about recent music. In a 1986 interview with Bruce Duffie, Tudor recalled: "I loved all the music I learned to play, and I still do. I used to play the organ, and I find that I listen to it very, very seriously."[2]

Source: A shorter version of this piece originally appeared under this title as Mumma's program essay to *The Art of David Tudor, 1963–1992* (7 CDs, NWR 80737), © 2013 Anthology of Recorded Music, Inc. Because of the revision, New World Records for ARM has graciously reverted the rights to the current version to Gordon Mumma.

Tudor's serious engagement with the organ continued throughout his life. During our performance tours with the Merce Cunningham Dance Company, particularly in Europe, Tudor would occasionally suggest that I accompany him on a visit to a nearby church that had a unique historic organ. When access to the instrument was possible, he would put on his thin leather-soled organ shoes, which he carried along in a little bag. He would begin by feeling out the instrument, testing the locations and sonorities of the stops and working the pedals for their physical responses. Then from memory he would launch into segments of the organ repertoire chosen according to the time and place of the instrument. There may have been some aspect of remembrance of things past, but equally evident was Tudor's vivid curiosity about sound sources and their interplay in space and time. He thrived on the time delays between keyboard activation and resulting sounds, the motion of overlapping sounds among separate ranks of pipes and their reverberation and cross resonances in the unique acoustics of each venue, and the vast possibilities of timbre and attack—what all organists work with, particularly in large spaces.

He prized the unique character of each instrument. During a free half-day in Hamburg in 1966, between sessions for the NDR filming of the Cage-Cunningham *Variations V*, we visited the Sankt Jacobi Church to see the famous late seventeenth-century Arp Schnitger tracker organ. It was a Baroque four-manual instrument that had been partially destroyed in World War II bombings, still being restored but very playable. The panels of stops, each stop with a decorative chimera, had some names unfamiliar to me, but not to Tudor. When I mentioned that the tuning of the instrument was a major-second higher than the standard A-440, Tudor replied: "Perhaps it helped them to keep warm." He performed excerpts from his early organ repertory, exploring contrasts of timbre and placement.

Back at the NDR studios later that day and still speaking about that wonderful organ, we were overheard by someone who said that we must also see their Welte-Funkorgel. It was a special organ designed in 1930 to produce "orchestral" sounds for radio and theater performances. Its large collection of stops fascinated Tudor for its many sound possibilities. He played fragments of Rimsky-Korsakov's "Flight of the Bumblebee," a staple of theater organ repertoire, adding ornate sound effects. Elsewhere we visited an early Welte Recording Organ, an automatic player organ notable for its use of paper player-rolls related to the technical mechanism of the Welte player piano.

Tudor's ongoing fascination with the complex timbre relations of wind-driven resonating pipes and reeds was further augmented in the mid-1960s by his introduction to the bandoneon. This bellows-driven instrument, with its resonators of wind-driven reeds, was technically a distant cousin of the small reed organs of his childhood—with the distinction of portability and close physical connection between its sounds and the performer. As with the organ, each bandoneon is often unique, with a wide range of dynamics and articulation gestures, long sustaining durations, and a broad spectrum of sonorities, harmonics, and sub-harmonics.

His bandoneon soon became a sound-maker to be processed with electronic means, a frequent performance practice for Tudor after 1965. One particular electronic configuration with time-delay processing of the bandoneon can be seen in a photo from Christian Wolff's Burdock Festival in Royalton, Vermont, in August 1971 [fig. III-9]. The instrument also featured in Tudor's commissions from others (Pauline Oliveros, Stanley Lunetta, and myself),[3] and in his own theatrical *Bandoneon!* (1966), an interactive sound and visual collaboration with Lowell Cross.

In 1967 Tudor was under pressure from Columbia Records to re-record Karlheinz Stockhausen's *Klavierstücke* at their 30th Street studio to replace Tudor's earlier recording, which had proved unusable due to defective tape. By that time Tudor's priorities had shifted. He persuaded Columbia to issue a contract for a very different project—three recent works for wind-driven reeds. These included my *Mesa* for Tudor's bandoneon and cybersonic processing [see fig. III-4] and works for organ by Mauricio Kagel and Christian Wolff.[4] The recording of Kagel's *Improvisation ajoutée* for organ at St. George's Episcopal Church in New York City [fig. III-10] took the "added" aspect of its title as an invitation to include three additional performers (Alvin Lucier, Michael Sahl, and myself). Our function was to activate the stops selected by Tudor among the eighty-six available on this large four-manual Möller instrument. Tudor thus extended Kagel's work from solo to ensemble in order to increase the complexity of sonorities beyond the already considerable ones available to the soloist. Wolff's *For 1, 2 or 3 People*, by contrast, was recorded on the two-manual Baroque tracker organ by Schlicker in Richard Lippold's sculpture studio on Long Island. The choice of two very different organs was Tudor's decision. It is notable that he again performed on the organ in the premiere recording of Wolff's *Burdocks* at Dartmouth College in 1971. Tudor never re-recorded the Stockhausen.

Many aspects of Tudor's creativity have roots in his early experience with historical organ cultures and repertoire. The "structured improvisation" central to organ performance practices was fundamental to him, and with it the idea of the composer-improviser who rearranges and further develops sound materials retrieved from past experience. From his years as an organist Tudor had also developed prodigious skill in the simultaneous overlapping of multiple contrast-

Fig. III-9. David Tudor and his bandoneon with electronic processing at Christian Wolff's Burdock Festival, Royalton, Vermont, August 1971. (Photo © Gordon Mumma.)

Fig. III-10. David Tudor the organist, recording Mauricio Kagel's *Improvisation ajoutée* at St. George's Episcopal Church, New York, July 1967. (Photo © Gordon Mumma.)

ing layers of sound sources. The extended resources of timbre and sonority, as well as the properties of time delay and spatial sound placement of the organ, were second nature to him. These skills nourished the sound environments of his *Bandoneon!*, *Rainforest*, and the ongoing Merce Cunningham Dance Company collaborative Events, and contributed to the breadth of his evolving achievements in the electronic-music arts.

Fig. III-11. David Tudor the composer, on tour in Chicago with the Cunningham Dance Company, January 1971. (Photo © Gordon Mumma.)

CHAPTER 18

David Tudor the Composer along the Path to *Rainforest*

(2006/2013)

David Tudor's performance life as organist and pianist was supplemented and eventually supplanted by his developing activities as a "composer of sound resources" during the 1960s (his own phrase when speaking to me in 1966). Although *Rainforest* (1968) is generally considered to mark Tudor's emergence as a composer, its creative roots run deep into his collaborative creative work of that decade with John Cage, the Merce Cunningham Dance Company, Pauline Oliveros, Lowell Cross, Alvin Lucier, myself, and others. This was a garden of shared ideas with minimal fences.

The genesis of the sound-processing ideas that Tudor used in *Rainforest* extends back to his contributions to Cage's *Cartridge Music* (1960) and *Variations II* (1961). Cage's premise for *Cartridge Music* was the use of amplified small sounds from resonating objects. In assisting with its preparation and rehearsals, Tudor obtained many obsolete transducers from lower Manhattan junk shops, applied them to resonating devices such as suspended "slinkies," and worked with elementary mixers and amplifiers. He was also attentive to electronic music gadgetry being developed by others. He visited the Space Theatre during his first concert with Cage in Ann Arbor in May 1960, and ordered two of my Cybersonics units, which I built specially for him. He would use them extensively over the following years.[1]

Source: This substantially new essay of 2013 incorporates materials from Mumma's program notes to *David Tudor and Gordon Mumma*, NWR 80651-2 (2006): 13–17, © Anthology of Recorded Music, Inc., with major revisions and copious additional material. Accordingly, New World Records for ARM has graciously reverted the rights to the current version to Gordon Mumma.

In order to realize *Variations II* as instructed by Cage, Tudor also developed technical procedures that extended those of *Cartridge Music*. Tudor's performance of *Variations II* at the February 17, 1963, ONCE Festival in Ann Arbor, Michigan, treated the piano as a sound source with most of the action inside the instrument.[2] In both projects, Tudor was creatively involved in building the interactive small instruments and realizing Cage's performance intentions. But although Tudor had studied composition with Stefan Wolpe, he did not yet consider himself a composer, any more than the young organist had thought of himself as a pianist when he had begun studying with Wolpe's wife, pianist Irma Wolpe Rademacher, in the late 1940s.

The year 1964 was a significant one for Tudor's sound explorations. It witnessed the first of the ongoing series of Cunningham's choreographic Events in Vienna that June. These Event performances developed over the following decades into unique music-dance collaborations that involved both structural planning and improvisation. Several months later, in September, Tudor produced the sound installation *Fluorescent Sound* for Robert Rauschenberg's *Elgin Tie* theater-sound production in Stockholm. This event was a notable step in Tudor's expansion beyond the piano and in establishing his creative independence from Cage. In it he electronically amplified and distributed the mechanical resonances of the fluorescent light fixtures in Stockholm's Moderna Museet. He said of the project that he was happy doing something entirely of his own. Although *Fluorescent Sound* is often listed as Tudor's first composition, he remained uncertain whether it had established him as a "composer."

Several events of 1965 brought Tudor closer to that goal. He worked closely with Cage in the realization of the electronic tour de force *Variations V*, premiered in July. It was for Tudor a massive experience of collaborative composition. He would expand his creative contributions in touring versions of *Variations V* over the following years, constantly selecting and recombining materials in performance and experimenting with amplified small sounds, acoustical resonances, and feedback processes.

Two months after the premiere of *Variations V*, Cage and Tudor performed *Talk 1* with Ashley, Rauschenberg, and myself at the September 1965 ONCE AGAIN Festival in Ann Arbor. Through our earlier connections Tudor knew what I was doing with electronic sound modifications. In the wake of his recent experience he was interested in discussing my use of cybersonic processing. He had also brought along his newly acquired bandoneon, and we played long, sustained acoustic sounds back and forth, comparing his instrument with my horn and with electronic sound. The bandoneon seemed to have a liberating effect on Tudor—its portability, sustained wind sonorities, and freedom from the historical weight of the piano. During this period he developed as an electronic composer by following paths similar to those with the organ and bandoneon: trying out sounds and shifting from wind-driven to electronic modifications.

Tudor's imagination was now evolving beyond simple amplification to the use of acoustical objects as resonating devices to modify sounds of electronic origin. This interest was stimulated in part by his collections of defective and low-grade small loudspeakers that produced "distorted" sounds. He was also enthusiastic about similar ideas in the work of others, notably Pauline Oliveros in her *Applebox Double* (1965), which Tudor and Oliveros performed together at a ONCE recording concert on March 28, 1966, in Ann Arbor.

Tudor was still considering the question of whether he was a composer in the summer of 1966 when I stayed with him at his Stony Point, New York, home for about a month before the upcoming European tour of the Cunningham Dance Company. These were intense workdays. Tudor and I had to make major preparations to complete my *Mesa* for his bandoneon and my cybersonic processing before its August premiere with Cunningham's choreography *Place*. Cage and Tudor were also desperate for solutions to the disastrous technical problems of touring with *Variations V*. We set up the *Variations V* equipment in Tudor's living room, and Cage occasionally dropped by to urge us on. I managed to reduce the technological overload by a half, while maintaining all the basic functions.

Although I was new to the Cunningham circle at that time, trust developed between us. Tudor was especially interested in talking with me about his compositional interests. He spoke especially of his work with Lowell Cross, Fred Waldhauer, and others for the *9 Evenings* project of E.A.T. (Experiments in Art and Technology) to be premiered in October 1966. That collaboration became Tudor's *Bandoneon!* (read "bandoneon factorial"), an interactive sound and visual production with Cross's system that rivaled *Variations V* in extravagance. It was a "combine" of programmed audio circuits, moving loudspeakers, TV images, and lighting, activated by the acoustic signals of a bandoneon. For this work Tudor developed special "instrumental loudspeakers" with which he exploited the unique resonant characteristics of sounding physical materials.[3] He was already establishing working patterns of intense technological collaboration with others.

In 1968 Cunningham commissioned Tudor to create music for his forthcoming choreography *RainForest*. Tudor was ready to accept the challenge. The Events with their opportunities for experimentation in sound recycling had helped him gain confidence as a composer. For the music—for which he adopted Cunningham's *Rainforest* title, minus the capital F—Tudor would extend Oliveros's example of working with sounds from resonating wooden boxes, to which he added metal objects activated by his developing electronic audio resources.

Rainforest is an example of acoustic modification of electronically generated sound. In its earliest form, the sounds of *Rainforest* were electronically generated and applied by special transducers to various resonant objects of wood, metal, and plastic. Each of the combinations of transducer and resonant object was an "instrumental loudspeaker" that added and subtracted harmonics and occasionally created complex inter-modulations with the electronic sound sources. Further, attached to each "instrumental loudspeaker" was a small microphone that allowed the acoustically modified sound to be further amplified and resonantly distributed by conventional loudspeakers throughout the performance space. He recycled his acoustical sounds through the mixer as if within an ecological system, returning them to the resonating objects and adding more sounds to the widening cycles. Tudor's lyrical music shared the success of the March 9, 1968, premiere of Cunningham's *RainForest* at Buffalo State. Around that time, Tudor spoke with me at his place in Stony Point about his *Rainforest* experience: "I am comfortable with the idea of being a composer."

Thereafter *Rainforest* grew, and different versions emerged over the years. In the late 1960s *Rainforest* was generally performed by two performers and a "forest" of four or more instrumental loudspeakers and four conventional loudspeakers. The performers articulated the electronic system and created combinations that were heard by the audience from the conventional loudspeakers.

The first concert performance of *Rainforest* took place in March 1969 at a large conference center at Cornell University in Ithaca, New York.[4] The equipment was set on tables in the center of the space, with the audience seated around the performers. Four separate channels of sound were used (not always possible in Cunningham touring performances), widely spaced with two in the foreground and two in the background. The sound sources had also expanded from those used in the earlier Cunningham performances, with Tudor now adding recordings of small sounds from insects and birds in conjunction with the previous electronic sounds, all modified by his acoustical resonant devices. The interactive circuitry was fundamentally the same as that used previously, a system of one to eight input and output sources, but expanded with new devices and interactive connections. We rehearsed parts of this concert performance for assurance that we could fly by ourselves in the absence of dancers and floating pillows. With regard to the duration, just before we started Tudor said to me: "We will end at the right time." Knowing one another as we did, that was all that was needed. For me the lyrical gentleness still predominated, even with Tudor's occasional celebrated sound-bursts. The resulting performance was about twice the length of the danced version.

Fig. III-12. David Tudor with participant Susan Palmer at summer courses, Chocorua, New Hampshire, July 1973. They are seen preparing the premiere of the large ensemble version of *Rainforest 4*. (Photo © Gordon Mumma.)

At the summer courses of 1973 at Chocorua, New Hampshire, Tudor directed an "experimental electronic workshop in sound transformation without modulation" with a group of twelve student participants. The end product was the first performance of *Rainforest IV* in its expanded concert version. Tudor brought along a lot of equipment and guided the participants through the stages of building their own instruments and realizing the work in performance—a learning process similar to that which Tudor had experienced with Cage over a decade earlier [fig. III-12]. Under his direction they also extended the sound materials to include prepared sounds of non-electronic origin. The Chocorua performance was presented in a large barn as a six-hour sound environment.

Tudor and I worked well together, sharing space, time, ideas, and production activities with minimal conflicts. Yet our compositional procedures were largely different from one another. Whereas I explored the electronic modification of acoustical sounds, Tudor explored the acoustical modification of sounds of electronic origins, often by resonating objects to which small loudspeakers were physically attached. Yet we also crossed paths, overlapped, and sometimes used each other's sound-resources for further creative work with our own procedures. In every sense of the word, David Tudor had become a composer.

PART IV

Not Wanting to Say
Anything about John (Cage)

Editor's Introduction

The 2012 John Cage centenary unleashed a worldwide celebration of concerts, exhibitions, and conferences. As a longtime creative associate of Cage and a first-hand witness of his daily life for many years, Gordon Mumma was invited to participate in several of these, in Berlin, Lublin (Poland), Washington, D.C., New Orleans, and Victoria, B.C. The resulting harvest of words about Cage promises a burgeoning crop of evaluation and re-evaluation of Cage's legacy in music, poetry, philosophy, and the visual arts.

Mumma had met Cage in 1953, but their first work together was in the early 1960s, mostly in Ann Arbor, Michigan. Following his engagement with the Cunningham Dance Company in 1966, Mumma worked closely with Cage and Tudor on the expanding technology of their live-electronic collaborations into the mid-1970s. During this time he also performed regularly with Cage, both with the Cunningham Dance Company and in separate concerts and events. After Mumma accepted a teaching position in 1973 at the University of California, Santa Cruz, they continued working together on various projects until Cage's death in 1992.

Mumma's personal relationship with Cage, always warm and appreciative, was also somewhat guarded. Even after Cage's death Mumma has remained reluctant to disclose the details of their personal conversations, because Cage himself was private about them. On the professional level Mumma has distanced himself repeatedly from attempts to fabricate a "school of Cage" or to posit himself as a "follower" of Cage—or of any other aesthetic movement or herd. Rather than Cage the composer, it has been Cage the *performer*—of piano, percussion, voice, and live electronics—that has provided Mumma with the more durable "nourishment of discovery" and an inspiring model of discipline and independence in the collaborative creative process. Hence the focus of the three following contributions on Cage as performer and innovator in the field of live electronics. The close friendship between Cage and Mumma also emerges in controlled doses in the twenty-five vignettes of their shared experience culled from Mumma's private diaries. Modeled after Cage's famous indeterminacy stories,[1] they provide photographic glimpses of the humor, wonder, and intensity of life on the road with John Cage.

CHAPTER 19

Cage as Performer
(2001)

In the last part of his life, John Cage's performance virtuosity was mostly vocal: reading (or singing or chanting) from his writings and responding to questions in lively public encounters. Most currently available recordings of his performances were made during this time. And since his work seems to have had greater impact on people younger than himself, most of those who heard him are probably less familiar with his earlier instrumental and live-electronic performances.

The performances in the earlier part of his career were unique and as memorable as his later vocal performances. Typical of musicians who have considerable playing experience, he had developed a reliable technique while accompanying modern dance classes and during many years of concerts. Though at no time in his career was he primarily a performer (as was the composer Serge Rachmaninoff), his performances were always remarkable.

Cage made use of four performance resources in the course of his career: piano, percussion, electronic-music equipment, and voice. His performing life, which began in 1933, divides roughly into three periods, each about two decades long. In the first period, 1933–53, Cage was primarily a performer with piano and percussion; during the 1940s, he also conducted percussion ensembles. In the second period, after 1953, Cage continued as a pianist (and sometimes as

Source: Reprinted with minor adjustments from "Cage as Performer," in *Writings through John Cage's Music, Poetry, and Art*, ed. David W. Bernstein and Christopher Hatch, 113–19 (Chicago: University of Chicago Press, 2001), © 2001 by The University of Chicago, with permission of The University of Chicago Press.

conductor) and developed skill in performance with electronic equipment and with his voice. In the third period of his creative life, after 1973, he performed mostly with his voice.

Cage's early formal musical training was as a pianist. After the five-finger exercises of his elementary school years, he studied nineteenth-century piano music with his aunt, Phoebe James, and during the mid-1920s with pianist-composer Fannie Charles Dillon in Los Angeles. His formal study of piano concluded in the 1930s with Richard Buhlig in Los Angeles. As a performer of percussion and electronic resources and with his voice, Cage was essentially self-taught. He did not develop his performing skills as a percussionist by learning the classical rudiments of the orchestral or band percussionist. Rather, he learned what was necessary for each situation. Cage developed as a percussionist as one does in gamelan traditions, by progressing through levels of skill from relative beginner to mature virtuoso. The development of his creative skills with electronic equipment resulted from a disciplined exploration of possibilities (rather than a formal background in science and engineering), nourished by his productively unorthodox imagination. His vocal skills developed from his love of writing and speaking and grew out of his major innovations as a poet with the written word. (It was also in this third period that he extended his creativity as a graphic artist.)

Throughout his first period, Cage performed as a pianist in concert and as a dance accompanist. His repertory included his own compositions. He had good sight-reading proficiency and considerable technical skill, sufficient for his notably challenging pieces such as *The Perilous Night* (1944) and the *Sonatas and Interludes* (1946–48). He also performed with piano virtuosos such as Maro Ajemian, Grete Sultan, William Masselos, Marcelle Mercenier, and David Tudor. With these colleagues he performed his *Experiences No. 1* (1945), *Music for Piano 4–84* (1953–56), and *34'46.776"* (1954).

In the late 1940s, Cage was formally introduced to Tudor by composer Stefan Wolpe.[1] Merce Cunningham was at work on choreography (*Pool of Darkness*, premiered in January 1950) for a technically difficult piano piece of the same title by the American composer Ben Weber. Cage engaged Tudor to perform the Weber piece when he saw that it was beyond his abilities. As a pianist Tudor established benchmarks for performance of the challenging, innovative piano music by Cage, Pierre Boulez, Karlheinz Stockhausen, Christian Wolff, Wolpe, and many others. Tudor's association with Cage and with the Cunningham Dance Company relieved Cage from a sense of obligation about performing as a pianist.

Cage continued to perform as piano soloist with the Cunningham Dance Company into the late 1960s, notably in the choreography *Nocturnes* (1956;

the music was Erik Satie's *Three Nocturnes*). Cage's approach to the Satie work was lyrical and gently liquid rather than markedly articulated, with a subtle lilt like a barely perceptible perfume. In this second period, several Cunningham repertory works involved Cage and Tudor as duo pianists; these included *Minutiae* (1954) and *Suite for Five* (1956), both of which used Cage's *Music for Piano 4–52*. The piano duo of Cage and Tudor also performed Morton Feldman's *Ixion* (1958) for Cunningham's choreography *Summerspace* (1958). After the early 1970s, Cage performed as a pianist mostly in one work, *Cheap Imitation* (1969).

The context of *Cheap Imitation* offers insight into an aspect of his creative life. In the late 1960s, Cage and Cunningham returned to work on a project begun many years earlier, a choreography for Satie's *Socrate*. The situation was extraordinary for the Cunningham ensemble: the choreography was coordinated with the music, and the dancers rehearsed with the music. (In most of the Cunningham repertory, the dance and music are independent of each other, created, rehearsed, and performed separately, though in performance their independence occurs simultaneously.) Cage had made a two-piano transcription of *Socrate*, intending that he and Tudor would perform it.[2] Unforeseen legal issues interfered: the Satie estate denied permission for the use of Cage's transcription. Cage resolved the problem by composing *Cheap Imitation* for solo piano, in which he maintained the architecture of *Socrate* but, by using chance operations, replaced Satie's music with his own. In response to the situation and to Cage's title for the music, Cunningham gave the title *Second Hand* to this long-gestated choreography (1970).

Cage's *Cheap Imitation* is now well known. It is a half-hour single melodic line in three movements for solo piano. Cage performed it widely on the Cunningham tours into the early 1970s. He also made other versions of it, including one for solo violin and an orchestration. Playing *Cheap Imitation* was the last substantial performing that Cage did as a pianist.

As a percussionist during the first period of his creative life, Cage was encouraged particularly by Henry Cowell and inspired by compositions of Amadeo Roldán and Edgard Varèse. His collaboration with Lou Harrison is celebrated, both for their percussion ensemble and for the collaboratively composed *Double Music* (1941). The members of this percussion ensemble included Doris Dennison, Margaret Jansen, and Xenia Kashevaroff (to whom Cage was then married). His work with percussion media continued after the 1950s primarily as a resource for live-electronic music.

In the late 1930s and continuing through the second period of his creative life in collaboration with David Tudor, Cage developed performance skills with live-electronic resources. His *Imaginary Landscape No. 1* (1939) and the classic

Cartridge Music (1960), as well as the works using amplified plant materials—*Child of Tree* (1975) and *Branches* (1976)—are important examples. He also performed with live-electronic resources in Cunningham repertory with music by other composers, such as Pauline Oliveros's *In Memoriam: Nikola Tesla* for the choreography *Cantfield* (1969) and Alvin Lucier's *Vespers* for *Objects* (1969).

The reasons for Cage's progression from piano to percussion to electronic instruments to voice were both practical and artistic. Though the practical circumstances may seem mundane, they were important. His contributions to the percussion genre declined as he grew weary of travel with a cumbersome menagerie of heavy instruments. One reason for his development of the prepared piano was to have a multi-timbral resource of sonorities without the heavy labor of moving percussion instruments.

Cage's gradual retirement as pianist was due to arthritis. By 1960 his hands were already troubled with this affliction. He had increasing difficulty performing the music for *Suite for Five*, an exquisite choreography that had an unusually long life in the repertory. In 1961, following the performance I saw of this work with Cage and Tudor as duo pianists, I expressed my appreciation to Cage at intermission and shook hands with him. He said, "Please be careful," and continued: "The sponsor worries that we are hurting the pianos by playing inside them, and some of the audience think the sound hurts their ears." Then, with his unique grin: "But this piece hurts me more than it hurts them."

By the late 1970s Cage had changed his diet to minimize fatty foods and alcohol and had given up smoking. Though his arthritis improved for a time, it gradually became a burden again, along with sciatica, in the 1980s. But by this time he had developed his activities as a vocal performer into a major effort and had also extended his prolific creative life as a writer and graphic artist, activities that were less physically stressful. I last saw Cage in May 1992, between a rehearsal and a performance of *Music for* (1984) by the San Francisco Contemporary Music Players. Cage, Betty Freeman, and I had to take a taxi for the five blocks to a vegetarian restaurant when Cage's arthritis made the journey by foot impossible.

Cage's performing voice and the writing that he performed with it in his third creative period are well known.[3] An early example is his reading of the one-minute stories from *Indeterminacy* (1958). He also read these stories to accompany Merce Cunningham's celebrated choreography *How to Pass, Kick, Fall, and Run* (from the 1960s repertory). Some of his vocal skills were developed with the Cunningham Dance Company's many Events, which date from 1964. Events were not repertory works but were collaboratively conceived for single performance occasions, often in non-proscenium spaces, using materials from

Fig. IV-1. John Cage performing his *Mesostics* with David Tudor's live-electronic *Untitled*, Pro Musica Nova, Bremen, Germany, May 8, 1972. (Photo © Gordon Mumma.)

the choreographic repertory. By 1995 the Cunningham Dance Company had made several hundred unique Events. The music for Events was often a collaboration of several musician-composers. Cage sometimes performed with electronic equipment and sometimes used his voice.

The vocal contribution Cage made to Events was concurrent with the development of his *Mureau* (1970), *Sixty-two Mesostics re Merce Cunningham* (1971), and *Empty Words* (1974), which he commonly performed as a solo vocalist. In these works Cage addressed the syntax of language and applied chance operations to its restructuring and abolition. On occasion he presented these works in other contexts, such as a simultaneous performance of his *Mesostics* with David Tudor's live-electronic composition *Untitled* (1972). In the premiere performance of this collaborative work with Tudor at Pro Musica Nova in Bremen on May 8, 1972, Cage stood before four microphones, each of which was amplified to a loudspeaker in a different corner of the performance space [fig. IV-1]. He spoke close to each microphone and moved from one to another, sometimes rapidly. The sound of his voice moved weightlessly around the space.

Cage was usually comfortable as a performer. In show-business vernacular, he was a "trouper." But some circumstances made him anxious. One of these was his performance in Lukas Foss's clever production of Stravinsky's *L'Histoire du soldat* in New York in July 1966. The three speaking parts were to be performed by the "three C's of American music": Aaron Copland as the narrator, Elliott Carter as the soldier, and John Cage as the devil. Cage accepted the invitation with misgivings. He told me that he did not think he would be able to do the rhythmic co-ordinations between his part and the instruments. He said: "It should be devilish, not foolish." Cage overcame his apprehension, partly because he wanted to meet Stravinsky to ask for a manuscript for his in-progress book *Notations* (1969). Perhaps Cage thought that his participation in *L'Histoire* would give him some cachet. And they did meet in Stravinsky's New York City hotel suite. The *L'Histoire* performance was a glamorous success, and Cage had no trouble with the rhythmic co-ordinations. He was a brilliant devil, equaled only in devilish virtuosity by Vanessa Redgrave's recorded performance.[4]

With the Cunningham Dance Company, Cage often played the music of other composers, including, for example, the work of Toshi Ichiyanagi for *Scramble* (1967) and Pauline Oliveros for *Canfield* (1969). Separate music concerts were sometimes presented as part of the dance tours. On one of these, at Cornell University in Ithaca, New York, in the spring of 1968, Cage and I played one of my works titled *Swarmer*.[5] This music was for two vernacular—or "folkloric"—instruments, concertina and bowed saw. Cage played the concertina.

The Cornell concert was a last-minute arrangement. We had time for only one rehearsal. *Swarmer* was a new piece, and Cage said he had never before played the concertina. He learned what was necessary during a morning rehearsal that preceded our afternoon concert. *Swarmer* required close and responsive connections between the two players. We did not play from a notated score; as with much folkloric music, *Swarmer* was a music of "oral tradition." I explained the piece to Cage at the beginning of the rehearsal. The rules of *Swarmer* specified a limited number of choices. Each player could choose a single pitch or at the most two pitches played simultaneously. When two pitches sounded together, a limited number of pitch intervals could be used.[6] After each choice was made, it could not be used again. Thus each player had to remember what had been previously played in the performance. This is similar to chess and some card games, and Cage was an avid player of both.

During that one rehearsal Cage chose only single pitches. He said, "I'll make the easy choices first." Because he was unfamiliar at first with the concertina, he made a few incorrect choices. But he was from the very start skilled in matters of continuity, grasping immediately when sounds occurred in time, and how they overlapped. Owing to limited time, Cage did not use the two-pitch sonorities in rehearsal. Just before the performance was to begin, I assured him that it was legitimate to play only the single-pitch choices. He smiled (again with his unique grin) and said, "I think it will be fine."

We began the performance. Cage's first choice was a two-pitch sonority. After my responding sound from the musical saw, he continued with the next choice—a single pitch. As the performance continued, Cage used, variously, single pitches and two-pitch sonorities. He followed securely the logic I had explained during the rehearsal. By the end of the performance he had included many of the possible two-pitch sonorities, including some that were quite difficult. I never heard him repeat a choice that he had already used. The continuity of his concertina part with my musical saw was excellent. He was bold with choices and subtle with musical nuances. It was as though he had learned the concertina and we had rehearsed the piece many times.

This performance of *Swarmer* contradicts the legend that Cage had no ear for pitch or melody. Cage encouraged this legend. He enjoyed saying that he could not do solfège and that Schoenberg had told him that he had "no sense for harmony." I do not think this is the truth—certainly not the whole truth. Cage told those stories about his being "unmusical" because they were good stories. He was a virtuoso storyteller, a happy raconteur. But Cage was also quick with complex ideas and structures, and a fast learner. As a performer he was disciplined, reliable, and imaginative with creative decisions.

Cage loved performing. He was nourished by the performing experience, even under difficult circumstances. He usually found an appropriate match of his technical proficiency with a given situation. Indeed, quite often his unique performance virtuosity—with music, with words and verbal repartee, and with graphic materials—was astonishing, even to practitioners of those arts not easily astonished.

CHAPTER 20

John Cage, Electronic Technology, and Live-Electronic Music

(2012)

Electronic technology was a lifelong pursuit for John Cage. After around 1960, interactive live electronics became his preferred approach. For the most part his activities in electronic media involved productive working with others in a process of shared decisions. The details of these "others" are essential to understanding the evolution of Cage's use of electronic technology and his creative expansion into writing, theater, and the visual arts in his later years.

Cage's first significant collaborator in the field of electronics was his father. John Milton Cage Sr. (1886–1964) was a pioneering structural and electrical engineer with significant achievements in the establishment of patents for his innovative work in electronic communications and related military applications. During my years working with Cage, he sometimes spoke to me about his father. One memorable occasion was a lunch in 1965, the year after his father's death, when he was still at work settling the estate. Cage spoke in detail about the complexities of his father's patent ownership and assets, of particular relevance to Cage Jr., who at the time was contributing to the support of his mother.

John Cage Sr. and Jr.—father and son—developed their creative work by designing things. They also worked together. From 1931 onward (in Los Angeles and later in New York), Cage Jr. followed his father's work and actively assisted

Source: This essay merges materials from two conference lectures presented during the Cage centennial: "John Cage and Live-Electronics" (Berlin, Germany, March 20, 2012), published in *Cage & Consequences,* ed. Julia Schröder and Volker Straebel, 95–100 (Hofheim, Germany: Wolke Verlag, 2012), © The Authors; and "John Cage's Work with Electronic Technologies from the 1930s to the 1960s" (Lublin, Poland, May 16, 2012), unpublished.

him with legal analysis and library research for the patent applications. For Cage Jr. this research activity provided both occasional income and the roots of his understanding of electrical engineering. From these experiences he developed sufficient skill with the concepts and vocabulary of the field to communicate with professionals and to put this knowledge to significant use in his later live-electronic collaborations.

Cage's creative work was also fostered by his early fascination with the rapidly evolving technologies of radio transmission, silent film and sound cinema, sound recording, and early electronic musical instruments such as the Theremin and ondes Martenot. While living in Michigan with his parents (1916–21), Cage had followed the pioneering development of radio broadcasting in Detroit. Back in Los Angeles, he presented weekly Boy Scout radio talk programs at station KNX from 1924 to 1926.[1] Radio broadcasting until the early 1940s was a "live-performance" medium; most of the music and spoken word broadcast in the United States at that time was transmitted live, with recordings used mostly for re-broadcast purposes and advertisements. This early experience would form the basis for Cage's lifelong comfort in the studio, whether speaking or performing his music live for radio (or later, television) broadcasts, and for his skill in audio recording and editing procedures and in operating the technological apparatus of the radio studio. The radio would remain an important compositional resource for much of Cage's life.

Cage also interacted intermittently with the developing field of sound films. In 1937 he worked briefly as a film-editing apprentice in Los Angeles with the innovative filmmaker Oskar Fischinger, whose experiments with optical film soundtracks would influence Cage's later development. He worked on the synchronization of sound with the visual animations for Fischinger's film *An Optical Poem* (1937), using a process of cutting and splicing that would later prove a basic technique of tape music. In the 1940s he worked with Maya Deren, Hans Richter, and Herbert Matter.[2] From these projects, Cage learned many aspects of film technology essential to his early tape sampling works beginning with *Williams Mix* (1952), including sound-effects collections and the procedures of optical soundtrack recording and editing with film.

By the late 1930s Cage had gravitated toward music performance and composition. During these years a primary impetus in Cage's early electronic music was his use of percussion sonorities in the context of modern dance. In the summer of 1938 he was at Mills College in Oakland, California, with Lou Harrison, with whom Cage later collaborated on the 1941 *Double Music* and other performing and recording projects in San Francisco. At Mills, Cage was an accompanist for the innovative modern dance department, working as a pianist and developing a percussion ensemble—all typical activities for a dance-studio accompanist.

In the fall of 1938 Cage was at the Cornish School in Seattle, where he met Merce Cunningham for the first time. Cornish had both a modern dance program and a radio station, as well as the first American college-level curriculum in radio broadcasting. There, Cage developed a percussion ensemble from the Dance Department collection previously assembled by his Cornish colleagues Bonnie Bird and Lora Deja. To this collection of idiophones[3] he added resonating metal objects that he found at local junkyards. Cage also explored the possibilities of adding radio-station electronic equipment to the ensemble in live performance. The Cornish percussion ensemble often performed music by other composers, notably Johanna Beyer's *Three Movements for Percussion* (1939), dedicated to Cage. Beyer had envisioned a live-performance electronic-music synthesizer well before its time for her visionary *Music of the Spheres* (1938). Cage knew that score and used it as a prime example in his unsuccessful efforts to establish a center for electronic music research and development. He mentioned to me that Beyer's concept for a sound synthesis device reminded him of how his father thought so futuristically.[4]

"Electronic" ideas were in the air in the 1930s and 1940s. Other musicians besides Cage were exploring those possibilities before the acoustical disc–sampling *musique concrète* of Pierre Schaeffer in the late 1940s. In the early 1930s Les Paul was amplifying acoustical guitars with phonograph-cartridge transducers and established the solid-body electronic guitar. In 1941 the virtuoso saxophone and clarinet performer Sidney Bechet made multiple-disc recordings with different instruments. He then played them at synchronized varied speeds as "samples," mixing them for his classic "Sheik of Araby" (1941). Les Paul and Mary Ford followed with similar tape-sampling procedures in their now classic "How High the Moon" (1951).

Cage's first significant music using electronic technology was the series *Imaginary Landscapes*, beginning with *Imaginary Landscape No. 1* (1939). The instruments included two variable-speed phonographs used to perform with radio sound-testing records, a large Chinese cymbal, and a "string piano" in the manner of Henry Cowell.[5] In the performance instructions provided in the Peters edition,[6] Cage recommends that it be performed live in a radio studio, confirming that he already considered live-radio broadcasting a viable medium for musical performance. With *Imaginary Landscape No. 1* the use of the two record players as live-performance instruments is an early instance in the history of "disc-jockey" culture, an extension of the techniques that originated in the 1930s with the insertion of recorded advertisements in live radio broadcasts. More

Imaginary Landscapes followed in the next few years, each including electronic sound-making instruments as part of the percussion ensemble. *Imaginary Landscape No. 2* of 1942 was Cage's first use of amplified small sounds. A resonating coil of wire was attached to a phonograph cartridge and amplified, as a practical replacement for the large metal gong that Lora Deja had taken with her when she left Seattle for New York.

By the early 1940s the broadcasting of music in the United States was complicated by union disputes requiring that performers be paid when recordings of their music were broadcast, by the unavailability of the materials used to make records due to wartime restrictions, and by military guidelines on the kinds of music that could be broadcast during wartime. Thus Cage's broadcast disc recordings, such as those previously made with Harrison, ceased by 1942.[7]

In 1941 Cage's activities moved eastward—to Chicago and eventually to New York City. By the late 1940s his life was mostly in New York, except for his increasing touring activities in the United States and Europe. Most significant to Cage's new work of this period was the rapid expansion of electronic musical technology in the early 1950s. By the late 1940s transistor technology had appeared, and by the early 1950s magnetic tape recording was entering general commercial distribution. Neither of these technological developments replaced the previous vacuum tube or disc-recording technologies, but they expanded the resources of creative artists such as Cage. His engagement with electronic sound technology was a natural outgrowth of his exploration of other sound sources during these years, including the prepared piano in the 1940s and his introduction of chance operations around 1950.

Cage's experience with film editing and new recording technologies was put to use in his first tape-sampling work, the *Williams Mix* project of 1952. Its tape-recording and editing of sound materials also exploited chance operations and the newly developing magnetic-tape technology. Its complex editing process was possible because Cage had enlisted the dedicated assistance of several others, notably Earle Brown and David Tudor. The work was done at the New York City studios of Louis and Bebe Barron, who would compose the electronic music for the now classic science fiction film *Forbidden Planet* (1956). *Williams Mix* also initiated the music-technology activities that involved significant collaborations between Cage and others. Another collaboration followed in 1955, when excerpts from Cage's *Sonatas and Interludes* for prepared piano (1946–48) provided music for *In Between*, the first color film by his friend Stan Brakhage.

A turning point in Cage's career was the formation of the Cunningham Dance Company at Black Mountain College in 1953, and with it Cage's primary commitment to its development for the rest of his life. The Cunningham Company provided an enormously productive and durable venue for Cage's collaborative exploration of electronic technology in live performance. Central to this creative process was his association with pianist David Tudor beginning in the early 1950s. By the end of that decade their working relationship had become essential to Cage's live-electronic music, notably in the series of *Variations* beginning in 1958.

By the late 1950s Cage had Tudor searching for a variety of electronic transducers, which were then becoming commonplace in the development of solid-state transistor technology. These transducers became part of the instrumental "ensemble" for Cage's iconic *Cartridge Music* of 1960. By this time, Cage had already composed several works using amplified "small sounds," often performed with Tudor as pianist. These small sounds, usually inaudible to an audience without amplification, were derived from live acoustical sources (piano, percussion, invented or found instruments). Electronic amplification and equalization were also used to project Cage's music from *Atlas Eclipticalis* and *Winter Music* in Cunningham's choreography *Aeon* (1961). This was done with a rapidly burgeoning assortment of small equipment—transducers, preamplifiers, equalizers, and mixers. This equipment collection would soon become a space- and time-consuming menagerie for Cage and Tudor.[8]

Working with Cage would provide an early wellspring for Tudor's own evolution from pianist-performer to composer with live electronics. Tudor developed his own technical procedures for Cage's *Variations II* (1961), which extended those of *Cartridge Music* by enhancing the complex internal acoustical resonances of the piano. Tudor often performed *Variations II* as a solo for piano with live electronics, notably at the 1963 ONCE Festival.[9]

The use of electronic music in the Cunningham Dance Company increased throughout the 1960s. Cage's *Variations* compositions expanded into the extravagant theater-dance-music-video collaboration *Variations V* (1965), created with Cunningham. Its basic idea was that the choreography, music, and decor, though occurring simultaneously but separately from one another, would have an additional technological component.[10] For the *Variations V* project Cage enlisted the help of engineers from Bell Laboratories and the pioneering music synthesizer designer Robert Moog. Cage approached Moog concerning the possibility of adapting the "Terpsitone," a special device that Leon Theremin had designed in the 1930s for use in activating musical sounds with dance. The Terpsitone was a younger sibling to Theremin's more famous "Thereminvox," a capacitance-technology proximity-sensor from the late 1920s that produced solo melodic lines without physical touch.[11] Cage had heard the Thereminvox in Los Angeles while doing research for his father's electronic inventions in the 1930s.

Cage thought that Moog would be the right person for the task: through the early 1960s he had been manufacturing a transistor version of the basic Theremin. Moog later explained to me the situation of this meeting with Cage. At that time, Moog was very busy in the early stages of designing and building his own electronic-music synthesizers. At first unsure whether Cage really understood what was wanted, Moog was reassured when Cage specified that he was interested in an instrument such as the Terpsitone to be used with dancers, and described his clear understanding of its basic electronic technology. Moog accepted the project and produced the Terpsitone-related vertical antennas that were used in the performances of *Variations V*.

At the premiere of *Variations V* in New York, its extravagant wealth of complex and fragile equipment filled the massive stage and orchestra pit at Lincoln Center to overflowing. Given its complexity, it is no wonder that there were technical problems resulting from inadequate installation and rehearsal. Nevertheless, the premiere was a huge theatrical coup, and Cunningham wanted to take it on tour. When I was engaged by the Cunningham Company in 1966, it was initially to provide the technological support for touring performances of *Variations V*. Tudor and I stripped the technical equipment down to a workable touring package for the 1966 European tour. Cage approved, advising us: "Be practical." A major part of my contribution to its touring performances was just that—repairing fragile equipment and minimizing redundancy. It also included working with both Cage and Tudor to design procedures for packing and unpacking the *Variations V* equipment, reducing where possible chance operations. The setup came to require only about six hours. Our "virtuosity" really showed *after* the performance, when we could strike the musical parts of the set and load it into the shipping containers in less than two hours.

Until 1973, when I left the company, the threesome of Cage, Tudor, and myself, occasionally with the addition of David Behrman, Toshi Ichiyanagi, or others, worked together on the music for numerous Cunningham choreographies and Events, including several notable Cage collaborations with electronic media. Tudor and I provided technological skills that complemented Cage's primarily *creative* involvement with emerging electronic technologies. Already in *Variations V* Cage's performance role was primarily as a tape-jockey, as can be seen in the studio performance filmed in Hamburg, Germany, by NDR in August 1966.[12] Figure IV-2 shows Cage in rehearsal on the film set at NDR, adjusting one of the light sensors at the base of an antenna unit. Thereafter he increasingly left the design and operation of technological equipment to others.

In 1968 the Cunningham Dance Company was involved in an elaborate outdoor film production with the title *Assemblage*. It was a project for KQED

Fig. IV-2. John Cage adjusting a light sensor at the base of an antenna unit during a rehearsal of *Variations V* at NDR Studios, Hamburg, Germany, August 1966. (Photo © Gordon Mumma.)

television in San Francisco. The music was co-composed by Cage, Tudor, and myself with magnetic tape editing in a separate facility near Ghirardelli Square, where the outdoor choreography was filmed. For the *Assemblage* music the three of us planned a structure for the fifty-five-minute duration of the film. We also defined the differences of our individual compositional procedures, so that we had an overview of what each of us would be doing. Cage collected recordings of worldwide weather sounds, Tudor used insect and small animal sounds, and I traveled the San Francisco streets and ferryboats recording the natural ambience. This process worked well because we knew each other's practices and had agreed upon the structural disciplines necessary to yield coherent results from our independent decisions.

A similar compositional process evolved in the music components of the Events performed with the Cunningham Dance Company. In 1964 Cunningham and Cage established the "Event" as a flexible performance situation for tours of the company.[13] The collaborative music and the separate choreographic structure of each Event were often planned by chance operations. The music for each unique Event was always a collective creation by the composer-musicians performing with the Cunningham Dance Company. Generally the musicians drew on previous sound sources or original material as opportunities for live-electronic interaction. Cage and Tudor were the two performers for the first Event in Vienna in 1964, as part of the world tour that brought the Cunningham Company major international attention. For Cage the experience of the early Events was an inspiration for the 1965 *Variations V*. In 1966 the music components of the Events became a joint venture of the three of us—Cage, Tudor, and myself. During those years the music for the Events was predominately live-electronic, although acoustical instruments and sound sources were also used into the 1970s.

Event no. 24 (1972) at Zellerbach Hall in Berkeley, California, was a grand example of the process. We had a large venue, a massive collection of acoustic and electronic instruments, and a whole week to prepare. We generally decided on structural proportions in advance of each Event. Cunningham provided detailed guidelines on the duration of the various choreographic ingredients. We took his proportions and established our own proportional relationships as part of our structural discipline. We rarely discussed the musical devices we would each use in performance, largely because we knew each other so well and what we were working on at the time. Within our planned structure we each had creative freedom in the ensemble and made our musical decisions independently. The sound connections were also guided by circumstances. Cage occasionally surprised me with something quite new, as he did in *Event no. 24*. At the time, his arthritis limited his use of the piano and electronics, and he was in transition to using his voice in readings from such works as his written *Mesostics* over the following years. But on this occasion he got into deep chant-like singing, a whole world of sound that I had never heard from him, developing his voice as a new instrument.

By 1968 Cage's collaborative work in live electronics expanded beyond the Cunningham milieu to other electronic engineers and computer programmers. *Reunion* was a sign of the times.[14] Where the initial idea came from is now obscure, but it seemed to have descended upon us at the same time. It was to be a live-electronic performance ensemble of several people in which the sounds of the music would be heard as the result of the moves of a chess game. The chessboard was to have sensors that sent electrical signals to trigger the electronic sounds of the ensemble of musicians. The design of the chessboard was by

Lowell Cross, and the three other musicians were David Behrman, David Tudor, and myself. The chess players were John Cage, Marcel Duchamp, and his wife Alexina (Teeny) Duchamp. Composer Udo Kasemets organized the project, the performance of which took place at the Ryerson Theatre in Toronto on March 5, 1968.[15] The technological functions of the *Reunion* chessboard, as with *Variations V*, involved control signals that were sent to the sound-producing apparatus. For *Reunion* they were activated by the chessboard moves by the chess players, and for *Variations V* by movements of the dancers performing Cunningham's choreography. In both, the signals influenced the articulations of the music.

The *Reunion* performance and its preparation were filmed by the Canadian Broadcasting Corporation, resulting in a twenty-minute documentary film that has not yet been released commercially. Some of that film was devoted to the complex setup of the electronic equipment and its connection to the chessboard circuits. The musical outcome was mostly beyond the control of those of us performing our own music. By using headphones we could hear what we were doing individually, but much of what we did was unheard by the audience, except when the chess moves released our individual or aggregate sounds. The audience filled the theater, seemingly engaged with the occasion, even though some left before the end of the four-hour performance.

Two chess games had been planned, the first with Marcel Duchamp and Cage, the second with Teeny Duchamp and Cage. The *Reunion* performance concluded when Teeny and John stopped before the end of their game, intending to complete it another day. Afterwards each performer was paid, but Marcel Duchamp refused the money because it would have ruined his amateur status as a champion chess player. Someone asked Duchamp what he thought of the music. His poetic reply: "Oh oui, beaucoup de bruit."

A high point of Cage's engagement with electronic technology during these years was his collaboration with Lejaren Hiller for the theater-music event *HPSCHD*, completed at the University of Illinois in 1969. Hiller, originally a chemist, had been a pioneer in the development of computer programs for music compositions such as his 1957 *Illiac Suite* for string quartet (a collaboration with Leonard Isaacson). The Cage-Hiller *HPSCHD* took nearly two years to complete, with substantial support from the university. It was an extravagant theater piece with multiple harpsichords and image projections and sufficient publicity that the performance in the covered sports stadium was attended by thousands of people, some of whom had traveled from as far away as Europe.

The intensity of Cage's exploration of electronic media tapered in the 1970s as his creative activities broadened to embrace other areas. At this time other musicians joined forces with Tudor and Behrman in expanding the use of electronic music in the Cunningham milieu, especially after my departure.[16] The reasons for this shift are complex. With Cage's growing fame came major commissions for compositions for *acoustic* instruments (encouraged by his publisher, C. F. Peters). A growing number of engagements for concert performances and lectures also took him away from the Cunningham Company for extended periods (but also contributed substantially to its financial support). By that time as well, Cage had come to depend on Tudor and me for most of the technological aspects of electronic music for the company. His growing arthritis also encouraged him to turn to writing and to the use of his voice as a performance medium. Even when electronics were used—as in some readings from his *Mesostics* for amplified voice (1971) or in *Voiceless Essay* (1986–87)—they were supervised by others. Moreover, after the death of Duchamp in October 1968 and Cage's exquisite memorial plexigram of the following year, *Not Wanting to Say Anything about Marcel*,[17] Cage was stimulated to expand his work in the visual arts. By 1975 Tudor had assumed the leadership role with the Cunningham Company in the field of state-of-the-art live electronics previously supplied by Cage. Finally, the 1970s also marked Cunningham's growing interest in other media, especially film and video in collaborations with Charles Atlas and later with Elliot Caplan.[18] Composer collaborations still occurred, however, as in the epic *Five Stone Wind* (1988) with music by Cage, Kosugi, and Tudor.

Cage's last major collaborative work was in many ways an inverted summary of his life's work with electronic technology. In the last year of his life he made a "film without subject" titled *One[11]* (1992) with Henning Lohner, Van Carlson, and Andrew Culver. Cage established the basic structures and procedures for both image and sound but depended substantially on the support of his associates for their implementation. The visuals depend on a combination of historical and cutting-edge technologies. The classic 35mm motion picture camera with black-and-white film of Cage's youth was mounted on a moving crane in an empty room. Both the lighting and the camera positions were determined by chance operations controlled by an elaborate computer program contributed by his associates. The visual aspect has no referential content other than the fluid motion of light and shadow. The sound is an orchestral score that evokes the tradition of symphonic accompaniment to the early epic films of Sergei Eisenstein and others: Cage's 1991 composition *103* performed by full symphony orchestra.[19] *One[11]* is considered by many to be among the most important creative works of Cage's life, a closing magnum opus.

John Cage's imagination always followed the technological developments of the times—exploiting and expanding the creative possibilities of those resources. All of his work related to evolving technology in the arts from the early

1950s onward was deeply and essentially collaborative. The 1960s marked the high point of Cage's creative work in collaborative live electronics. Even if he left the technical equipment increasingly to others in the 1970s and 1980s, with the expansion of computer and digital technology, he remained active in inspiring and creating electronic music in association with other musicians, sound technicians, and computer programmers. Collaboration always involves risk. Cage's risk-taking produced results that have changed the ways of thinking and working in the creative work of now so many others.

Fig. IV-3. Gordon Mumma performing Cage's *Diary: How to Improve the World (You Will Only Make Matters Worse)*, University of California, Davis, December 6, 1967. (Photo © David Freund, with his permission.)

CHAPTER 21

Twenty-Five Minutes with John Cage

Indeterminacy

In 1958 John Cage brought together thirty one-minute stories under the title *Indeterminacy*.[1] At Columbia Teachers College in 1959 he added another sixty stories that he read, this time with electronic accompaniment by David Tudor.

In 1965 Cage used them as the spoken score for Merce Cunningham's choreography *How to Pass, Kick, Fall, and Run*. Cage's reading was a performance in itself. Seated at the side of the stage in full view of the audience, he began with the careful ritual of opening a bottle of champagne, dispensing himself a glass, and inserting a cigarette into a long holder. Regardless of the number of words, each story was read within the duration of one minute, with pauses between the stories for lighting another cigarette, sipping some champagne, or refilling the glass. Because of their uniform duration, the stories (like the dance itself) occurred at varying tempos of articulation, from extremely slow to very rapid. In its first year in the repertory, the stories were increasingly obscured by Tudor's electronic modification procedures, which often resulted in a montage of sonic fragmentation that increased in verbal unintelligibility with each performance.

Source: This substantially new contribution expands an earlier version containing twelve of these vignettes in "Fourteen Visits with the Cage: Persönliche Vignetten," published in German in *MusikTexte* 127 (December 2010): 47–50, © Musiktexte, with their permission. A segment of *HPSCHD* was published as "From Decade 6, Tour Process, years 6–9," in *John Cage,* ed. Jacques Bekaert (Brussels: Algol, 1971), © Gordon Mumma. The additions draw on Mumma's manuscript Cage journal from the years of the Cunningham tours (GMC), recent interviews with him, and several new entries written in 2011–12.

Less well-known, however, is that *Indeterminacy* had reached 128 stories by May 1960, when Cage and Tudor presented the expanded version at the University of Michigan's College of Architecture and Design. I helped them cobble together the equipment for the performance and made a personal tape recording. This may have been the last performance of the full sequence, which was sensational. I recall one story about Leonard Bernstein and Karlheinz Stockhausen exchanging undershirts at a party. Cage would soon destroy the more outrageous additions, believing that they could be viewed as unnecessarily aggressive. I loaned my tape to someone. It was never returned.

Erdös Questions

In the question-and-answer sessions that often followed a Cage concert or lecture, the subject of his "using chance" and "indeterminacy" as a way of making compositional choices usually came up. Sometimes he spoke in detail about his disciplined creative process. On one occasion Cage said: "My choices consist of choosing what questions to ask."

This response reminded me of Paul Erdös (1913–96), renowned in the esoteric field of theoretical mathematics. It was uncommon for Erdös to develop proofs for abstract ideas; instead, he asked probing questions of his colleagues. The "Erdös questions" were so original and inspiring that they reshaped many directions of theoretical mathematics in the second half of the twentieth century. Many papers published in this field include Erdös's name along with that of the primary author.

Like those of Erdös, Cage's questions have generated responses that have reshaped artistic concepts and have nourished many creative individuals.

Some Answers

The conventional concepts and definitions of "music" were a regular topic in such discussions. Cage's responses to the "same old questions" were rarely the "same old answers." Following one concert of Cage's music, a person from the audience said with some agitation: "Mr. Cage, I just don't see how you can call that music." Following an appropriately dramatic pause, Cage replied: "Well, don't call it music if the word bothers you."

He had remarkable skill with difficult questions. In London in December 1968, someone in the audience asked him if he was schizophrenic. Cage responded: "I have managed to function in society." In Pittsburgh in 1970, he was asked about the function of "good art" in those times of social turmoil, citing the recent brutalizing of black children by white racists on a school bus. After a moment's thought, Cage answered: "Art is a means by which people change their minds."

Notoriously, on a few occasions he prepared answers in advance for unknown or imaginary questions. He then read those answers without relation to the questions. The results were sometimes spectacular.

Discipline and Cicadas

I have always been impressed with Cage's discipline as a performer, particularly under unusual or difficult circumstances. On my first tour with the Merce Cunningham Dance Company in the summer of 1966, we performed in Saint-Paul de Vence on the French Riviera. We had traveled by train from our previous engagement, crossing the border from Spain that day. It turned out to be a national holiday, and the customs offices were closed. All our equipment, costumes, and musical instruments would have to be held at the border until customs opened the next day.

The performance was that night in an outdoor space at the Fondation Maegt to a sold-out house. I considered the situation a disaster. Cage, on the other hand, undertook a careful exploration of the gallery and outdoor stage, experimenting with its inherent sounds. He dragged pieces of wood across the soggy, splintered stage. He considered the results in the context of the natural sounds of the space: screaming cicadas in the noonday sun and a croaking chorus of tree frogs that emerged later in the day.

In the end we did get some of our equipment by a small private plane, chartered from Corsica, and the performance could proceed almost as originally planned—though without the cicadas and frogs.

Tramway

Following a rehearsal of the Cunningham Dance Company in the Spanish town of Sitges in July 1966, we discovered that it was siesta time and the tractor-tram to our hotel was not running. A few dancers conceded to the long, hot walk; the rest of us decided to wait. A nearby store was ignoring siesta, and Cage purchased a rare heavy sherry, Sandeman's Brown Bang. Boarding the idle tram, Peter Saul and John resumed a previously suspended game of travel-board chess, sharing with the kibitzers the Brown Bang. A half-hour passed, the air grew hotter, the Brown Bang was finished, and the chess moved more slowly. David Tudor opened a secret bottle of coconut liqueur. The chess game stopped and unnoticeably the tram began its now quite surreal journey down the long beach to the Terramar Palace Hotel.

Escher

Cage's visually innovative musical scores, in draft form, sometimes appear to be closely related to his visual arts engravings. Both often use graphic structured patterns, mathematical procedures, or the *I Ching* as part of his creative discipline.

Here is an aside concerning the visual artist M. C. Escher, who explored graphic interrelationships that have opened new theoretical areas in mathematical topology. Some of Escher's early sketches are published in recent books on his work, often placed next to reproductions of his final paintings and drawings. Differences of process aside, Cage's work-pages are sometimes nearly indistinguishable from Escher's but for the latter's German notes.

John Meets Igor

In connection with the Stravinsky festival in New York in 1966, in which Cage, Elliott Carter, and Aaron Copland performed the acting roles for *L'Histoire du soldat*, Cage was eager to ask Stravinsky for a manuscript for his *Notations* collection. John was a little nervous about the occasion. After the meeting, he happily reported that Stravinsky had promised a manuscript for the collection. I asked what else they had talked about. John replied that Stravinsky had asked him what he thought about "tempo."

Cage replied: "There isn't any."

Stravinsky asked for an explanation.

Cage responded: "Imagine that the window is open and we hear from outside several sounds spaced far apart in time. We don't say it is slow; we say it is quiet. But if we hear several sounds very close together, we don't say it is fast; we say it is noisy."

Notations

In London later in 1966 Cage arrived late for lunch at a coffeehouse. He explained that he had just met the Beatles.

"All of them?"

"No, just Paul Lennon and John McCartney."

We straightened that out. Carolyn Brown asked how he had arranged it.

"Through Yoko Ono."

Carolyn remarked how Toshi Ichiyanagi had changed when he was married to Yoko. I asked John if he had got a manuscript from the Beatles for his *Notations*.

"Do they notate their music?"

"It doesn't matter," I almost shouted. "Get Yoko to arrange another meeting and get a manuscript; that'll really make your collection!"

In spite of my overexcitement, John listened seriously and promised to see the Beatles again. A year later two packages for the *Notations* collection arrived by the same day's mail. One contained Webern manuscripts, the other several versions of "Eleanor Rigby."

Flowers at the Saville

In late November and early December 1966 John Cage, David Tudor, and I performed Cage's *Variations V* at London's Saville Theatre with the Merce Cunningham Dance Company.[2] The elaborate electronic setup before each performance was always a huge challenge. When it was at last completed, we left for dinner. On our return we found the orchestra pit full of flowers. Tudor was rather annoyed that someone had tampered with our gear. One of us found a note: "From the Beatles."

Party Line

In November 1971 I crossed paths with Cage one afternoon on Bank Street in New York. He said that he was looking forward to the end of a long telephone installation strike. "John Lennon and Yoko Ono have rented the apartment next door, and my telephone has become a global village."

Paparazzi

In June 1972 I conducted Cage's *Atlas Eclipticalis* with percussionists Max Neuhaus, Philip Corner, James Fulkerson, and Gregory Reid at the New School in New York. Because it was Cage's sixtieth birthday year, the place was swarming with photographers. Our performance was very quiet and gentle. Nothing much to see: me making the slow clock, small sounds, silence, occasionally a page turn. Seven photographs would have done it. But the moment the piece began the clicking started and never let up. We had placed the microphones very carefully to record the concert, but somehow the photographers were always nearby. Even Peter Moore, that veteran photographer of the avant-garde positioned backstage to keep out of the way, happened to be standing next to a critical microphone. A number of people asked for their money back because of the racket, and I got a letter from John Vinton complaining bitterly about the "publicity mongering." I had to agree with him. New York has become a publicity town, with Cage the man of the moment.

Indo-Ceylon

Shortly after the Cunningham Dance Company arrived in Boulder, Colorado, in the summer of 1968 for a four-week high-altitude preparation for the South American tour, Cage discovered a little restaurant, the Indo-Ceylon. The idea of finding Ceylonese food in Boulder seemed incredible. David Tudor determined that it was open for lunch. The Indo-Ceylon proved superlative: David suggested it was one of the three best Indian restaurants in the Western world, comparable with the Agra and Kwality in London. We ate there every lunch and many dinners and became admiring friends of the owners, Mike and Kusuma Ford. After we'd tried the entire menu, Kusuma prepared special menus for us. On one occasion John brought a selection of wild mushrooms he had picked in the nearby mountains and asked her to prepare them. Kusuma was skeptical. We assured Mike that John really *did* know his fungi. To no one's surprise she prepared a heavenly dish. Our parting dinner was at the Indo-Ceylon.

Our next meal was with the entire company aboard a jet from Denver to Dallas, en route to Mexico City. As we contemplated how to liven up the muzak-cuisine, John produced from his attaché case a bottle of mango pickle, a parting gift from Mike and Kusuma Ford.

More Mushrooms

Yes, Cage won the big Italian TV game show prize in 1959 by naming all the known species of white-spored mushrooms.[3] The much-needed money went to support the Cunningham Dance Company tours. Yes, he became internationally recognized as an amateur expert on mycology, and was called upon by professionals to share his experiences. To speak here about Cage's involvement in mushrooms requires that I add something new.

Alexander Smith, a professional mycologist of international stature, experimented in collaboration with the University Medical Emergency Division of the University of Michigan. Smith ate deadly poisonous mushrooms while medically wired up to test their complex biochemical interaction. The Medical Emergency Division attended with carefully timed resuscitation. Cage and Smith became very good friends and met every few years to hunt mushrooms together in Ann Arbor and elsewhere.

Difficulties in Latin America

What were the most difficult times when touring with the Merce Cunningham Dance Company and John Cage? They were usually related to the interactions of people under stress, but Cage mostly participated in ways that dissipated the bumps and stings.

At times the circumstances could press to extremes. Touring Latin America in 1968, the Cunningham Dance Company encountered many surprises. In Rio de Janeiro a preliminary performance was required for the police in advance of our opening public performance. This was a censorship requirement to clear the "plot" of our production of any "political difficulties." At that point, the circumstances of politics and survival in Latin America were becoming increasingly complicated—years later it was referred to as the time of *los desaparacidos*. Cage and the Cunningham people decided to refuse the censorship and were supported in this decision by the U.S. Cultural Attaché in Rio de Janeiro. The previous performance in that theater by a European Shakespeare ensemble had had parts of Shakespeare's text censored. Cunningham told the police there was "no plot" and that the dancers moved "as in sports." The censorship was revoked and a precedent made for later performing groups.

Earlier on that Latin American tour, the Cunningham Dance Company had performed in Mexico City. Because it was the time of the Mexico City Olympics, the U.S. government had put up money to support this "American Art." When the word spread that the company had received government funding, invitations to parties and other occasions diminished. Later, at a news conference in Rio following the Brazilian censorship incident, Cage and Cunningham publicly renounced and returned the U.S. government sponsorship money for the Mexico performances. Cage added ambiguously: "You have to remember about the country we come from."

Revolution

On tour with the Cunningham Dance Company in 1968, Cage and I met in Buenos Aires with a group of young composers from all over Latin America. Most were there on stipends, working with electronic and other contemporary media in lavishly equipped facilities. They were an aristocracy of artists, uncomfortably aware of their privileged positions in an underprivileged and politically repressed continent. Cage spoke enthusiastically to them of the composer's responsibility to use the growing abundance of technology and of the likely impact of technology on reactionary institutions, which would need to change or fall of their own accord.

An Argentine composer asked: "What if they do not fall? And if the majority continues to be denied access to this abundance, how are we to bring about change?"

Cage replied: "Then your responsibility is not to a revolution of music, but to one of society." Cage's remark would become a legend among Latin American artists and composers.

Beograd

In September 1972 the Cunningham Dance Company performed at an international theater festival in Belgrade, Yugoslavia. Both ballet and modern dance were represented. The famous Cuban National Ballet of the esteemed choreographer and dancer Alicia Alonso was also in the festival. But as a U.S. citizen I was advised not to attend the Cuban performances—it would be an illegal action in the category of "trading with the enemy." The Belgrade theater technicians, with whom I'd shared several local beers, brought me into the theater through a back door, out of sight of the U.S. "intelligence observers" at the public entrances.

The Cunningham Dance Company had several performances there, one of which was Cunningham's choreography titled *Canfield*. Its elaborate live-electronic music was by Pauline Oliveros, her *In Memoriam: Nikola Tesla, Cosmic Engineer* (Tesla was an early twentieth-century electrical inventor and a cultural hero in Yugoslavia). Of all the performances at the Belgrade festival, the first prize was awarded to the Cunningham-Oliveros production.

Now the absurdities begin. The international press stumbled over the name of Pauline Oliveros and reported that the music was by John Cage. Cage was dismayed. It took months to correct that historical error. And because the Cunningham Dance Company was on tour, we left Belgrade before the end of the festival for our next engagements, including one in Germany at the Cologne Opera House, where *Canfield* provoked an ugly riot and police intervention. The Belgrade festival prize was given to a representative of the U.S. government, who was to forward it to Cunningham. But the prize was sent first to Washington, D.C., "for inspection." Several months later it arrived at the Cunningham Dance Studio in New York, requiring all postage due.

HPSCHD

In Rio de Janeiro in 1968, vellums of blue-penciled harpsichord solos were spread about Cage's hotel room. All that late summer, South American hotels were full of score pages of *HPSCHD*, still a year from its premiere.

A year later in Urbana, Illinois, Cage reflected with Edward Kobrin on the trio-like creation of *HPSCHD* by the ensemble of Cage, Lejaren Hiller, and the computer. Kobrin brought to my attention certain differences between Cage's aesthetic and that of Hiller when working with the computer, citing the philosophical concern of others that man may ultimately lose his control over computers and become their servant. We reflected on further implications for societies that depend on artificial intelligence. I think Cage already understood. Perhaps the computer has a radical personality for democratic societies. It is neither controlled nor controller, but an intelligence to be allowed to be itself.

In St. Paul, Minnesota, in 1969, we arrived at an after-performance reception for the Cunningham Company. Interspersed with sounds of the crowd is a bouncy, *jig-jog-clink-twank* music, as jocular as the occasion itself, a music for people of many minds—the host's recording of *HPSCHD*.

Money

In general, Cage's relationship to money was simply a matter of finding resources for life and work. Before the early 1950s, he was concerned with his own survival and his sense of responsibility to close friends. Most of his meager income came from various odd jobs, some performance fees, the occasional patronage of an institution, or a surprise windfall. His writings and scores through the 1960s were published at a time when performance royalties were minimal. Cage paid ongoing alimony to his ex-wife Xenia and supported his mother after his father died.

To establish the 1964 world tour of the Cunningham Dance Company, Cage spent the year writing letters seeking financial support. From 1938 to 1992, 1964 is his only year without other creative work. The 1964 tour brought substantial attention to the Cunningham circle. Robert Rauschenberg received the Venice Biennale visual arts prize (some of which went to pay for the Cunningham Dance Company tour), and the French government was involved in the commission of *Variations V* for the Lincoln Center premiere in 1965. By then Cage had qualified to obtain his first credit card.

In the Cunningham milieu from the 1950s through most of the 1960s, whatever money was made for a performance would pay for transportation and ac-

188 · Part IV. . . . Say Anything about John (Cage)

commodations; the remainder was divided equally among the participants. The composers of new music and designers for decor received a flat $25 commission. Everyone agreed with this financial equality.

By the end of the 1960s, Cage's income from lectures, performances, commissions, residencies, and royalties became more than sufficient to support his own work. Besides money, sales of his visual arts and other documents added to his support "pantry" for access by others. He established procedures for supporting other creative artists—particularly in his efforts to establish the Foundation for Contemporary Performance Arts and later the John Cage Trust. In those philanthropic activities, as usual, he enlisted the support of others.

Cage was always generous.

Other Composers

Cage sometimes spoke to me with appreciation about other composers. Sometimes he was notably enthusiastic, often asking if I knew a particular composition. Among the composers who were returning topics for him are (in alphabetical order): Johanna Beyer, Henry Cowell, Alan Hovhaness, Charles Ives, Alvin Lucier, Wolfgang Amadeus Mozart, Erik Satie, Edgard Varèse, and Christian Wolff. Most frequently he mentioned Hovhaness and Satie.

Library

In the mid-1970s I was in Ann Arbor, Michigan, on a performance tour. I had been a student at the University of Michigan in the early 1950s. Following a nostalgia trail, I visited the university's general library, where twenty years earlier I had spent hours in intense reading, particularly in history and literature. The Reserve section had multiple copies on hold for a large survey class on the "ten influential authors" of twentieth-century English literature. Among them were books by James Joyce, Ezra Pound, William Butler Yeats—and John Cage. Three of Cage's books were there: *Silence* (1961), *A Year from Monday* (1967), and *M* (1972).

Continuing my sentimental tour, I crossed the campus to the university music library. There I inquired at the circulation desk about scores of Cage's music (which were published by C. F. Peters continuously from the 1960s). The response: "I don't know why we carry them. They aren't music."

Museum

In the early 1990s I visited the old San Francisco Museum of Modern Art, then at the War Memorial Building next to the Opera House. It was to see a special collection of very large paintings from Richard Diebenkorn's "Ocean Park" series. They were on display in a large, high-ceilinged open room. Off to one side was a large corridor with a separate display of smaller works, both newly acquired and on loan. There I saw for the first time John Cage's drypoint and aquatint etchings collection, titled *Seven Day Diary (Not Knowing)* (1978).

While pausing to examine these etchings, I was approached by an elegantly dressed woman who inquired why I had stopped at the *Seven Day Diary* series. I replied that I had always been interested in Cage's creative work, and this was the first time I'd seen this collection.

"Well, I collect beautiful art," she continued, "and I'm going to buy one of those portfolios. There are several remaining sets of them here in a San Francisco studio. I'm pleased that you like them, too. And you might be interested in this: someone told me John Cage is also a composer."

Accolades and Guilt by Association

On April 4, 1968, Cage was given an award by the American Academy of Arts and Letters. Rather than addressing the awards banquet, he had decided to play his *Cartridge Music* in the duet version for amplified piano and cymbal. He asked me to play the cymbal part. The banquet began as an auspicious occasion, attended by many notable writers, artists, and musicians. As we were preparing to begin the performance, word reached us backstage that Martin Luther King had just been assassinated. John decided that we should begin the performance immediately, before the news reached the audience.

I was surprised after the performance to be greeted by Ross Lee Finney, with whom I had studied composition during my student days in Ann Arbor, and with whom I had remained on modest if not always cordial speaking terms. He said to me: "You know, Mumma, I wasn't sure that you'd get your musical talents in order, but you've certainly come along in the world and met the right people."[4]

In the 1970s I was offered a professorship at a major university in the United States, albeit to serious objections from one evaluator. Many years later I was shown a document, apparently written by the dissenter:

I consider that the musical circle with which he [Gordon Mumma] is often strongly identified is a minor part of current musical developments. This group, led by John Cage, has been effective in mocking and deriding the basic assumptions of musical tradition, and has been successful in the reshaping of attitudes. While I appreciate a little fun and occasional absurdities, I am uncertain about what positive achievements will emerge from more of the same, and am concerned that our recent graduates think it is a significant activity.

Hooray for Cage

Pauline Oliveros had worked with Cage for the first time in 1964 at the "Tudor-fest" performances in San Francisco produced by radio station KPFA and the San Francisco Tape Music Center. One of the events was an honest performance of Cage's *Atlas Eclipticalis*, which had recently been sabotaged by members of the New York Philharmonic.

But in 1982 Oliveros told me that it was not until 1980, when Cage was in residency at the University of California, San Diego, that she had come to understand the depth of his "discipline in his own work and his interactions with others. Many people are struck by the novelty of Cage's sounds and ideas," she observed, "but I was very impressed by his example of how one's life can be changed by such a discipline."

Her reaction to his seventieth birthday: "Hooray!"

Love Letter

Framingham, 28 February 1988
Dear John,
    In the winter noontime sun of Massachusetts, this day after the Arditti's incomparable performance of your three works for string quartet, I am still hearing in my memory your quietly Olympian, transcendental music. At intermission, Dick Higgins and I stood silently together for a time. He then said: "I've heard the *Quartet in Four Parts* so often—I thought I knew it." Later with William Brooks, our eyes misted, he said: "I want to tell John 'Please wait for me.'"
We are all so grateful to you.
With love,
Gordon

Ananda Fuara

My last visit with John Cage was on May 7, 1992. He was attending an eightieth-birthday celebration concert by the San Francisco Contemporary Music Players at the Herbst Theater of the War Memorial Performing Arts Center. One of the compositions was *Music for 14*, and two of the guest performers were the wonderful soprano Joan La Barbara and myself performing on horn.

Between the afternoon rehearsal and evening concert Cage invited Betty Freeman and me to dinner. Betty was sponsoring our recording of *Music for 17* the following week at George Lucas's Skywalker Sound Studio.[5] Cage, who maintained a strict vegetarian diet in these late years of his life, suggested that we go to a nearby restaurant aptly titled Ananda Fuara—The Fountain of Delight. It was obvious as we walked to the theater exit that Cage's increasingly debilitating arthritis would make it very difficult to walk to the restaurant. We traveled the five blocks by taxi and settled into the delight of lively conversation in its otherworldly atmosphere. In spite of his physical impediments, Cage in his usual lively youth of mind was enthusiastic as always about the future and his next creative projects.

PART V

Latin America

Editor's Introduction

"American" music for Gordon Mumma has always included that of Latin America.[1] The contacts he made in Mexico City, Rio de Janeiro, Buenos Aires, and Caracas during the 1968 tour of the Cunningham Dance Company developed into close professional relationships with many Latin American composers during the volatile 1970s. During the 1968 Cunningham tour, Mumma, Cage, and Tudor also spent a memorable day with Conlon Nancarrow in the player piano studio of his Mexico City residence. The friendship was renewed in late December 1974, when Mumma visited Nancarrow for several days of intensive discussions of his player piano technology and compositional processes.

The 1974 Nancarrow visit documented here was the first leg of the long trip to Montevideo, Uruguay, where Mumma served on the faculty of the Fourth Curso Latinoamericano de Música Contemporánea (Latin American Course of Contemporary Music) in January 1975. These two-week summer courses were held almost every January from 1971 to 1989, variously in Argentina, Brazil, the Dominican Republic, Uruguay, and Venezuela.[2] Mumma was invited to participate yearly beginning with the first Curso in 1971, but competing professional engagements and his resistance to accepting travel funding from U.S. foundations "with complicated stipulations of questionable political purpose"[3] allowed him to participate in only three of the Cursos: Montevideo, Uruguay (1975), Buenos Aires, Argentina (1977), and Santiago, Dominican Republic (1981). He would be the only United States–born composer ever to serve on the composition professorate of this important Latin American cultural institution. His free agency and cultural openness made the participation of this "yanqui californieño" welcome, in spite of his spotty Span-ish.[4] The Cursos proved to be among the most significant musical experiences of Mumma's career, nourishing his lifelong friendships with its directors Coriún Aha-ronián and Graciela Paraskevaídis and his passionate interest in the panorama of Latin American electro-acoustical music. Mumma regularly featured Latin Ameri-can repertoire, especially by Aharonián, Oscar Bazán, Leo Brouwer, Mario Lavista, Joaquín Orellana, Paraskevaídis, and Héctor Tosar—much of it from rare scores and recordings squirreled away in his returning baggage—in his university lectures during the 1970s and 1980s. This was at a time when this music was both little known and politically charged in the United States.

Mumma kept detailed journals of his Latin American trips with the intention of writing extended articles. Only two were completed. His survey "Innovation in Latin American Electro-Acoustical Music" proposes a taxonomy of Latin American music based on Mumma's travels and conversations. Written for the Pacific Rim Festival at the University of California, San Diego, in May 1986, it represented a terra incognita for most of his U.S. readers at the time. "Briefly about Conlon Nancarrow's *Studies for Player Piano*" was developed on the basis of extensive notes and interviews with Nancarrow in Mexico City in December 1974. His candid "Uruguayan Diary," about the Fourth Curso in Uruguay in 1975, profited from the relative freedom of the remote Cerro del Toro, in comparison to the relentless military surveillance of the January 1977 Curso in Buenos Aires, which impaired the frankness of his journal for that trip. The result is a vivid re-creation with photo documentation of the daily rounds of a little-documented creative community, unpublished until now.

CHAPTER 22

Innovation in Latin American Electro-Acoustical Music

(1986)

Latin America shares with North America a long history of musical innovation. Latin American composers include innovators with musical timbre, chromatic and serial syntax, and microtonal tuning. Historical figures in this area include Juan Carlos Paz (Argentina, 1901–72), Walter Smetak (Brazil, 1913–84), Acario Cotapos (Chile, 1889–1969), Amadeo Roldán (Cuba, 1900–39), and from Mexico Julián Carrillo (1875–1965), Augusto Novaro (1891–1960), and Silvestre Revueltas (1899–1940).

Electro-acoustical music has also flourished in Latin America, in spite of chronic political difficulties, erratic institutional support, and the limited availability of electronic equipment. One extraordinary center, the Torcuato Di Tella Institute in Buenos Aires, was active for about a decade. But many composers have also worked in shorter-lived institutions or have established independent, private facilities (often outside Latin America) in order to make their electro-acoustical music. The innovative Latin American composers best known in the northern hemisphere are usually émigrés or exiles.

The first important Latin American electro-acoustical music appeared in Chile at the Catholic University in Santiago, where the Experimental Sound Guild established a studio in the late 1950s. José Vicente Asuar (Chile, b. 1933) composed his *Variaciones espectrales* (Phantom Variations) there in 1959. In 1958 the Estudio de Fonología Musical (Studio for Musical Phonology) was established at the National University of Buenos Aires; it was adjunct to the study of

Source: Program brochure of *The Pacific Rim Festival, April 29–May 9, 1986* (Department of Music, University of California, San Diego [private publication]): 23–25.

architectural acoustics. Though very little music was made there, one remarkable exception based on a Tunebo Indian text was the evocative *Creación de la tierra* (Creation of the Earth, 1972) by Colombian composer Jacqueline Nova (1935–75). Other early institutional studios were established in Argentina (the Center for Experimental Music at the National University of Córdoba, 1965), in Venezuela (Studio of Musical Phonology, Caracas, established by Asuar in 1966–67), in Brazil during the 1970s by Jorge Antunes (b. 1942) and Conrado Silva (Uruguay, 1940–2014), and in Mexico by Héctor Quintanar (1936–2013). In Cuba the composers Juan Blanco (1919–2008) and Leo Brouwer (b. 1939) and others worked with the Experimental Sound Group of the Cuban Institute of Cinematic Art and Industry (ICAIC).

Some of the institutional studios were technologically extravagant or imitated European and North American facilities; they rarely produced much quantity or diversity of compositional results. Usually more productive were the private studios established by individual composers such as Jorge Rapp (Argentina, 1946–2010), Joaquín Orellana (Guatemala, b. 1937), or the cooperative studio ELAC in Montevideo, under the guidance of Coriún Aharonián (Uruguay, b. 1940).

The Torcuato Di Tella Institute of Buenos Aires established an electronic music laboratory as part of the Latin American Center for Advanced Musical Studies (CLAEM). Over the period it was operative (approximately 1963–72), stipends for one or two years of study were available for composers from all over Latin America. The director of the center was Alberto Ginastera (1916–83), an Argentine composer of international stature whose reputation and guidance secured some continuance of its operation. Among the various people responsible for its technical direction was Fernando von Reichenbach (1931–2005), who not only supported a diversity of compositional directions but also applied his inventive genius to the development of extraordinary electronic music instruments. One such device converted graphic images into control voltages for sound synthesis. His application of this "high-tech" idea was notably in advance of its development in the affluent countries of the northern hemisphere.

Operation of Di Tella ceased in about 1972, concurrent with the decline of a relatively liberal artistic and political decade in Argentina (and in Latin America generally).[1] The studio itself was moved to new quarters under the auspices of the Center for the Investigation of Mass Communication, Arts, and Technology (CICMAT). Von Reichenbach was joined in its technical direction by Francisco Kröpfl (b. 1931), who had been the technical director of the National University studio, José Ramón Maranzano (b. 1940), and composers Gerardo Gandini (Argentina, 1936–2013) and Gabriel Brnčić (Chile, b. 1942). By 1976 artistic innovation was badly constricted by the deleterious political climate. Stipends were no longer available. The name of the studio shifted evasively to become the less-provocative Center for Acoustical Musical Studies, while non-Argentine composers had reduced access to the facilities.

A remarkable diversity of music was produced during the halcyon decade of the Di Tella Studio in Buenos Aires. The first major work was *Intensidad y altura* (Intensity and Height, 1964) by the Peruvian composer César Bolaños (1931–2012). Other important compositions include *Metéora* (1968) by Joaquín Orellana and the witty *Parca* (1974) by Oscar Bazán (Argentina, 1936–2005). Aside from fostering compositional achievements, the major impact of the Di Tella studio was the cross-fertilization of ideas and the creative momentum nourished in the composers who studied and worked there. Some of their major accomplishments occurred after they had returned home. Several of the Di Tella alumni developed studios or produced significant work elsewhere. Besides those mentioned above, they include Eduardo Bértola (Argentina, 1939–96), Eduardo Kusnir (Argentina, b. 1939), alcides lanza (Argentina, b. 1929), and Graciela Paraskevaídis (Argentina, b. 1940).

Orellana studied at the Di Tella Institute in 1967–68. After his return to Guatemala, he bypassed the distractions of technological opulence as inappropriate to the Guatemalan context. Instead, he explored indigenous acoustical resources, developed extended performance techniques with local ensembles, and built new musical instruments. He established a robust electro-acoustical studio and gathered the sounds of his experiments and of life in city and countryside. Using these materials, Orellana produced a stunning group of electro-acoustical compositions during the 1970s, some of which employed theatrical or projected images. They include *Humanofonía I* (1971), *Malebolge (Humanofonía II)* (1972), *Primitiva I* (1973), *Rupestre en el futuro* (1978), and *Imposible a la "X"* (1980).[2]

The musical accomplishments of Orellana's work are radical and profound. His sense of musical time comes from a Guatemalan and Latin American reality (indigenous or *mestizo*) rather than from cultivated European models. He employs sounds as themselves rather than as artifacts; his "primitive" elements are authentic rather than exotic. He juxtaposes and overlaps blocks of sound in an intuitive rather than discursive continuity (analogous, perhaps, to *cinéma vérité*). His sound montages, even at their most complex, manifest material and aesthetic austerity.

Public access to musical innovation in Latin America has been mostly through the efforts of metropolitan new-music organizations (for example, in Bogotá, Caracas, Mexico City, and Montevideo) or at occasional international festivals such as the notable Third Art Biennial in Córdoba, Argentina, which was co-sponsored by Kaiser Industries in October 1966. Its "New Music Days" presented an extraordinary panorama of contemporary electro-acoustical and chamber music documented in publications and LP recordings.[3]

Among the most significant new-music endeavors have been the Cursos Latinoamericanos de Música Contemporánea (Latin American Courses of Contemporary Music), held almost annually since 1971.[4] These courses have an international faculty and include in their curriculum musical performance, analysis, composition, technology, and critical studies, with attention to cultivated and vernacular genres. The Pan-American faculty of the courses has included Gerardo Gandini, Hans-Joachim Koellreutter (Germany-Brazil, 1915–2005), Mario Lavista (Mexico, b. 1943), Emilio Mendoza (Venezuela, b. 1953), José Maria Neves (Brazil, 1943–2002), Cergio Prudencio (Bolivia, b. 1955), and Héctor Tosar (Uruguay, 1923–2002).

A comprehensive selection of Latin American electro-acoustical music, titled *Música nueva latinoamericana*, is recorded on the Tacuabé label [now Ayuí/ Tacuabé]. Its eight volumes[5] include electro-acoustical or instrumental music by many of the composers mentioned above as well as other new music for instrumental and vocal resources.

CHAPTER 23

Briefly about Conlon Nancarrow's
Studies for Player Piano
(1977)

Several experimentalists have managed to survive in the predominantly conservative musical culture of Mexico. Julián Carrillo (1875–1965), an early experimenter with microtonal scales, is perhaps best known. The little-known Augusto Novaro (1891–1960) designed and built pianos with innovative tuning arrangements and guitars and other string instruments, and published his treatise *Natural System of Music* in Mexico City in 1951.[1] And then there is Conlon Nancarrow.

The music of Conlon Nancarrow is only recently becoming known beyond a small group of admirers.[2] Nancarrow is the composer of an in-progress magnum opus called *Studies for Player Piano*, which now number more than forty.[3] The studies explore complex rhythmic relationships with the same kind of thoroughness that J. S. Bach brought to problems of chromatic keyboard music in *The Well-Tempered Clavier*.

Though Nancarrow is a Mexican citizen and has lived in Mexico City since he began work on the *Studies for Player Piano*, he was born in Texarkana, Arkansas,

Source: Unpublished manuscript journal written in Mexico City during Mumma's stay with Nancarrow in late December 1974 ("Mexico City and Montevideo, 12.74–1.75"). Much of the current text was revised from the latter and published as "Briefly about Nancarrow," in Conlon Nancarrow, *Selected Studies for Player Piano*, ed. Peter Garland, Soundings Book 4 (Berkeley, Cal.: Soundings 1977): 1–5, © 1977 Gordon Mumma; German trans. in "Programmheft *Pro Musica Nova*" (Radio-Bremen, May 6–12, 1980): 20–23, and as "Conlon Nancarrow," *Neuland: Ansätze zur Musik der Gegenwart* 1 (1980): 123–30. The current text also incorporates some supplementary material from Mumma's program notes for the 1969 Columbia recording of twelve of the studies (MS 7222), later adapted in his "Nancarrow Notes," in Zimmermann, *Desert Plants*, 247–52.

on July 8, 1912. His father was a businessman from the north, sent to Arkansas to establish a manufacturing business. As a young man Nancarrow played the jazz and popular music of that era on trumpet and composed for piano and various small ensembles. According to Nancarrow, his early music for traditional instruments was rarely played, apparently because of its rhythmic difficulties, and is now mostly lost or abandoned.

In 1940 Nancarrow moved to Mexico City. Whatever neglect he had experienced from musicians unable to cope with the rhythmic and performance difficulties of his earlier music, he found himself almost completely isolated in the conservative musical milieu of Mexico.[4] A Sonatina for Piano dating from as late as 1941 has survived; it was performed in concert for a time by the pianist James Sykes. The score and parts of a string quartet from around that time were once in the possession of the Léner Quartet, from Hungary but also active in Mexico. They never performed the work.[5]

Nancarrow soon began his experiments with player pianos, and also spent several years building a mechanical-pneumatic apparatus to play an assortment of percussion instruments that he was collecting. The problems of his "player percussion instrument" were unending. By the early 1950s Nancarrow had abandoned the project, disposing of the apparatus and most of the percussion instruments. As one of his final efforts with these instruments, he composed a now-abandoned "musique concrète" *Piece for Tape* on magnetic tape. In the meantime he continued his experiments with player pianos and began composition of the *Studies for Player Piano*.

The first of these was composed in 1948. Since then he has completed forty-one studies as of 1977. Three types of rhythmic procedures are prominent in the *Studies for Player Piano*: (1) intuitively determined relationships, (2) rhythmic canons of fixed proportions, and (3) specific rates of acceleration and deceleration. In the early studies 1–5, 12, and 13, his rhythmic, melodic, and harmonic vocabulary is essentially intuitive, established by the circumstances of each piece. Some of the early studies have a flavor of ragtime or boogie-woogie. Study 3, for example, is a five-movement work that was composed separately from the other studies as "Boogie-Woogie Suite," replacing a different Study 3 that Nancarrow has now abandoned. Studies 10 and 11 are blues, and Studies 6 and 12 have a decidedly Spanish flavor. Studies 6–11, though essentially intuitive in their composition method, also employ canonic procedures.

Of the canonic studies, nos. 15–19 are rhythmic canons of fixed proportions. For example, Study 17 is a three-voice canon with the proportions 12:15:20. This procedure of fixed proportions also applies to Studies 24, 26, and 31–37. Some of the higher-numbered studies are extremely elaborate: Study 37, for example, is a twelve-voice canon with rhythmic proportions spread between 150 and 281¼.

Only Studies 22 and 27 exploit fixed percentages of acceleration and deceleration as a fundamental characteristic of their structure. Study 22 is "Canon 1%, 1½%, 2¼%," and Study 27 employs the relationships 5%, 6%, 8%, and 11%. Some of the later studies exploit specific irrational relationships in which the effects of acceleration and deceleration are present but elusive. For example, Study 33 has the ratio of 2:√2, and Study 40 explores the ratio of "e" to pi. These studies could be placed in either the second or the third category outlined above.

Study 21 is a special case. Subtitled "Canon X," it is a two-voice tour de force in which the higher of the two voices begins at great speed and decelerates, while the lower voice begins very slowly and accelerates. The two voices meet "in tempo" for a brief moment at the center of the piece before continuing on to complete the X shape at the conclusion.

The *Studies for Player Piano* also exhibit a wide variety of musical devices and effects beyond their rhythmic procedures. Some have diatonically oriented key centers; others are polytonal, and most of the later studies are fundamentally chromatic. Study 24 has the characteristics of an orchestral concerto grosso, with alternating solo and full ensemble sections. The demonic fantasy of Study 25 is achieved with massive, sweeping blocks of sound. In some of the later studies the sonority of the player piano is transformed, making it barely recognizable when taken out of context. The high speeds of certain passages and the complex durational relationships between individual notes within the passage deceive one's sense of acoustical perception. Some of the studies are made for special resources: Study 30 is for prepared player piano, while Studies 40 and 41 are for two player pianos operating simultaneously.[6]

For his work on the now-abandoned player-percussion instrument as well as his continuing work with piano-roll composition, Nancarrow built a sound-proof studio separate from his living quarters. The main room of the studio is approximately twenty by thirty feet, and about thirteen feet high. An adjoining workshop area approximately six feet wide extends around two sides of the studio. The inside walls of the studio are lined with shelves filled with books, journals, and piano rolls. Part of one wall has a long, wide table equipped with a track that enables him to notate directly in pencil on the unpunched paper rolls. On each end of this table is an apparatus for dispensing the paper along the length of the table from its supply roll to a take-up roll. An upholstered stool, with its own carriage and wheels, moves along the length of the piano roll table, easing the long hours Nancarrow spends seated at work on his notation.

Two player pianos occupy one end of the studio. They are both Marshall and Wendell uprights with Ampico Reproducing Piano mechanisms. Nancarrow has modified the hammers of both pianos. One piano has wooden hammers that have been covered with steel strips: its timbre is hard-edged and brilliant. The other piano has wooden hammers covered with leather. Into each leather cover, at the point where it strikes the piano strings, is anchored a small metal tack. The timbre of this second piano is mellower than that of its steel-reinforced neighbor, but it still has a crisp attack. The specially built machine on which he punches the rolls is located in the adjoining workshop.[7]

Nancarrow had several player pianos previous to the two he now uses. One of these, also an upright, had standard felt hammers that he hardened by soaking them with a varnish (this is the instrument on which his first eighteen or twenty studies were recorded for the tapes later sent to John Edmunds of the New York Public Library). Another upright was used with its hammers unmodified, though it had an accessory "mandolin" attachment.[8] Nancarrow liked the sound of this second piano, but it worked unpredictably. The mandolin attachment was abandoned, but he recalled that this is otherwise the same piano that now has the leather-and-tack hammers.

During the late 1950s Nancarrow obtained a grand piano with a player mechanism for work on a study for prepared player piano, now called Study 30. This innovative work was apparently inspired by John Cage. Its process was not without challenges. The strings of an upright player piano are virtually inaccessible, since the player mechanism itself fills the usually empty space. Furthermore, the hardware of preparation—bolts, screws, rubber strips, and the like—is easily dislodged from vertical strings. The horizontal strings of the player grand were accessible and quite satisfactory for preparation, but the player mechanism proved unreliable. Nancarrow eventually disposed of the player grand.

In his first experiments with player pianos, Nancarrow punched his rolls with a hand punch. He realized that a less time-consuming procedure was needed, and in 1947 he made a trip to New York City. There he had a machine specially built to punch his player piano rolls. He brought it back to Mexico City and used it for Studies 1–21. The design of this machine followed the traditional practices, including that of moving the punch-carriage along a notched track. The punching machine was a great improvement in efficiency over the hand punch. However, its notched-track mechanism limited punching to multiples of discrete steps, thereby limiting the shortest interval of duration or attack between two different pitches on his rolls. Within a few years he had a Mexican machinist make a modification to the apparatus that enabled him to punch anywhere along

Fig. V-1. Conlon Nancarrow demonstrating his modified punch machine for the preparation of piano rolls in his Mexico City workroom, December 1974. (Photo © Gordon Mumma.)

the length of a piano roll. This was the mechanism that I observed and photographed at work during my December 1974 visit with Nancarrow [fig. V-1].

The paper for the Ampico mechanism is 28.6 cm wide (on the piano roll it is 4 to 6 cm in diameter). When installed on the player mechanism, the paper unspools from the supply roll at the top, over a pneumatic aperture bar that extends the width of the paper, and onto a take-up spool below the aperture bar.

The speed of the roll (and thus the tempo of the piece) is determined by a lever calibrated with standard metronome markings. Because the speed of the roll is dependent on the rotation of the take-up roll (rather than a capstan-and-idler mechanism, as on a tape recorder), there is a slight increase in the speed of a roll from start to finish, due to the slight increase in diameter of the take-up roll as it gathers the paper. Because of this effect all of the studies will have a slight *accelerando* from beginning to end. Nancarrow explained to me that it doesn't really bother him because gentle acceleration is "probably a natural phenomenon in all rhythmic music," and referred to the same thing occurring in long African drum performances. Only in Study 27, which because of its length required two rolls, did this slight increase in take-up speed pose a serious problem. It was clearly apparent at the beginning of the second roll that the tempo was less than at the end of the first. He calculated the amount of change and increased the tempo regulator by that amount when he was playing the second roll. Still dissatisfied, he revised Study 27 by re-punching it to fit on one roll.

Most of the openings in the pneumatic aperture bar correspond to hammers of the piano. A hammer strikes the piano strings only when a hole punched in the paper passes the corresponding opening in the aperture bar. On the extreme right and left of the aperture bar are openings that, according to corresponding holes punched in the paper roll, control the damper-raising (sustaining) and muting pedals of the piano. Besides the pedal holes, there are three holes on each side of the aperture bar for the control of loudness, or the force with which the hammers strike the strings. The three holes on the left control the dynamics for the lower register of the piano, while the three holes on the right control the dynamics for its upper register. The dynamics of each half of the piano are controlled factorially: a code of eight dynamic levels is thereby possible from the various combinations of the three holes on each side. It is also possible to control crescendo and diminuendo, though Nancarrow does not often use these effects, depending more commonly on ingenious pitch doublings for this purpose. The Ampico mechanism has a bellows-and-spring apparatus that acts as a pneumatic governor to preserve the loudness specified by the factorial code regardless of the number of hammers in use.

In the late 1950s, John Cage received tape recordings of the *Studies for Player Piano* from John Edmunds, who had received them directly from Nancarrow. The Edmunds tapes had been made on the varnished-hammer player piano in Nancarrow's studio. In 1960 Cage arranged the tape-recorded performances of six of these studies, in the order 1, 2, 4, 5, 6, and 7, as the music for Merce Cunningham's *Crises*, a work for five dancers with decor by Robert Rauschenberg. Its premiere at Connecticut College in August 1960 was the first public hearing

Fig. V-2. Conlon Nancarrow in his Mexico City residence, late December 1974. (Photo © Gordon Mumma.)

of any of the studies in the United States. *Crises* remained in the Cunningham Dance Company repertory for five years, performed widely in the United States and on the six-month world tour in 1964. It was revived briefly in 1970. This prolonged exposure, though only to a small number of Nancarrow's *Studies for Player Piano*, spawned a considerable, though rather arcane, legion of admirers.

In August 1968 the Cunningham Dance Company, with musicians Cage, David Tudor, and myself, made a tour of Latin America. During a meeting in his Mexico City studio, Cage, Tudor, and I discussed the *Studies for Player Piano* with Nancarrow, and we were treated to a short demonstration of the equipment that he had created for this project. We also discussed the idea of electronically modifying a group of the *Studies for Player Piano* in some future live-performance situation. Nancarrow was receptive to the idea, and on January 18, 1969, the project was realized in a collaborative theater performance at the Billy Rose Theatre in New York, featuring dancers Viola Farber and Peter Saul along with Cage, Tudor, and myself. In this special performance the musical articulation and rhythmic structure of the Nancarrow studies retained their original form. Electronic variations were made only to the pitch and timbre characteristics of the music.[9]

In late December 1974 I again visited Nancarrow in Mexico City on my way to Montevideo, this time alone, partially in preparation for this essay. Over a four-day period, fortified with delicious meals prepared by his Mexican cook, trips to the nearby café, and periodic libations, Nancarrow and I examined and discussed in detail the instrumental resources and musical aesthetics of his *Studies for Player Piano*. The portrait of Nancarrow in figure V-2 shows him during a thoughtful pause in our discussions.

Toward the close of our time together, I wrote the following in my journal: "Imagination often surpasses reality. For composer Conlon Nancarrow the problem is easily defined. His imagination and music are filled with complex, often irrational rhythms, most of which are beyond the performing skills of musicians. The solutions to this problem have occupied much of his creative life" (Mexico City, December 29, 1974).

CHAPTER 24

Uruguayan Diary
The Cuarto Curso Latinoamericano de Música Contemporánea, Cerro del Toro, Uruguay
(January 3–17, 1975)

Gordon Mumma to Coriún Aharonián, Executive Secretary, Sociedad Uruguaya de Música Contemporánea, Montevideo, Uruguay, November 22, 1974

Because I must return to San Francisco by January 12 [1975], I plan to arrive in Montevideo several days before the Cuarto Curso Latinoamericano de Música Contemporánea [CCLAMC] begins, perhaps as early as December 30 or 31 [1974]. During those first days I hope to learn about Uruguayan music activities and meet musicians and artists who live and work in Montevideo. During the CCLAMC I would like to participate in any seminars where interchange of ideas about new music and art will occur. These are good ways for me to learn about your part of the world, perhaps the most important reason for me to join you in the CCLAMC.

Coriún Aharonián to Gordon Mumma, December 13, 1974

Do you think you can do a series of six lectures-seminars-workshops-but-more-live-and-practical-than-a-german-audience-herr-doktor-lecture about both subjects of multimedia and of the relationship between music and other languages? And if you can do some extra sessions . . . on the application of electro-acoustical resources to the instrumental media, we will be very happy. Remember that we need, in the third world, to destroy the myth of the divine and

Source: Assembled from Mumma's unpublished manuscript journal "Mexico City and Montevideo, 12.74–1.75" (GMC).

unknown forces of technology, and to help our people to master in the measure of possibility these mysterious forces.

Coming to technical equipment: you will have three Revox tape recorders, four or six loudspeakers, two microphones, one or two mixers, one Uher portable tape recorder, one Synthi A mini-synthesizer, one audio generator, one or two turntables, two slide projectors, one 16 mm film projector (an old RCA with optical sound), one Steinway half-grand piano, one destroyed old upright piano, and some guitars and other instruments, if people are carrying them. Not much more.

Gordon Mumma to Coriún Aharonián, December 21, 1974

A most important part of my trip to Uruguay is to write an article about the CCLAMC and the contemporary music activities of Uruguay and the surrounding cultures (Argentina, Brazil, etc.). Perhaps I can begin work on the article as soon as I arrive.

Coriún Aharonián to Gordon Mumma, December 22, 1974

If you can bring with you one or two blank tapes, it will be nice. Here in Uruguay we have no tapes at this moment.

Journal

December 30, 1974, Mexico City

Several days with Conlon Nancarrow in Mexico City. I also took a side-trip to visit composer Héctor Quintanar and viewed the impressive electronic studio of the National Conservatory of Music, the first of its kind in Mexico City [fig. V-3].

Two bottles of dark Noche Buena beer last night before retiring. Eight hours of sleep to begin the long flight to Montevideo, with a 12-hour layover in Rio. There are always unexpected things on difficult flights that cause drain. Like discovering one of my fiber cases has a split along its side. It must hold together until the end of the trip, as it is heavily packed.

I arrive at the Mexico City airport two hours early because of heavy security precautions. I have packed my two cases very carefully. One goes with the baggage. The other I carry on the plane after some argument. It contains my most valuable materials: cameras and film, slides for lectures, tapes, and an extra pair of socks. I wait in the departure lounge, grateful to be alone. How often am I disrupted in airports when I see old friends who are also traveling—unlikely in this remote spot! Then a mirage: out of the crowd, dancer Barbara Lloyd and

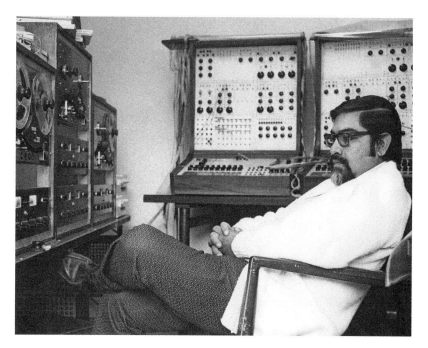

Fig. V-3. Mexican composer Héctor Quintanar in the electronic studio of the National Conservatory of Music, Mexico City, December 1974. (Photo © Gordon Mumma.)

her extended family. We talk and I nearly miss my flight to Rio. I am already exhausted. The jet is only half-full. We fly over the volcano Popocatepetl. It seems to be sleeping. A good idea.

Hot towels on the flight. Nice. I relax. Then a flight packet with map, stationery, etc. The map has a caption that reads: "This map has been specially edited by Varig Airlines for your information during the flight and, though topologically accurate, has no political significance."

December 31, 1974, arrive Montevideo, Uruguay

I have been invited to stay at Coriún Aharonián's apartment in the Parque Posadas until the Curso begins. A substantial part of it is occupied by his private lending library of books, music scores, and recordings.

January 1, 1975, Montevideo

We eat lunch at the home of Coriún's parents in a very old neighborhood, still middle-class but run-down, with the look of a movie set. They are Armenians who escaped the genocide by the Turks. There we eat Armenian food prepared

Fig. V-4. Uruguayan composer Coriún Aharonián making preparations for the CCLAMC at his parents' apartment in Montevideo, January 1, 1975. (Photo © Gordon Mumma.)

by his mother. She speaks very good English and French, having studied at the American School in Beirut, Lebanon. She was a translator for ITT years ago. His father is retired, and both are on pensions. They had built a house outside Montevideo, but lost it in the inflation. They rent their present place. They also have a phone, an expensive rarity in Montevideo. Coriún does not have his own phone, a nuisance in this final planning stage for the Curso, and takes advantage of theirs to call various people [fig. V-4].

Montevideo time is six hours east of California. We have just passed the summer solstice here, and it is still light at 11:00 P.M. The sky is very blue, the air clear, with brilliant ocean light. Coriún says: "It is this Uruguay that I miss most when I am in Europe, this light, this ambience." Last year he made a trip to Brazil by bus to "collect the cultural milieu" (and to save the advanced air fare money). Two days and nights continuous from Montevideo to Rio, then on to Brasilia. "I know Argentina well," he says, "at least the central and Buenos Aires parts, and the central part of Chile, but only half of Uruguay, nothing of Paraguay, Bolivia, etc. It takes much time. It is very important for us to learn about ourselves. The South American intellectual still goes to Europe instead of learning this continent."

Political slogans are painted on street walls throughout most of the city. Every week the military brings the work-prisoners to remove the slogans. Over the next few days new slogans reappear. Some are quite partisan, clearly the work of a specific faction. But most are poetically referential to the specific time of the year or living conditions of a locale, or to circumstances in the country or the world.

Very slowly the popular music of Latin America is being disseminated from one country to another. It is a complicated political and poetic process. Brazilian popular music is known to only a few intellectuals here, but some Argentine and Chilean popular music is available. Popular singers are often politically suspect. Their poetry is complex and full of allegory, most of it too subtle for the military occupation censors to grasp immediately. So recordings are made, initially passed by the censors. After many thousand copies of a pop tune are on sale, the military finally comes to understand its implications. They attempt first to intimidate the record companies (which are owned mostly by foreign money interests, such as Philips, who also supply electronics to the military). The company is making money and answers: "But we have the permission paper." The same answer from the radio stations. When the singer appears in public before a large audience, the police finally obtain a paper that prohibits the singer from singing the song. So the singer plays the accompaniment and the audience of thousands sings the words. Next the police prohibit "*singing* and *playing* of the song." The audience sings alone, without accompaniment. The song is whistled in the streets. Eventually one of the whistlers is arrested on some obscure charges. Soon another singer makes an allegorical song about the whistler who is in jail. Finally the military realize that their prisoner has become a martyr. He is released, but is forced out of the country. The process continues in one way or another, gradually expanding public consciousness.

The quality of the street and commercial folk musicians here is very high, and some of the best guitarists in the world now are Uruguayan. One conservatory has changed its policy to include guitar and folk music as serious courses of study. But the director of this conservatory is in exile for reasons I am unable to determine.

At Coriún's apartment we listen to South American tape and electro-acoustical music, some of which will be played from tapes at the Curso. I am most impressed by Coriún's *Que* (1969), *Gran tiempo* (1974), and *Homenaje a la flecha clavada en el pecho de Don Juan Díaz de Solís* with indigenous flutes (1974), Joaquín Orellana's *Humanofonía* I (1971), Jacqueline Nova's *Creación de la tierra* (1972), and Oscar Bazán's *Parca* (1974). I wish I had brought more blank tapes with me. They are needed for the conference, and Uruguay has just run out. The next shipment from Germany is not due for several months.

Coriún returns to a question that in one form or another has been asked before: "Why does John Cage not become a part of the social necessity of the Cursos? Am I wrong in suspecting that he has basically aristocratic or 'bourgeois' ideas?" I wonder: Would Cage comprehend where these people think *they* are? Would he bring to this situation his *different* and *useful* attitudes?

January 2, 1975, Montevideo

Last day before the Curso begins. Coriún works through the night without sleep. His rationality suffers from time to time. We have lunch with his parents and with composers Eduardo Bértola (from Buenos Aires, Argentina) and Carlos Pellegrino (from Montevideo), who will also teach at the Curso [figs. V-5 and V-6].[1] Virtuoso *La Plata* humor abounds, with surreal plays of language.[2]

Coriún and I walk through Montevideo, doing necessary tasks and still attempting to make telephone calls—very difficult. The telephone system has recently been automated with Siemens equipment that does not yet work properly. We go to the Bar los Estudiantes to try their telephone, for which we wait in line. I order a yogurt (very good). Bars such as this, with lunch menus, owe much business to people in line, eating and drinking while waiting their turn to use the telephone.

After lunch we stop by at the printing press for the Tacuabé recording works, a small letterpress shop in an impressive granite building.[3] They execute excellent artistic designs with one or two colors only. For some clients they do seven-color process with offset techniques, painstakingly registered by hand on the old letterpresses. All glue work is done by hand, wet process, by beautiful young people who seem very glad to have employment. They work by dim light from dying fluorescent tubes. More than half their records are out of print.

Coriún is getting frustrated. The truck to carry equipment to Cerro del Toro is not available. The driver is ill (does being "ill" mean "in jail," as it sometimes

Fig. V-5. Argentine composer Eduardo Bértola, Montevideo, January 2, 1975. (Photo © Gordon Mumma.)

Fig. V-6. Uruguayan composer-poet Carlos Pellegrino, Montevideo, January 2, 1975. (Photo © Gordon Mumma.

does here?). It is not possible to arrange for professional transportation: even if the Cursos had sufficient money, the bureaucratic paperwork requires several weeks to complete. The Fourth Curso begins tomorrow. A plan is being hatched to borrow a small van in the middle of the night and make two trips from Montevideo to Cerro del Toro, a 90-minute trip each way.

We stop by the offices of the Sociedad Uruguaya de Música Contemporánea [SUMC]. Its famous address, Casilla de Correo 1328, turns out to be a small box in the antique Montevideo post office, a typical colonial building. Mail censorship and mismanagement slow communication to a minimum. Packages mailed to the SUMC from Europe or the United States take three to nine months. (I mailed two recordings from New York to Montevideo in early August; Coriún received them last week. My last letter, mailed air express from San Francisco, arrived two weeks later, the morning of my arrival here.)

Last night the brother of Conrado Silva, a Uruguayan composer who has been working in Brasilia for the past five years, came to Coriún's apartment with his wife. Conrado is one of the organizers of the CCLAMC and an important administrator. They bring news that Conrado has been denied exit papers by the Brazilian government, on suspicion of his intent to go to Uruguay. These exit papers are really re-entry papers, without which he would not be allowed back into Brazil. Because there are no employment possibilities in Uruguay, he has no choice but to cancel the trip. Thus the CCLAMC will be without this important composer and administrator for the first time.

January 3, 1975, Montevideo

The night transport of the heavier equipment to Cerro del Toro takes place with an Indio, a kind of Uruguayan Landrover with a Bedford diesel engine. It left at 9:00 P.M. last night and was back by 3:00 A.M. Because of its military look, the Indio survives many illegal maneuvers in the chaotic traffic of Montevideo. When Carlos returns from these critically necessary rides, he is always speaking in his surreal La Plata humor of anything but the miracles he has just accomplished.

Telegrams, panic, packing scores, tapes, manuscripts to meet the scheduled bus to Piriápolis, for which the CCLAMC has bought many tickets. A taxi jammed with cases full of our stuff takes us from Coriún's apartment to the bus. We make the bus within two minutes of departure, but the person with the tickets has not arrived. Suddenly, in bright red pants and blue top, as ever mysterious—the dancer Graciela Figueroa with the tickets. We pause, then a long, tearful hug. We do not know each other well, but share an enormous emotional involvement with the same and similar friends and activities in the

Fig. V-7. Dancer-choreographer Graciela Figueroa in conversation with dancer Gregorio Fassler in the lush landscape of Cerro del Toro, Uruguay, January 1975. (Photo © Gordon Mumma.)

United States.[4] Graciela spent several years in New York on a student visa. She has been away from the United States for four years, and is not yet eligible to return. She spent the first two years of her return to South America in Chile, working with theater and dance there. While in Chile she had a son, and the Allende government "fell." Graciela and her son barely escaped Chile with their lives, returning to Uruguay. She is here with a friend, Gregorio Fassler, who looks familiar to me. He speaks very good English, and I learn that he was in New York last year, studying dance with Joffrey (for legal reasons related to his visa) and with Cunningham (for artistic reasons). He is from Chile, now in exile in Uruguay, participating in the long bureaucratic wait for papers to return to the United States [fig. V-7].

We make the bus trip to Cerro del Toro, the name of a hill near the YMCA camp outside Piriápolis that is this year's home for the Curso. I sit with Graciela and we talk; mostly I talk, cautiously at first because I do not remember her comprehension of English (which is very good). It is an emotional talk. She asks about friends and artists we have shared lives with. She immediately asks about Barbara Lloyd, and we go on to others: Twyla Tharp, Sara Rudner, Sheela Raj, Yvonne Rainer, Douglas Dunn, Steve Paxton, Gus Solomons Jr., Merce Cunningham, on and on, often stopping briefly to let our tears dry and relax from the tension of this verbal re-living. Graciela smokes, from time to time asking for a cigarette from Gregorio, who sits a seat ahead of us. By the end of the trip, about two hours, I am not very much more relaxed with her. She is still a mystery to me.

During the pauses I take in the landscape, gently rolling hills typical of Uruguay, agriculture primarily and an occasional resort. We are traveling the route to Punta del Este. We are near the ocean; the land is of sand and sand vegetation. The military is in posts every 20 kilometers or so, manned by the automatic-weaponed and uniformed teenagers common to all colonial and ex-colonial countries.

Cerro del Toro [January 3 cont.]

I am listed in the publicity as a "compositor norteamericano." Here the term means someone from the United States.

The introductory meeting of the Fourth Curso begins thirty minutes late in the large meeting room at Cerro del Toro. Just beforehand I meet the composer Héctor Tosar.[5] The session is opened by Coriún, followed by Tosar, who reviews the history of the Cursos and the problems of past, present, and future relations with North American culture. The first objections emerge from the students, some of whom have misunderstood the descriptive information. One participant objects to the dance workshops because she "can't dance."

It is not yet clear how many students will be at the courses. I have seen only twenty so far. On one occasion there were ninety, on another forty-five. One student tells me it is expensive, the equivalent of about $120 for the two weeks, all-inclusive—it's at least twice that for anything similar in the U.S. The participants all carry cassette recorders and record everything, including the recorded concerts and discussions. One I talked with had saved his money for a year to buy the cassette recorder and the plane ticket for this Curso. The inflation and unemployment conspire to reduce attendance. And the postal service has seriously delayed publicity, giving little time to reach potential students.

Present today are most of the composition faculty, including Coriún Aharonián, Joaquín Orellana, Carlos Pellegrino, Eduardo Bértola, and Graciela Paraskevaídis, pedagogy professor Violeta Hemsy de Gainza, and dancer-choreographer Graciela Figueroa. The French composers from the Groupe de Musique Expérimentale de Bourges [GMEB], Christian Clozier and Françoise Barrière, have not yet arrived.[6]

After dinner, which at least is better than at Darmstadt, we have our opening *Audición*, or recorded concert, beginning at 22:30, to be followed by a *Debate*, or discussion. The meeting room is excellent for listening to recordings, with an ideal amount of liveliness. The repertoire tonight consists exclusively of studio electronic music from the early 1970s. Two works are by Latin American composers: *El Glotón de Pepperland* (1970) by the Uruguayan Ariel Martínez, produced at the Di Tella studio in Buenos Aires, and *Canto del Loco* (1974) by the Argentine Beatriz Ferreyra, produced at the GMEB. The remaining two works are by Europeans, Catalan composer José Luis de Delás (*Aube*, 1971) and French composer Fernand Vandenbogaerde (*Brumes*, 1972). This sampling will prove representative of the scope and character of the repertoire at the Fourth Curso, much of which is new to me. Representative as well are the intermittent electrical failures, which Coriún navigates with skill.

The Debate begins with vigorous discussion over whether technical explanations should be scheduled before or after hearing the music. Previous years have preferred after, while this year the participants seem to prefer to have the explanations in advance. A good discussion about the specific pieces follows. Latin Americans *really* do like to talk! I am struggling with the mixture of dialects of Spanish and Portuguese.

Following the open discussion, the faculty meets separately to plan the methodology of this Curso. Tosar, who translates for me, comments: "There are few composition students who bring their own work. It is not likely we can have a composition workshop; perhaps only an analysis seminar." The students who have requested composition instruction will be asked to submit their work, on the basis of which it will be decided tomorrow whether a composition workshop will be feasible. By 1:30 A.M. we are in the midst of a spectacular argument. Coriún is very powerful, even doctrinaire, but his humor is with him. Tosar proves an excellent moderator, with the quiet authority of an elder. The decision shifts without revolution, and by 2:00 A.M. a consensus is reached: one day of selective introductions, two hours each, all of which I will attend. Among these will be my first seminar on mixed media at 18:45.

January 4, 1975, Cerro del Toro

The day begins at 9:45 with Eduardo Bértola's introductory talk on aspects of contemporary electro-acoustical music.

Graciela Figueroa's dance workshop follows at 11:00. She first warms up with Gregorio, executing slow movements from yoga and Tai Chi. She speaks slowly to the audience in the course of it. Then on to quasi-Cunningham use of the back and rib cage, standing and angular. Graciela explains the "base of the spine centering" principle. Her arms fling outwards with the impression that they are being pulled from the trunk by the hands, with that same mysterious energy that I remember from her performances with Twyla Tharp. One recognizes Cunningham, Tharp, Limón, etc., although many techniques are easily hers. In the same sense (but not with the same look) as Viola Farber, she has a unique physical personality.

The floor is difficult for any dancer, Uruguayan tile on concrete. After an hour Gregorio and Graciela are warmed up; imperceptibly they begin an interchange, like an improvisation but obviously of material they have used before. Their movements use extremes of speed with unpredictable changes. Graciela stands motionless for nearly eight minutes, with every eye on her. Suddenly they engage in a high-speed martial arts fantasy. She flings her arms forward with a terrifying shout while shifting from one foot to the other. Each foot traces a pattern articulated with enormous energy and speed. They participate in it for only about one minute, with not fewer than twenty bursts interspersed with resting points in incredible positions, as though suddenly asleep. Then a verbal improvisation with movement follows, a duet of rhythm and reiterative melody, with loose-jointed movements shared between them.

Joined by two other men, they do a physically simple circular movement with spare verbal accompaniment. The rhythmic pattern is embellished collectively, punctuated with brief phrases in Spanish. The sound element grows. Phrase accents gradually shift across movements, lengthening, shortening, briefly heterophonic, then moving in parallel motion like an organum. The ritual closes comfortably. The dancers quietly move into the audience seated around the room. After a pause, the discussion begins. Graciela answers gently, with her special humor. Are her slightly Mongolian eyes a part of her mystery?

At 22:30 I attend the Audición of Brazilian music. Gilberto Mendes (b. 1922) is very strong among them. Brazil in all respects has such potential, and it may cost an awful lot of misery and life to achieve it. In the discussion afterwards, much time is still occupied with procedural issues—whether to discuss before or after the works, as a group or individually—and with "structure." The same questions and answers as everywhere else. How can I be so tolerant after all these years? Coriún is tired and short-tempered, but on very many issues he has it all together. His comprehension of the political and social perspectives of musical arts is formidable (even when one differs with him). He is in the thick of the debate, so I have lost my translator and must struggle alone.

Looking back over the first day, it appears that the enrollment of the Fourth Curso is about thirty. It is the worst year yet for numbers but not necessarily for diversity. Tosar and I talked today about the student composers. He is politely apologetic for the quality, though I am impressed by the craft of the works I assessed (and the very careful manuscript). We have composition submissions from at least three participants, sufficient for a composition workshop. I suggest that it is too bad that we have no instrumentalists to read through the variations for string quartet by the Argentine composer Ofelia Carranza. Tosar says there were more players in previous years, but is without suggestions about why so few this time. I wonder whether the current burden of monetary inflation and political difficulties has taken its toll.

Within the larger societies of Uruguay there are privileged areas such as Punta del Este and Piriápolis, with few police because there is no basic juncture of power. Montevideo is a power junction, and has many police. At Cerro del Toro we are isolated and secure without police because there are few revolutionaries here. It is a vacation spot, like the beaches of Rio. But nothing is simple. And who is the director of Cerro del Toro? One rumor is that he is the son of a high CIA official in Uruguay. Is everyone always paranoid here, or are such rumors usually true and these people simply live with them?

January 5, 1975

My schedule for the rest of the week has been set:

> 2 morning lesson introductions (9:45–10:45): Jan. 8, 9
> 3 composition workshops (12:30–14:00): Jan. 5, 6, 7
> Seminars (18:45–20:45): Jan. 5, 6, 7, 8, 9
> Audición and discussion of my music (22:30): Jan. 5

It is becoming difficult to write. There is too much work preparing for three classes each day, attending four others, and struggling with translation. To-night I will also have the Audición of my own music. I have chosen half of the program from my "student" works that I would not release to the general public:

> *Early music*
>   1959 *Vectors*
>   1962 *A Quarter of Fourpiece*
>   1963 *Say Nothing about This to Anyone*
>   1964 *Music from the Venezia Space Theatre*
> *Cybersonic Music*
>   1972 *Ambivex* excerpts
>   1967 *Hornpipe* excerpts
> *Communication Music* (works such as *Dresden Interleaf,*
>   related to political or historical events)
>   1974 *Wooden Pajamas*

Wooden Pajamas, with its echo of recent events in Chile, may make some people uncomfortable.[7] Politics are rarely discussed here in public—only in private, and very carefully. I learned from several of the Argentines that things have moved very far to the right: "It is a most critical period." One Argentine said to me: "Last year we were left, this year we are right." Another replied: "We were right both years, only more right this year." Discussing the theater of mixed media, I am told that a single group was at work in Buenos Aires, but "they were not very experimental." I asked if they could do anything they wanted. "Certainly." Must they be approved by the censor before they perform for the public? "Certainly." No one has anything else to add. Nothing is simple.

I am hearing interesting folk music of the interiors here. Some of the students make well-crafted if non-original work, particularly Gerardo Gandini's students from Buenos Aires, who exhibit substantial but narrow confidence. Their opportunities there are limited, as there are no public school instrumentalists available (only choral music). Thus they have access only to conservatory musicians. They know well what goes on elsewhere (substantially due to Gandini's influence), but their work seems mostly theoretical.

On occasion I wish I were not here, but back at work where I do not have to struggle with the language. After such a long day of esoteric theory, innovative music, and difficult talking, in order to find the energy to continue I finally sleep on the floor of a large tent, with an anti-mosquito "spiral" to keep away the bugs.

January 6, 1975

My very long and hard day yesterday included two lectures plus the audition of my own work. I did a Cunningham Dance Company lecture with slides, on collaboration and creative aspects of the artists. Only used twenty-five slides, but with the translations it was two hours long. It came after everyone had been to four previous two-hour seminars. Then dinner, and then my two-hour Audición, in the middle of which was another power failure. The last piece of the audition was my *Wooden Pajamas*, which as expected divided the opinion of the group dramatically. Many were very moved, and others felt that it was not a statement at all. Graciela Figueroa waited until most people had left. We went to the little bar for some Uruguayan beer. She said: "It's strong, but it doesn't do any good to make statements of any kind." Yesterday's Cunningham session, which at times demonstrated the conflicts between my commitment to those artists and my political reservations about the morality of bringing North American "high art" here, was emotionally charged for me as well as the audience. Afterwards, Graciela came up to hug me. She and I seem to be the only people here who really share the mystery of the modern dance experience, and certainly the only two who have been touched by the wonderful madness of the New York scene.

Graciela's dance classes continue to be excellent and well attended. Coriún was unhappy with the first class, sensing "false mysticism" in her words. "Words are mostly irrelevant in this dance-class process," I told him. She is aware of the problem, and in the real classes that are not intended as a "show" for others she uses the straight-ahead, non-verbal communication of people working together, with a minimum of verbal concepts.

I give a Nancarrow class this morning to provide an important example of working independently. Played the last movement of his Sonatina, Study 37, and Study 40a.

At lunch: This is the day for presents to the children in South America. Festivities are in the air. "Like Papa Noel," says pianist Nadeshda Darizcuren. We play a camp game, established during the First Curso, that all the participants loved; they have continued the tradition ever since. All those seated around the table make non-verbal cues. When the time becomes appropriate, all together fists strike the table, at the same time a short, loud shout. Occasional rhythmic tapping of the tables and dishes moves in waves around the large eating hall. It is quiet but complex, with cross-rhythms I have heard before only in African drumming. For a time our table is silent. Someone begins a quiet pulse on a plastic plate. I join with one of those catchy tango-like rhythms, produced by the elbows and clapping hands, which I saw Coriún do at Darmstadt last summer. I have been practicing it by myself ever since, and now I am rather virtuoso at it. I don't speak Spanish, but I can make a Uruguayan rhythm. My tablemates are impressed and pleased, and one by one join me with embellishments. It grows to a formidable spectacle, and the entire half of the room gradually joins us, perhaps 40–50 people. I drop out of the performance to listen and observe how the "voices" enter and leave, with glasses and fingers clacking, feet stamping on the hard earth floor, knives on the wooden tables, etc. Then I notice everyone is glancing around at each other, as the rhythmic performance continues on its complex course. Perhaps they are listening, observing, as I do—but they continue performing. I am unable to do both at once. Suddenly, with as much surprise as when the first shout-thump pulse had disrupted the eating and conversation, this vast rhythmic ensemble comes to an abrupt halt, everyone exactly together. Absolute silence follows. I did not see or sense the communal cue that brought it to an end. There are still many parts of their communication I do not comprehend.

Tosar has returned from a few days with his wife. He is not regularly on the faculty this year, but maintains his serious interest in the Curso. Tomorrow we will share the composition seminar.

Today it has rained intermittently, and with it the discovery that my roof leaks. Wet floor, bed, and some wet tapes.

Bértola does a seminar on Varèse, whose work, curiously, is not well known here. Varèse provides a particularly interesting study for this group: an independent with a severe, self-critical nature, whose life sets an example of an international "pan-American" consciousness.

The French musicians have arrived (Clozier and Barrière), with many stops via Air France from Paris. They are not yet in the spirit of the place. Carlos Pellegrino translates for them.

My afternoon seminar on synthesizers: too much to do in two hours. Explanation of general format of commercial synthesizers, then a brief history with slides. Pellegrino brings in a smuggled mini-synthesizer, the first in Uruguay. The discussion suggests that there are only a few synthesizers in all of South America. At the end of the seminar we discuss philosophical aspects of using synthesizers and the intimidations of new technology.

At dinner, I am seated next to Gregorio Fassler; across the table are Graciela Figueroa, Eduardo Bértola, and Carlos Pellegrino. Eduardo and Carlos get into one of their La Plata wordplays again, this time over the subject of the dessert, a very jiggly flan. Gregorio and I talk about New York, where he lived and studied dance the first year I was in California (we met briefly during a March 1974 concert at the Cunningham studio). He wants to return there to study dance. He works with Graciela and loves her very much, but realizes he must go to the "center" to learn and work outwards. We discuss the problem of loving people and not being in their part of the world all the time.

The taped concert tonight consists of Latin American music: Carlos Pellegrino, *Sin* (Paris, 1974); Eduardo Bértola, *Rouges* (1972); and Oscar Bazán, *Parca* (1974), produced at CICMAT [Centro de Investigación en Comunicación Masiva, Arte y Tecnología] in Buenos Aires. Coriún Aharonián's *Homenaje a la flecha clavada en el pecho de Don Juan Díaz de Solís* (1974), a tape music montage of indigenous flutes, elicits the following comment: "Don Juan Díaz de Solís was the first Spaniard to step on Uruguayan land, and this was his last step. He was writing in his diary 'I have just discovered . . . ' when the arrow pierced his chest." These musics are entrances to the soul, my soul, of course, and to the soul of the composer, perhaps, to the place from which they come and the place in which they are heard. I often have a feeling that an environment can be changed, even significantly, by the performance of music.

End-of-day reflection: The people in Graciela's dance workshops are doing the *whole* thing, real work without technology. In four days she has taken these amateurs from flabby urban indolence to the point that they are now throwing each other in the air, high above the stone floor, with skill, confidence, and love. The difference between what she does here and what I am doing is embarrassing. I bring these people alluring insights from having worked in technologically sophisticated cultures. I don't bring them the *real* technology, only the pictures and recordings of it. The new information is clearly of use to them, but compared to what Graciela is doing my contribution seems to be superficial, academic information (if perhaps more comprehensive than is common). I have never felt so uncomfortable, being a Yankee in the "old colonies." We all contribute what we can, but perhaps I could have done better.

January 7, 1975

Today is another composition seminar, with Tosar joining me. People bring their music, one listens and looks, expresses opinions. What more is there to do? A young woman from Buenos Aires, Ofelia Carrera, brings a set of short variations for string quartet written with the techniques of Schoenberg, but with some original rhythmic insights. She does not yet have a personal language, and if I am gentle I can perhaps offer her alternatives: play her some Nancarrow, or Varèse, or Robert Ashley. But she comes from a cosmopolitan city, after all, and has access to these things anyway. Coriún says I should "shake them up." I would rather offer them diversifying alternatives.

Armando Albuquerque, a man perhaps in his 60s, fascinates me [fig. V-8]. He brings his Toccata for piano, written in 1948, and his *Movimentos encadeados* for string quartet (1949).[8] He lives in Porto Alegre, an isolated provincial city in Brazil, and has been composing for decades. He has his own language, a sort of polyglot of European and urban Brazilian, with a decidedly original flavor. His music doesn't remind me of anyone else. It is also very well made. There is nothing more to say, for Armando is an authentic, isolated maker of music. It is perhaps a music that could (in European terms) be from any time between 1880 and the present, particularly around 1910. In my context, it is lovely, even quaint; but in *his* context, it is new and strange. He is in the middle of a vast difference of cultures, and has been working all these years with honesty.

This shy and beautiful man says he is an autodidact. One morning he asked me whom I had studied music with. I told him no one formally, and recounted the brief history of my failures at university education. He asked then: "Where did you get this way of analysis and perspective of music, which I like very much?" I answered: "From everywhere, to survive everywhere." Armando smiled in his eyes, as though he felt comfortable being, in this sense, somewhat like me.

Coriún has asked Graciela Figueroa and me to do a performance together. We have not made any plans yet. I consider some sound possibilities on my own,

Fig. V-8. Brazilian composer Armando Albuquerque, Cerro del Toro, Uruguay, January 1975. (Photo © Gordon Mumma.)

and suggest one to Graciela at lunch. She is not responsive. I suggest that we should do something not expected of us. For example, not perform at all. I find that idea appealing, and Graciela responds with bright eyes. We are now free.

In the afternoon, the first French seminar by Christian Clozier [fig. V-9]. Coriún translates from French to Spanish, while Graciela Figueroa, sitting next to me, translates for me into English. In many ways his sketch of experimental music in France from musique concrète to serialism is very interesting, especially the political implications of the move away from Paris of many experimental French composers. But it is also heavy-handed, laying on extravagant slides of glamorous light shows—all theirs, no one else's, as if they were at the center of the world. They're nervous, perhaps.

Fig. V-9. The first "French" seminar at Curso IV, Cerro del Toro, Uruguay, January 7, 1975. L to R: Françoise Barrière, Christian Clozier, and Coriún Aharonián. (Photo © Gordon Mumma.)

Graciela and I sit together at dinner, with Eduardo and Ofelia. Graciela buys the first bottle of wine and I buy the second. She is mixing Coca Cola with hers. It is a humorous dinner, with occasional rhythmic clapping and disruptions. Spanish language-humor has come as a revelation to me.

I ask her in the middle of dinner if she has given any further thoughts to our performance. The answer: "Not thoughts, just things coming through my mind." We have not yet made a firm commitment to each other, nor to Coriún. Perhaps it will not happen, but if we do it right it could be beautiful.

The Audición that night is devoted exclusively to music of Guatemalan composer Joaquín Orellana: *Metéora* (1968), produced at Di Tella, Buenos Aires; *Primitiva I* (1973), composed in Guatemala for instruments of his own design; *Entropé* and *Malebolge (Humanofonía II)* (1972). Joaquín is a mystery and so is his music, with its uncanny sense of how to mix and cross-fade sounds. He often works with real sounds, not in a concrete fashion but more like a hyper-evocative cinematic montage that flows forcefully. When he uses an obvious technique, such as a fractional speed change or a simple sound reversal, the continuity and context are so skilled that I am not distracted by the technique. And he uses reverberation in a special way, as a contribution to sonority, often ending abruptly, not as one would expect, but in a way that refocuses my attention on the sound-event that follows. His skill with human voices is in extracting essences from vocal gesture. This is especially true of *Malebolge*, which uses prison-songs to create combinations of sounds that are original beyond my imagination. I cannot remember when I have been so engrossed in listening to a piece of tape music. There is evidently a giant growing in Guatemala.

January 8, 1975

With Graciela Paraskevaídis at lunch, we discuss her life (born in Buenos Aires of Greek parents). There she was a school-time friend of Mariano Etkin and was in an early group at Di Tella. She became politically conscious by going to Germany for seven years, where her perception of the negative aspects of European culture was magnified. She knew Coriún before she went to Europe but their friendship was discontinuous during those years; they met occasionally when he traveled to Europe for musical activities.

For my class "Sounds of Evocation/Music of Political Nature," I reference Orellana's *Malebolge*, Luigi Nono's *Canto sospeso*, Christian Wolff's *Changing the System*, Frederic Rzewski's *Coming Together*, and Penderecki's *Threnody*, as well as my own *Dresden Interleaf* and *Wooden Pajamas*. Sounds seem to have evocative power in many cultures, though the same sound may not have the same implications for all individuals.

Comments to self for my upcoming class on high technology: We have looked at many aspects of mixed media as they are practiced in many places with different levels of technology and resources. It is important not to think too much about possibilities that are impractical where you are working. If you are interested in making high-tech music and you do not have access to that technology, then perhaps you should stop dreaming and go to where there are super-computers. But before you leave, you might consider whether some better social and artistic purpose might be accomplished by working innovatively with the resources you have.

High technology has solved very few basic human problems. Further, I am beginning to suspect that societies may be obsessed with technology not for the usual stated purpose—"to improve the conditions of people"—but rather to perpetuate by the force of technological power the brutality of colonialist or racist conditions. This statement is not a political gesture, but an expression of doubt about my own involvement with technology and what good it really is to anyone. This doubt has occurred to me only in the past few years, since I came to South America for the first time in 1968. Since then I have worked in many parts of the "third world," what in the United States we call the "minority countries," each new encounter increasing my doubts. My visit to South America this year has made my doubts even more significant.

Coriún wrote to me in a letter that I should "demystify the technology." I teach unorthodox ways of electronic technology in the United States, and have a reputation for demystifying electronic concepts. So I thought, should I bring my toys to South America, where I am a guest, and invite my hosts to play with them as if they were *my* guests? You have seen some of these toys in the slides I have shown you. The technology of these toys is rather difficult to duplicate without a massive industrial economy (much of that technology was developed for military purposes). I also have a reputation for making complicated things from simple resources. But those resources have to be available. In the United States I cannot duplicate many of the world cuisines that I appreciate because we do not have the resources. I cannot make a good Indian *masala* or Indonesian *rijsttafel* there, just as here many of you do not yet have the resources, the transistors and integrated circuits.

Orellana's seminar today includes a demonstration of the "sound utensils" or instruments of his own design used in his music: those made of wood or bamboo with resonators, such as the sonarimba [fig. V-10] or a kind of multiple pan flute called a "pre-Ar." He closes with a playing of *Humanofonía*, explaining that the different layers of his tape montages have specific symbolism for him.[9]

Christian Clozier appears not to be adapting well to the situation here. He is still wearing his winter clothes from France. I suggest to Coriún that this may be the problem; he replies that Clozier wears these clothes "because he is still in France." Françoise Barrière wears summer clothes, but they are *French* clothes. I don't usually notice such things, but she seems to wear them like a banner. The value of Clozier's viewpoint notwithstanding, he has been unable in these first days to relate his position to the situation of Uruguay. Several of the other participants have sensed that under his gentle, if not aloof manner, he may be just another conqueror. Just as the situation appeared to be mellowing, he presents his Audición.

Clozier is doing the setup for his mixed-media concert. He has brought his French studio toys along, without the necessary electrical adapters and connections. Clozier draws a sketch of how everything is to be connected, and Coriún gives it to me for my advice. It is an interesting sketch, partly real, partly fantasy. Ah, a poet! But Coriún needs the reality. Clozier's attempt to elaborate shows that his knowledge of basic principles does not go far beyond "entrée et sortie." He also seems confused by the different jacks and plugs (of which there are few here to begin with). I nearly abandon my attempts to assist, but there are the other participants to consider. I make a list of what is needed from the diagram and our conversation. Coriún will call Montevideo and Buenos Aires to see if he can hunt down the proper connectors. By now the problem has spread to the attention of the other participants and is being referred to as "the French connection."

Fig. V-10. Joaquín Orellana demonstrating the *sonarimba*, a bamboo instrument of his own design used in *Primitiva I*, Cerro del Toro, Uruguay, January 8, 1975. A glass ball in the central shaft rolls to contact resonators in the side tangents. (Photo © Gordon Mumma.)

At the start of the Audición at 22:30, Clozier declines to begin because some of the chairs are still unoccupied. When he is looking the other way, the empty chairs are removed from the hall and the piece begins. It is very "French," with an attractive use of children's sounds.[10] But we have previously heard the work of the Guatemalan Giant—a hard act to follow.

While the music is going on, I am thinking that Graciela and I must make a decision if we are to perform tomorrow night. We are sitting together, and she seems to be drifting in and out of consciousness. It is now the middle of Clozier's work. He is hiding his head in his winter jacket, smoking like a smudge pot. The piece is stretching out without Gallic wit. Armando Albuquerque is asleep in his chair, just as he was during my Audición, as beautiful as ever.

The kids are running by outside and shouting, even now at nearly midnight. They are real kids, Uruguayan kids. French kids wouldn't be out this late. I whisper to Graciela that we should share ideas about our performance. She replies cryptically: "There are some things I won't tell you." Now the war section of Clozier's piece, an infanticide: bang-bang mixed with kids. We have passed the one-hour mark. Clozier also seems asleep. I am becoming more objective about the Graciela "mystery." I could nourish a new mystery: the other Graciela, Para-skevaídis. Albuquerque wakes up with a burst of machine-gun fire. Look at them, this audience of relatively "together" people. They have listened quietly. No one has left their chairs. Yet somehow no one is here. Nadeshda is poised uncomfort-ably sideways in her chair behind me, with her cassette player running. Suddenly, grunt. The music is over. Someone has mumbled something—it is Carlos.

I meet a participant on the porch during the question and answer session. He says: "Boy, who does he think *we* are?" I respond: "Perhaps it is still too soon. We should give him the benefit of the doubt." He replies: "Oh no, not any more!"

Slight doubts in my mind again. Do I make a similar impression here? Are these people nice to me because I'm a nice guy in spite of my Yankee music? Then I glance about, savoring these wonderful people. Dear Armando is smil-ing at me. Nadeshda is rewinding her cassette to erase it. Orellana is sitting back in his Guatemalan jacket, with his dark glasses hiding his smiling eyes at midnight, *viva Zapata*!

Clozier is still answering questions, still behaving as if he were in France. His comments seem irrelevant to the situation. The Latin Americans follow the "conqueror" into his self-made jungle and watch him perish. I feel sorry about this unfortunate turn of events for the French representatives. It will likely make future communication more difficult.[11]

Afterwards I visit Graciela Figueroa in her tent to say that I think we shouldn't perform together. She brightens, looking relieved. Suddenly she is beside me and explains in brief phrases, with silences between, some of her fears. Some I had sensed, others were new. As it turns out, we will not perform.

Carlos Pellegrino has given me a book of his poetry. I am very pleased. Earlier today I discovered something else about Carlos: he plays the piano very well. It was Chopin I heard him playing, in the hall between classes.

The woods are full of wild morning glories. Last night Graciela found a lu-minescent bug. She remembered the fireflies from the USA, but had forgotten what they were called and asked me. Later we found the bug again; it was not a firefly but some creature I had never seen before. The spiders are as creepy as ever. I have never forgotten the first experience of standing under the southern hemisphere night sky and not recognizing it. On the tennis court at Cerro del Toro I study the summer sky, with Orion again, upside down.

January 9, 1975

In preparation for my departure I am copying addresses of my friends from Coriún's private files. He comments that some of the numbers are coded and I should ask him for the correct versions. I tell him about my occasional practice of writing addresses separately from the names, to protect my more celebrated friends from intrusions into their private lives. Coriún seems pleased. If he is paranoid, it is not apparent to me, although I may not understand his style of paranoia. But when he later gives me an out-of-print recording, he cautions me not to show it around to the other course participants: "For some people at the Curso it is really subversive." I wonder whether I will have trouble with it at the airport?

Most of us trust each other, we certainly love each other, and by evening everyone is feeling rather emotional at my leaving. At dinner I am greeted at various times with several long cheers, the traditional "oooo" for one who is leaving, and with chanting that I do not recognize. Coriún explains: "It is your name in our dialect."

January 10, 1975

I awaken to a moderate rain. It is 8:30, and I begin packing. One of my cabin people comes to my room. "Ah, you are up already," he says. "The whole world is weeping because you are leaving." Now I am weeping, too, and it is difficult to see my packing.

Graciela's dance group begins to work at 11:00. Her last words are: "We will begin soon." I nod. I watch the rehearsal a bit through a window, standing in the rain. I am glad to leave her while she is working. There is no chance of embarrassed formalities, no departure hugs, no tears. She is working, setting a beautiful example for her *campañeros*. It is nearing the time for me to leave this incredible world.

A group of people accompanies me to the road, carrying my baggage and chanting: "Don't go home!" We wait in the rain for the small bus to take us to Piriápolis. Great confusion! My bus ticket has been forgotten at the camp. Coriún runs to get it. The little bus arrives. I load the baggage aboard and climb on, accompanied by Zulema, Violeta, and Luiz. Coriún arrives back with the ticket and some more recordings, all of them out of print. This is inconvenient, as I could have packed them properly earlier. But I smile and get them into the larger case to be shipped with the baggage, with less chance of detection. He boards, says "gracias," and we embrace briefly.

In Piriápolis, Zulema accompanies me to find a map of Uruguay—no luck! I realize that I know nothing of their lives except for what we have done together this week. These people have other things they do, families, lovers, obsessions that I don't know about. It is fifteen minutes until the bus for Montevideo. They say they will leave me now, sad but also happy that we have met. Suddenly it is easy. My emotional tension disappears. My tears recede. I begin the long journey and short readjustment back to California.

Gordon Mumma to Coriún Aharonián and Héctor Tosar, Santa Cruz, California, December 15, 1975

I am again honored by your invitation to participate in the Quinto Curso [January 1976]. Because I have recently begun a new position at the University of California, it is with very many regrets that I cannot be with you personally. But I am with you in my heart. Your achievement in continuing these on-going courses is incredible and historic. This is particularly true for the North Americans who, as a result of your efforts, regard your cultural and social achievements with ever increasing respect. My own participation in the Quarto Curso was one of the most inspiring activities of my life. I am still humbled and a bit dazed by the impact that experience has had upon me.

PART VI

An American Gallery

Editor's Introduction

Working friendship is the theme of this series of short vignettes. Conceived as tributes to esteemed colleagues, some departed and many others still fully active in the American musical community, these sketches draw equally on previously published materials, manuscript notes, and newly crafted pieces. Whether devoted to the members of the Sonic Arts Union, Christian Wolff at the Burdock Festival, Pauline Oliveros, or Lou Harrison and Roger Reynolds chatting with Mumma about Charles Ives, the tone is personal and the content experiential.

CHAPTER 25

Nelson Mix for Gordon Mumma
(1966)

My good friend Richard Nelson, a scenic director from Philadelphia and a man of clearly reasonable sensibilities, returned to the United States from Paris recently. He wrote me the following:

> Fun and games on the flight home . . . took apart the "in-flight" headsets. The left side received half of the "Classical Specialties" tape, and the right side received "Music for Teenagers." This is truly clean sound: the package reads: "We are pleased to bring you the finest sterilized sound in aviation history." The headset has no conductors in it . . . it's plastic tubing. When you bend it in half the sound fades out. You can do a channel at a time, or both together. Or stick a pin through the plastic and effect a mechanical mix. Of course the effect is permanent. The favorite is splitting the plastic tubes apart so that you can plug one earpiece into the switchbox on SEAT A and the other into SEAT B; hence the "mung-mix" technique.

Source: Excerpted from Mumma, "Technology in the Modern Arts: Music and Theatre," *Chelsea* 20/21 (May 1967): 105, © Chelsea Editions, with their permission.

CHAPTER 26

Gordon Mumma's *Stovepipe* for Richard Nelson
(1970)

An ensemble of low-power lasers
each with a deflection system producing a horizontal scan
adjusted in length to the diameter
of a corresponding mirror-surfaced, gravity-balanced stovepipe damper
in an ensemble of operating chimney stovepipes
is arranged such that the vertical deflections
of the horizontal scans
are reflected by the undulating dampers
onto the various surfaces
within a commodious enclosed space,
dimly illuminated with winter afternoon light
and comfortably accessible to the public.
—Harwich, Cape Cod

Source: *Scores: An Anthology of New Music,* ed. Roger Johnson, 203 (New York: Schirmer, 1981), © 1970 Gordon Mumma.

CHAPTER 27

Good Times Up on the Farm

(1969/2013)

Atop a green mountain overlooking the site of the historic Royalton massacre lies Christian and Holly Wolff's farm—a real working farm settled in the Vermont hills and valleys. I spent numerous summers there, visiting them and their Burdock Festival of contemporary music and dance. The Wolff summer residence, an early nineteenthth-century farmhouse with wood-burning stove, served as headquarters for the Burdock Festival. Preparations for the first festival in August 1969 required that two pigs be moved from an old shed into a portable swimming pool. A lovely Guernsey cow, six months with calf, was moved out of range of the loudspeakers in the trees before I performed my *Hornpipe*. Apparently the cow was not moved far enough: the following day, she gave only half her quota of milk.

This was where the burdocks grow and things catch together. Christian's composition *Burdocks* had its festival premiere there in August 1971. Old friends came together to play it and other compositions in the out-of-doors, working hard to keep the scores from blowing away in the whistling wind—a special kind of *Hausmusik* on the farm. A bit later we all traveled to Spaulding Auditorium at Dartmouth to record *Burdocks* for Wergo.[1]

Walking through the streets of London years later, I heard someone whistling Wolff's catchy tune from *Burdocks*. It turned out to be a musician who had performed it in the large Scratch Orchestra.

Source: Typescript notes on the August 1969 Burdock Festival (GMC); new material supplied by Mumma in 2013.

Fig. VI-1. Christian Wolff at the Burdock Festival, Royalton, Vermont, August 1971. (Photo © Gordon Mumma.)

CHAPTER 28

Merce and Ludwig

(1971)

In the early 1970s a persistent analogy kept returning to me: Cunningham's choreography was like Beethoven's late music. In recent years Cunningham's work had been taking on an intensely polyphonic character, increasingly complex of gesture and weighty in its dramatic sweep. Some of the works were architecturally structured fantasias approaching the epic in duration. Thinking of Beethoven, who with increasing deafness gave up performing to devote his best energies to composition, I speculated on Cunningham's turning his energies increasingly to choreography. He was a very great dancer, but an even greater choreographer.

The experiences of *Canfield* and *Landrover* were for me as gripping as Beethoven's late piano sonatas op. 109, 110, and 111, or the late string quartets op. 131 and 132. *Changing Steps* had the easier accessibility, with the out-of-context character yet solid impact of the last quartet op. 135.

Source: Mumma, "Cunningham Company Notes," April 1971 (unpublished typescript, GMC).

CHAPTER 29

On the Ives Railroad

(1977)

Gordon Mumma: *Some Voltage Drop* (1974)

with minimum obtrusiveness
and adjusting to circumstances
remove teakettle and plastic canteen
from backpack under panel table
fill teakettle with water from plastic canteen
and affix whistle-top to teakettle spout

remove compact gasoline stove from backpack
and place on panel table
prepare stove for lighting (prime burner element
with gasoline drawn from tank with pipette, etc.)
light backpack stove with flint and steel
and adjust flame to appropriate height

place teakettle on backpack stove

Source: Excerpted from "Five Composers' Views," in *An Ives Celebration: Papers and Panels of the Charles Ives Centennial Festival-Conference,* ed. H. Wiley Hitchcock and Vivian Perlis, 203–8 (Urbana: University of Illinois Press, 1977), © Board of Trustees of the University of Illinois, now reverted to the authors. This panel discussion of October 21, 1974, was chaired by Roger Reynolds and included composers Charles Dodge, Lou Harrison, Salvatore Martirano, and Mumma.

interrupt remains of panel discussion
to announce slides of old wind-up train—"Ives Railroad"—
being projected on wall behind panel

remove crosscut saw and violin bow
from case under panel table
tighten and prepare bow with rosin

as the whistle-drone begins from the teakettle
and the slide projection is completed,
introduce a single, high-pitched sustained sound
from the bowed crosscut saw
in ensemble with the teakettle drone

establish a specific interval
including the possibility of a unison
and gradually increase the loudness of the bowed saw
to equal that of the teakettle drone

after an appropriate time
interrupt suddenly
the teakettle drone and bowed-saw ensemble
with the three-minute tape composition *Wooden Pajamas* (Salvador
      Allende: "de aquí sólo me sacarán en pijama de madera")
played at maximum, but undistorted, loudness
from loudspeakers surrounding the audience.

The Panel Discussion Continues

ROGER REYNOLDS: Gordon is extraordinarily responsive to local conditions, which is to say he is a dedicated observer of things. And I think
   this is a characteristic aspect of many American composers, perhaps
   all of the American composers who are of interest to me personally.
   They have this quality: extraordinarily responsive pragmatism. They
   work with what there is and overcome obstacles. Gordon's presentation of *Some Voltage Drop* was an example of that conception: translate
   an aim into relevant action without much interest in the historical
   roots. . . .

MUMMA: Who, me? You mean I'm not much interested in historical roots?

REYNOLDS: . . . that your actions don't necessarily depend upon them.

MUMMA: I was talking with Sherman von Solkema last night. I haven't seen Sherman in many years, so we don't have a sense of continuity in terms of our professions. In our conversation the matter of "what Ives means to me" came up. We both felt that this was very hard to describe because it was not a matter of direct influences, of the sort that can be traced from one composer to another in a given school of composition.

My first contact with "Ives" was that model railroad train you saw in the projected slides of my presentation. It was a hand-me-down, wind-up electric train given to me when I was only a few years old. Shortly after receiving a communication from Roger asking me to join this panel, I happened to be visiting my parents' home in Massachusetts. They reminded me that they still had the train. Now I wasn't discussing this panel with them at all, and I had forgotten all about the train, forgotten that its name was "Ives Railroad." It was just one of those things that goes into the back of your memory, and when you see it again there's that Proustian response of more than déjà vu; it becomes a mystical kind of experience. And so I took a few pictures of it, assuming it would get thrown out eventually. (After all, I am a grown boy.)

LOU HARRISON: I was delighted by the sound of the rhythm tape, and by the train, too, and I did not notice that it was an "Ives Railroad." Of course, this is the "Terrestrial Railroad." . . . But I'm somewhat alarmed at a "wind-up electric train"—that's what you said.

MUMMA: Is that what I said? But, you see, that's perfectly understandable. It's part of my mixed-up heritage. I was a kid during World War II, and we couldn't buy dry-cell batteries to make paper-clip motors and all those experiments you can do, and that's affected my life very much: I'm still playing with those toys that I couldn't have. . . .

HARRISON: electrically deprived . . .

MUMMA: It's all mixed up. . . . Whether I heated this kettle on an electric hot plate or with some solid-state heat transfer . . . there are any number of ways one could have done it. . . .

HARRISON: I liked that steam-drone section because it titillated me but did not cross my pain threshold, which is very low. It had a nice contour— just right. It also, of course, makes a political comment, just as Mr. Ives has done and all of us have to, sooner or later.

[. . .]

MUMMA: Ives has really been a spiritual influence on all of us, even though we're all quite different composers. I've had a thought, a concern about Ives, which is now being reinforced, particularly by people like Frank Rossiter and Robert Crunden, who are looking into the nature of his life.[1] I have the feeling that the man was undernourished, that he was not able to do, or chose not to do, the kind of experimenting that, say, Gustav Mahler did with *his* resources. A great deal of Ives's interest in ideas such as having more than twelve tones within an octave really remained very conceptual—celestial, if you will. In that sense, I feel we're all somewhat alike in that we're all quite different from Ives: we have apparently made the commitment to try it all out with the materials we have at hand. He used the materials he had at hand, but in fact, perhaps in some sort of laboratory sense, very consciously put himself apart from living with them. The reasons for that are undoubtedly very complex. But in that sense, I think, we stand apart from him. Now, I'm sticking my neck out here . . .

HARRISON: It's always a good thing to do.

MUMMA: . . . because I have the feeling that, in some respects, he didn't go on with things that *I* wish he had gone on with. He chose something else, in his ornery way, and . . .

HARRISON: . . . and that leaves us a bigger playground, too.

MUMMA: Yes, we have a bigger playground because he didn't nail it all down for us and tell us what to do. There's no "school of Ives," bless him.

REYNOLDS: Very few of us, I feel confident in saying, are in any scholarly sense aware of Ives. We're aware of him in a curious metaphoric and spiritual sense, and that is the force and variegated nature of his impact on present-day American musical practice. It is not an impact derived primarily from study of his scores, and frequently not even with aural contact except for a few works—*The Unanswered Question,* the "Concord" Sonata, "General William Booth Enters into Heaven"—certain formative things, that were available.

[. . .]

QUESTIONER: What if there had been no Ives? Would you be doing the same thing?

MUMMA: There were others. It's really a whole era. . . . One day, years ago, in a Boston music store I ran across thirty or forty volumes of [Henry] Cowell's *New Music* (which Ives was one of the persons responsible for) and came across all those other names in that uncanny music—that was when I realized that I had friends. I wasn't doing what they were doing, but there I found a nation with which I felt some affinity. And so, if there hadn't been an Ives . . . well, I don't know. There would have been a Ruggles, and there would have been . . .

REYNOLDS: Cage . . .

MUMMA: . . . Brown. There would have been a Nancarrow, and all the rest of them. It was all there and it's an incredible resource. That's my answer.

QUESTIONER: Are you finding in the electronic medium that kind of feeling that Ives talks about when he says that music does not have to be what you hear it to be?

HARRISON: My God! "What has sound got to do with music!" Unquote, Ives.

MUMMA: That's an interesting question. If Ives had had electronic resources, would he have worked with them in the same way he did with his acoustical resources? I'm sure he would have. There are some interesting people between Ives and us—for example, the composer Conlon Nancarrow, who, in his own quirky way, works with player pianos with procedures that are essentially related to what Charles Dodge is doing with digital computers. Player pianos were the resources Nancarrow had at hand. . . . I'm sure it's just a matter of working with what you've got.

CHAPTER 30

A Visit to Mount Olympus with David Tudor

(1996)

Early one afternoon in the late 1960s, at one of those old upstate New York colleges that had become part of the state university system, David Tudor and I were to set up the musical equipment for an evening performance by the Merce Cunningham Dance Company. I arrived at the theater later than planned, expecting to find David already busy with the wiring of our equipment.

I entered the still-unlit theater from the back of the audience—it was too dark to find my way to the orchestra pit. But from that pit came the sound of a well-mellowed piano. The music was one of Debussy's etudes. I sat at the rear of the theater waiting for my eyes to adjust to the darkness. After the Debussy was part of one of the Rachmaninoff *Etudes-tableaux*, with occasional missed notes and retries. Without finishing the piece, there was a rapid shift into a piece unfamiliar to me—stunningly virtuoso writing of nineteenth-century vintage, played with a shattering brilliance in spite of occasional halts and repeats of phrase. Then came a sentimental dance pattern that I recognized as Louis Moreau Gottschalk.

My first assumption had been that a student was practicing, but the unquestionable virtuosity challenged this assumption. The Gottschalk ended abruptly, spliced directly into fragments from Messiaen's *Catalogue d'oiseaux*. With my vision now secure in the darkness, I moved warily down toward the orchestra

Source: "David Tudor: A Historical Reminiscence," *20th-Century Music* 3 (1996): 6–7, © 20th-Century/21st-Century Music; German trans. as "Ein Besuch auf dem Berg Olymp: Historische Reminiscenz," *MusikTexte* 69/70 (1997): 94, © MusikTexte. Reprinted with permission of *20th-Century Music/21st-Century Music* and *MusikTexte*.

pit with the fantastic idea that it was David Tudor playing. I had not heard him play this repertory, though I knew it was a much earlier part of his musical life. At the edge of the orchestra pit the light was still inadequate to see more than the bare outline of a small grand piano. At a brief pause in the playing I inquired, "Is that you, David?"

"Oh, yes, isn't this a wonderful piano? It sounds and feels like an old Chickering, but there's not enough light to be sure. There's no electricity available in the house yet," he replied.

I realized he had been playing "by touch," alone in the darkness and rummaging through his memory for music he'd probably not played in a decade or more. I asked about the work I hadn't recognized, the piece after the Rachmaninoff.

He said, "Oh, was I playing Rachmaninoff? Don't ever tell anyone about it. I also played some Charles-Valentin Alkan; you really should know his music."

I never heard David play this repertory again. It was a unique experience—a visit to Mount Olympus. Many years later I asked him if he remembered that early afternoon in upstate New York. He replied, "Oh, really? I thought I'd put that aside years ago."

CHAPTER 31

On George Cacioppo

(2006)

As a creative artist, George Cacioppo (1926–84) was a gentle chemist. His life and work didn't move in straight lines from one point to another. After his early compositions of the 1950s, each musical work has its own unique identity and character. That uniqueness is heard in his individual overlapping of sound painting, his sense of forward motion in time, and the lyrical character and poetic implications of each composition. Cacioppo was careful with the details of mixing things, but rhapsodic in his large-scale thinking and poetic in the fanciful titles for his music.

Throughout his life Cacioppo was variously present: at times congenially gregarious, at others mysteriously absent or invisible. He had many devoted artist friends, particularly his occasional composition students. His primary money-earning profession was as a radio engineer and program director for an Ann Arbor FM station.

For medical or psychological reasons, Cacioppo was sometimes many months in rehabilitation, and few of his friends knew why or where he was. The medical conditions were due to Crohn's disease, for which he had recurrent surgeries. (This illness led to his death in 1984.) In the mid-1950s, after I had not seen him for nearly a year, he showed up at a bookstore where I worked. He was all smiles, and though he addressed me as "Gordon," he asked if I would verify my name. He had returned from several months of electroshock therapy. Nevertheless he was soon back at his radio occupation and the composition of new works.

Source: Written in May 2006 as CD liner notes for Mode 168, © 2006 Mode Records; reprinted with permission.

The works he wrote in the 1950s were made in the context of requirements for his academic studies. Of the four that have apparently survived, an early piano sonata exhibits his individuality even though it was made within an academic template. One of my special memories of Cacioppo was a 1952 performance of his master's thesis, "Overture," with the Royal Oak Symphony in Michigan, in which I played horn. The String Trio, begun in 1959, was the first of his works to be performed at the first ONCE Festival in 1961. A beautifully crafted work, though with echoes of an academic past, it is original and without a wasted note or gesture.

Cacioppo's full creative imagination emerged with *Bestiary I, Eingang* (1961). Thereafter he made one unique work after another, some so different from his preceding compositions that the character of his creative continuity was not easily apparent. The activities of the ONCE Festival in the 1960s provided the primary impetus for Cacioppo's extraordinary creativity in that decade. Everything he composed then was performed by the devoted ONCE musicians. *Cassiopeia* (1962) became an immediate classic, partly because of its mysterious but practical map-like score. As the ONCE Festivals continued, something of a fan club of performers developed, anticipating the rehearsals of his next piece.

Listening to Cacioppo's music now, many decades later, my memories still hold true. His use of instruments and voice is sublime. Each individual instrument plays with indigenous sense, as though he were performing it himself. His diverse ensembles are translucent and clear-sounding, even within relatively complex sound-textures. Within the limits of sonority inherent in his solo piano pieces—sounds articulated mostly from the keyboard—Cacioppo mysteriously extends the resulting sound spectrum without exaggerated physical foolishness.

Finally, it is Cacioppo's timeless imagination with the theatrical unfolding of sonorous events and textures that elevates each of his compositions, all of which bear well the passage of time.

Fig. VI-2. Earle Brown conducting a rehearsal at New York University, November 12, 1971. (Photo © Gordon Mumma.)

CHAPTER 32

Earle's Worlds

(2007)

Earle Brown was many. That confuses people who do not recognize the complexities of someone being many things. He was a composer, conductor, entrepreneur, recording engineer, photographer, writer, and teacher, always involved with many arts and artists, and always thinking anew in his own creative work. As a composer, he was an innovator in "mobile forms" for both small and large ensembles. His original work had notable influence and set new standards for other composers.

Earle Brown and I first met in his New York City apartment on Third Avenue in the early 1960s. Carolyn Brown was there—I had met her previously at a Merce Cunningham Dance Company touring performance in the Midwest. Over the years these unique artists became my very good friends.

Earle's creative beginnings were outside the general academic models for music composition, and were intertwined and nourished by his activities in the visual arts. He developed mostly on his own and was advantaged early in his career by the appreciative recognition of other influential artists such as John Cage, Alexander Calder, and Bruno Maderna.

As was typical of many innovative North American composers in the second half of the twentieth century, Earle's international reputation was first established in Europe, where his work had notable influence on various composers. In the last quarter of the century, he gradually received professional attention and appointments in the United States from the more adventuresome institutions,

Source: *Contemporary Music Review* 26, nos. 3–4 (2007): 427–28, © Taylor & Francis Ltd. [http://www.tandfonline.com/]; reprinted with permission of the publisher.

though performances of his unique music were not common. The evolution of performance-practice skills takes time.

Earle was very generous with helping other people in their artistic activities. His path-breaking and now historic recordings of works by other innovative composers were a major force in offsetting the narrow historical perspectives of contemporary music as formed by university-level history survey texts in the United States. Earle's generosity extended further in the connections that he facilitated between other artists.

We crossed paths often in recent decades. Usually after our initial greeting hugs, we were immediately engrossed in talking about music and creative ideas. I savored his mind; his ways of thinking were always fresh. Our last meeting was at the May 2001 David Tudor Symposium in Los Angeles. It was an impromptu late-evening gathering crowded into a hotel bedroom, with lovely things to eat and drink. Earle and I continued our absorbing discussions of topics both recent and past, and planned to connect again soon. Soon was not soon enough.

Three Sonic Arts Union Sketches

(2013)

Fig. VI-3. The Sonic Arts Union on their final tour in New York State in the late winter of 1977. L to R: Robert Ashley, David Behrman, Alvin Lucier, Gordon Mumma. (Photographer unknown.)

CHAPTER 33

Speaking Robert Ashley

Robert Ashley and I met in the early 1950s and began our collaborative work by 1957 with Milton Cohen's developing Space Theatre. Visiting at 1009 Granger Avenue, he played for me his newly completed tape composition *The Fox,* which first helped me appreciate the unique and subtle nuances of his speaking voice. The roots were there, unforeseen then, for the extraordinary verbal virtuosity of his later theater work, notably his operas. He was also a fine pianist and collaborated with other performers, including filmmaker George Manupelli and other visual artists.

By the early 1960s we had begun our concert performances together, with and beyond the ONCE Festival. Touring the Midwest in his old Lincoln Continental, we took our New Music for Pianos series on the road. Our repertoire included music for one and two pianos, percussion, horn, and sometimes integrated electronics. We played our own compositions and music by others, along with extras such as Manupelli's *Five Short Films* (1963), a prize-winning collaboration by the three of us. Our differences of personality and habits, such as Ashley's need to have coffee after midnight so that he could get to sleep, kept us lively.

This fox went out on more than nights, hunting out ensembles of performing friends. The ONCE Group theater performances would also nourish his eventual "opera for television" concept. Working with Ashley in the ONCE Group echoed for me Merce Cunningham's collaborative process, which trusted, appreciated, and encouraged the individual participants for their uniqueness. Strangely similar as well was their evolving practice of "hand choreography," Cunningham's in solo performances such as *Loops* and Ashley's in his TV operas, from *Perfect Lives* (premiered 1984) to his recent *Answers and Other Songs* (2010).

Ashley's major work is vigorous with conceits and figures of speech that revolve in feedback with his performers. Speaking cross-country, Ashley the musical wordsmith seems to en joy his un joyce's choices with the catch up of ketch up from a merry can, huh, mysteriously the miss steering becomes great A meri can a. He speaks with words that reason ate.

CHAPTER 34

Crossings with David Behrman

Memory has it that David Behrman and I first met at the historic October 1963 Morton Feldman–Earle Brown Town Hall Concert in New York City. Thereafter we continued our delicious conversations as pen pals, with ongoing correspondence in words and schematic electronic diagrams. We crossed paths again when Behrman performed his *Track* at the Ann Arbor ONCE Festival in February 1965 and his *Wave Train* at a March 1966 ONCE recording concert.

Our crossings increased rapidly with the emergence of the Sonic Arts Group (later Union) from its first joint concert in April 1966. The flow of his wonderful live-electronic compositions blossomed with our performances together of his *Wave Train* and *Players with Circuits* over the following years.[1] *Players with Circuits* allowed for two or more performers, and became a bulwark of the repertory of the Sonic Arts Union.

Behrman and I soon began collaborating in our own duo concerts, such as the March 1967 full-evening performance of our *Runway*, an elaborate soundspace event we designed and performed together at the Hunter College Playhouse in New York City. Within a specific time frame the internal structures were variable and used closely cross-related sound sources. In March 1968 Behrman was part of the Toronto *Reunion* ensemble with Cage, Lowell Cross, Marcel and Alexina Duchamp, David Tudor, and myself. The first act of that historic collaboration began as we crossed the border by car into Canada with our elaborately wired electronic equipment during the worsening separatist crisis in Quebec. Cage had just obtained a new credit card, and he maxed it out for the bond to guarantee that we would return with our "instruments." Behrman speculated dryly on what might happen the next time we performed it. When we did, in Toronto in 2010, Behrman and I were the only original performers there. By then a Canadian resident, I at least endured no border crossing.

Behrman works wonderfully with others. I remember the fruitful interactions in our many Event performances with the Merce Cunningham Dance Company. Perhaps our most expansive collaboration was in the quintet "Communication in a Noisy Environment" with Anthony Braxton, Leroy Jenkins, and Robert Watts in New York in 1970. In his *She Has a Mission and She Is in Motion* (1990), virtuoso flutist Maggi Payne interacted with his unique computer-response designs. I filmed a rehearsal, which was memorably embellished with their back-and-forth commentary and ready smiles. One of Behrman's later compositions, *My Dear Siegfried* (2005), uses spoken words from the writings of his father, S. N. Behrman, including the latter's anxious wartime letters to Siegfried Sassoon. It has never really ended, our cross-nourishment of shared ideas, toy boxes, stimulating events, and parties with creative friends, often bolstered by elegant food and drink.

CHAPTER 35

Becoming Alvin Lucier

In the mid-1960s Alvin Lucier moved beyond the early musical pathways that he had traveled well and set out to explore the unknown. What he found was himself.

His experience as a choral conductor and director of the Brandeis University Chamber Chorus in the 1960s provided a compass. His repertoire in that realm included more contemporary music than some of his university colleagues were comfortable with. Some of this music explored extended vocal techniques and acoustical resources beyond the Euro-American institutional traditions of choral singing; one such work was Pauline Oliveros's 1961 *Sound Patterns* for a cappella chorus.[1] Lucier toured widely with the Brandeis ensemble, performing Earle Brown's *From Here* (1963) at the Brown-Feldman Town Hall concert in New York in October 1963 and appearing at the February 1964 ONCE Festival in Ann Arbor. Touring with a chorus requires skill in adapting to different acoustical venues. This experience provided an impetus for Lucier's growing exploration of the acoustical resonances of diverse materials, places, and sound-making resources.

In such works as *Music for Solo Performer 1965*, *North American Time Capsule* (1966), and the live-performance process *I Am Sitting in a Room* (1969), Lucier created living sound-space sculptures of his own unique design. His *Vespers* (1968) is particularly notable for the articulation of acoustical space by the use of clicking echolocation devices. These works are at once gemlike in their exquisitely defined concept and large-scale, even vast, in their theatrical presence. In these works Lucier put aside many of the "classical" ideas of what a musical composition is and opened his imagination to a world of diverse musical cultures. In 1970 he moved to the supportive environment of Wesleyan University, where he found further stimulation in the innovative curriculum that embraced the music cultures of the world.

Lucier has a special humor as a raconteur playing with words. His powerful performance in George Manupelli's *Dr. Chicago* film trilogy reveals his unique theatrical speaking skills under unusual circumstances. His stage presence is both modest and mysterious, whether he is hunched over a small singing teapot in *Nothing Is Real* (1990), poised over a shifting, resonating sand tableau in *The Queen of the South* (1972), or wired for brain-wave sound in *Music for Solo Performer 1965*. The simplicity of concept in these works, eliminating all but the most essential, conceals a powerful originality that reveals the beguiling wonders of the everyday.

CHAPTER 36

Working with Pauline Oliveros
(2013)

Pauline Oliveros—I heard the name about 1960 from Milton Cohen, who had connected with her and her work in San Francisco during the early years of the San Francisco Tape Music Center. Initially beguiled by her origins in the State of Texas, he was soon impressed by her unique states of imagination.

On an eastward trip from San Francisco in the early 1960s Oliveros stopped in Ann Arbor. We met and connected immediately; it was the start of a lifelong friendship. Both of us were horn players, and she specialized in the accordion. A few years later David Tudor asked each of us to compose music for his bandoneon, that second cousin to the accordion by way of the concertina. The *Duo for Accordion and Bandoneon, with Possible Mynah Bird Obbligato* (1964) was her contribution, which she performed on a revolving seesaw with Tudor. I performed it with her at the Victoria Theatre in San Francisco in 1988 when Tudor was not available.[1]

When Oliveros and I were independently performing at the Metamusik Festival in Berlin in 1974, we experienced a wonderful instance of synergy. One weekend I crossed over to East Berlin and visited an isolated old music shop, where I bought an Alfred Arnold bandoneon from the 1940s. The same weekend Oliveros showed up with a different model of Arnold bandoneon, which by coincidence she had found at the same shop, but on a different day.

It seemed inevitable that we should work together with these instruments. One memorable occasion was a project for a Cal Arts contemporary music festival in 1980. Oliveros invited me to co-compose and perform with her for Beatrice Manley's multi-scene theater fantasy titled *Fwyynghn*. Over the course of several days at Pauline's southern California house, surrounded by its families of chickens, we co-composed a duo for our sibling bandoneons titled *Fwyyn:*

Fig. VI-4. Pauline Oliveros and Gordon Mumma with their bandoneons on a rifle range in Santa Cruz, California, in the summer of 1981. (Photographer unknown.)

Ex. VI-1. Gordon Mumma and Pauline Oliveros, *Fwyyn: Lament for a Princess Enchanted into Death.* (Autograph by Gordon Mumma, © Gordon Mumma and Pauline Oliveros.)

Lament for a Princess Enchanted into Death. We worked together at our bandoneons in back-and-forth interchanges of different button patterns, memorizing the overlapping chord progressions by rote. A bit more than five minutes in duration, in three sections, this interlude fit nicely into *Fwyynghn*. Later I made a notated musical score from the live performance [ex. VI-1], and we also recorded it.[2] *Fwyyn* was a little marvel of working with Pauline Oliveros.

PART VII

Mumma on Mumma

Editor's Introduction

Usually reticent about discussing himself, Gordon Mumma reluctantly provided a short set of responses to the "recalcitrant questions" of his creative life at John Zorn's request in 2009. "Notes on My Creative Procedures" from 2013, the last-completed essay of this volume, expands that earlier essay significantly. It may come as a surprise to some that the ever-developing and varied musical output of this singular artist in many diverse media stems from a consistent collection of aesthetic premises, as illustrated in a handful of his works from fifty years of his creative life. Scores are provided for several, and most are available on commercial recordings. It seems fitting that this book, devoted to Gordon Mumma's view of so many of his creative friends and associates, should end with a rare glimpse into his own compositional workshop.

CHAPTER 37

Notes on My Creative Procedures
(2009/2013)

About Composing

Composing for me is performing. I compose for myself and for other people who will perform my music, alone or with others, or in theater, dance, film, and other contexts. In composing I am always conscious of an eventual live performance, even when composing studio electronic music. As a performer with acoustical sources—first as a singer, then as a player of the horn and the wind-driven bandoneon, breathing is embedded in my compositional consciousness. I was also a keyboard performer on the piano, harpsichord, and clavichord, and studied carillon and organ. I later developed innovative skills performing the musical saw, which involves sustained, bowed sounds that contributed to my concepts of musical and acoustical durations.

Composing for me is building. The composition process starts with the basic sound sources, whether acoustical instruments or electro-acoustical sounds. Restriction of these ingredients—of material, rhythmic gesture, and pitch or sonority choice—is a basic design procedure that can stimulate fresh musical possibilities and liberate my imagination from learned habits. From the pantry of my experience I then select creative processes with which to assemble the ingredients, including structures, materials, developmental techniques, and other concerns.

Source: The opening sections of this essay are adapted from Mumma, "Aggregate Replies to Recalcitrant Questions," in *Arcana IV: Musicians on Music*, ed. John Zorn, 227–31 (New York: Hips Road, 2009), © Hips Road/Tzadik, reprinted with revisions with permission of John Zorn. The second major section, "Speaking of My Music," was added in 2013.

I use the word "structure" here instead of "form" because form is often overloaded with historical baggage. Using a classical form as a template, however, can be a healthy learning experience, a type of creative calisthenics. Much of the creative fun comes from warping the boundaries of such concealed templates and bending their formal gravity, or from indulging in the past as if viewed from a distance through my own refractive lens.

I work with all sorts of systems, some derived from my experience and others invented for a specific composition. Systems can provide a flexible sort of discipline that allows for subversion and diversion. They open fields of exploration both orderly and disorderly, nourish discovery, and surf the waves of serendipity. A system can be specific, such as avoiding a certain sound or pitch altogether or until a structurally significant place in a composition. A system can also be expansive, such as sustaining resonant sounds from any source and suspending them in resonant space.

My composing mind works within extremes of time duration. My compositions for acoustical instruments are often short in duration, as condensed as poetry, with multiple layers of activity and internal relationships. Sometimes I assemble groups of shorter compositions that are somehow related to one another into larger collections, occasionally giving the performer some choice in the order of their presentation. Since about 2000 I have used the term "construction set" for this structural design principle, although the modular concept has been part of my creative thinking for much of my life.

My compositions of longer duration often involve electronic media. Some of these are cinematic or "sonomatic"; others are flexible sound sculptures or mobiles. Often they explore multiple layers of sound. Transitions between sound materials and spectra can be elaborate or subtle, not unlike the transitions of colors in paintings. A good example is the electronic *Pontpoint* (1966–80): crucial to its process is the duration of the essential silences that bridge each of its eight movements.

Some of my compositions were completed quickly, in days or weeks. Among these are works for electronic media such as *Epifont* (1984) and *Cirqualz* (1980), as well as instrumental cycles such as *Graftings* (1990–96) and the individual *Songs without Words* (1990s). My *Song without Words* for David Tudor was conceived in a single day in 1996 after hearing of his death on August 13. Others were worked, reworked, and adjusted over a long period of time. Perhaps the most extreme example is *Pontpoint.* Work on its music began in Pontpoint, France, in August 1966 while the members of the Merce Cunningham Dance Company were the guests of Bénédicte Pesle, to whom the music is dedicated. The compositional work for *Pontpoint* continued with interruptions over the course of many years before its completion in 1980, with ongoing adjustments of its eight sections in its overall canvas of time. The *Sixpac Sonatas* (1985–97) provide a special example of extended gestation, to which I return later.

Many of my live-electronic compositions also evolved over time because they involved my building and modifying of electronic instruments. Building of instruments, whether hand-made electronics, functional modifications of established instruments (such as the horn), or the historical keyboards that I built beginning in the late 1970s, has always been an important part of my creative activity. Ancillary is my interest in the acoustics of tuning and temperament.

The arena of the creative process is not unlike the cambium layer of a tree, the vital buffer between the solid wood and the surrounding bark. The cambium of the creative mind is the layer of the imagination. It can be fully awake, but often is dozing or in partial sleep. Even when fully awake, the creative focus often excludes all awareness outside itself.

About Performers and Collaboration

Composing for me is an ongoing celebration of the way materials and people work together. Collaboration can be challenging to the ego for many creative artists, and is impossible for some. When egos recede, the results can be scintillating.

Working with others has provided significant stimulus for all my work, stemming from my early experience as a small ensemble performer making creative decisions with other musicians. Even my solo music is conceived collaboratively as a projection of my self into its multiple roles. The other performer does not even need to be human: the cybersonic systems in my live-electronic music are interactive performers as well. The most meaningful performances often have no audience but include only the performers in variants of the *Hausmusik* tradition or the "jam session."

Theater and modern dance usually involve intense collaboration. Modern dance, for example, the work of the Strider group in London and Jann McCauley Dryer's Portland Dance Theatre and Cirque in Oregon, has been predominant for me. The Cunningham Dance Company productions were theatrical collaborations in which coordination between the dancers, stage decor, lighting, and music required adjustments and changes—perhaps more collective than collaborative. Others were fundamentally collaborative, as with our productions of *Loops* (1971) and my *Telepos* for Cunningham's choreography *TV Rerun* (1972). Working with Cunningham has provided substantial nourishment for my perspectives of musical time and space.

The composers, dancers, artists, and performers with whom I have worked, diverse though they may be, have been known, trusted, and generally comfortable in our playground. But even well-defined creative games must allow space for each unique performer and room for surprise.

About Audiences

Audience reaction has no bearing on how or what I compose. I expect nothing from an audience except that they not disrupt or subvert a performance. They are free to leave if they wish. Audience reactions to some of my music, and to that of colleagues such as Ashley, Cage, Lucier, Oliveros, and Tudor, have occasionally included hostility, outrage, and sabotage, or simply a not-so-gentle disrespect, particularly in conservatory venues. I am pleased if someone appreciates my work, but not disturbed if others dislike or think badly of it.

The word "audience" is infinitely plural; there are only audiences, of many cultures and groups. I observe the audience less as a composer than as an anthropologist interested in its particular social culture. I have often been an audience to learned people arguing over some composition of mine—about "how well or badly it is composed"—"is it real music?"—that sort of thing. These arguments have sometimes been so intense that my presence as the composer of the music has gone unnoticed, putting me in the surreal position of an anthropologist observing angry tribes at battle.

I have no interest in trying to control an audience. My work may have some influence on the thinking of others, but that is not my compositional intention. With few exceptions, the audience is an unreliable mirror with which to evaluate one's own creativity. I have learned more from the performers of my music.

About Listening to Music

Attentive listening to music is an essentially creative activity, accumulating the passage of sounds in conscious memory and anticipation. Music can also enhance an experience, whether unique to that person or closely shared within an existing culture. Music for winter or for ceremonies of death and life can have validating functions in certain cultural contexts. There is, for example, music for dancing, preparing for war, planting and harvesting food, drugging the mind for predatory marketing commerce, preparing the mind for sleep, and even imposing psychological or physical torture for political and punitive reasons.

My responses to music are mostly a personal experience. As a composer or performer I become emotionally involved in what I am doing. But music itself does not have emotions. Emotions are responses that people have to events and experiences in life. If a person responds with emotional pleasure to a flower that has just bloomed, it is the person who is emotional and not the flower. Thus I try not to impose my ways of hearing any music on others, and resent the inverse.

Speaking of My Music

 The recalcitrant question, then, is how—and why—one speaks of music, even one's own. What is there to say about it, beyond speaking about its structure, systems, and function? In introducing the following discussion of a handful of works that I composed over the course of fifty years, I offer Cage's famous dictum: "I have nothing to say, and I am saying it."

Large Size Mograph 1962

The *Large Size Mograph 1962* for solo piano is one of seven Mographs for one or two pianos composed in 1962–64. *Large Size Mograph 1962* is system-based. Its large template structure is derived from seismographic charts of earthquakes or underground nuclear tests, the latter a topic of concern at the height of the cold war. The pacing and time-placement of the musical gestures within its structure are determined by the P- and S-wave activities on the original seismographic chart and their intersections in time. The chart also provided the structural outline of the composition, resulting in two sections roughly equal in duration, the second of which begins at the point of greatest rhythmic activity and musical density [ex. VII-1], tapering off to quieter motion toward the end. The musical motifs are mostly brief, except when accumulated into short, energetic bursts, and are internally related by variations of pitch and register.

I established additional limitations for my sound ingredients so as to explore further relationships among them.

1. The musical intervals were predominantly widely spaced beyond the octave, interspersed with occasional clusters of narrow intervals (e.g., m2 and M2), dramatic in their contrast.
2. A few specific notes served as "anchor pitches," recurring as single short or sustained sounds, mostly in the low register.
3. Sonorities accumulated variously across the keyboard, sometimes reaching more than eight voices that are sustained with use of the sustaining and sostenuto pedals.

Although the notation of the score is basically traditional and specific regarding pitches and dynamics, meter signatures and bar lines are absent. "Timing" is the result of visual spacing of the notes and the general metronome marking

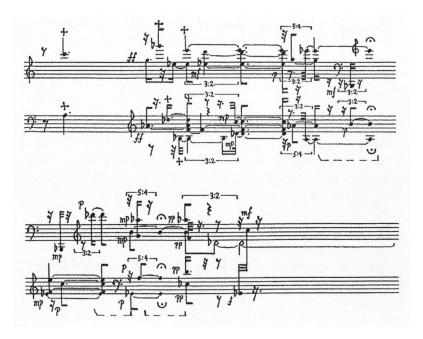

Ex. VII-1. Mumma, *Large Size Mograph 1962* (autograph), central climax of musical density

of quarter note = c. 54 beats per minute. Nevertheless the recorded performance of *Large Size Mograph 1962* by Daan Vandewalle (2007) independently reached results almost identical to my own unreleased recording made in the late 1980s regarding overall duration (8:03) and placement of the central climax of activity [ex. VII-1] near the "halfway point" (4:03). Our unplanned congruence suggests to me the presence of an internal proportion in this composition, however un-balanced its immediate effect for some listeners.

Eleven Note Pieces and Decimal Passacaglia for keyboard (1978)

I have always been a builder of instruments, electronic or acoustical. While at the University of California, Santa Cruz, I collaborated with others in building a single-manual Flemish harpsichord. The historical roots of this instrument in the eighteenth century were secondary, however, to its value for me as a new sound resource. I wrote several brief pedagogical etudes initially for my own use in learning to play the harpsichord. What had started as a practical performance tool became a larger creative project when I noticed that the pitch of G-flat was absent in the first few studies. The resulting set *Eleven Note Pieces and Decimal Passacaglia,* with its generic reference to the baroque keyboard suite, systematically explores limitation of resources: its eleven pieces use only eleven of the possible twelve notes in an octave scale. The absent G-flat appears in only one (no. 10 for Coriún Aharonián), which consists exclusively of the pitch G-flat heard eleven times with alternating timbre. The order of the pieces allows some defined choices for the performer (as do the harpsichord suites of François Couperin, for example), with nos. 1–2, 6, and 10–11 fixed and the others symmetrically interchangeable. Most of these works explore issues of contracting or expanding rhythmic patterns, a musical issue of considerable interest to me.

Piece no. 1 for Luigi Dallapiccola [ex. VII-2], a miniature homage to his *Quaderno musicale di Annalibera* of 1952, is a two-measure cross-hands etude exploring two patterns: an eighth-note rotary pattern for the right hand consisting of four pitches in five-note (pentameter) groupings, and an intertwined melodic line for the left hand. The pitch material for each hand is different. The second measure inverts all the functions of the first and closes tightly and purposely with the lowest and highest pitches.

Piece no. 4, dedicated to Graciela Paraskevaídis [ex. VII-3], is a "time-condensing" piece in three large gestures, each beginning with a six-note descending pattern contracting to five, four, three, and two notes. As seen in its first gesture, the eleven notes are purposely distributed between the hands, followed by free variation of its motivic implications.

Piece no. 9 for Linda Burman-Hall is a tricky perpetual motion of expanding and contracting patterns. When the performer decides to end its repeating process, one is confronted by the eleven G-flats for Aharonián (no. 10), followed by the final "chord" for Robert Ashley (no. 11), a single event consisting of a

Ex. VII-2. Mumma, *Eleven Note Pieces and Decimal Passacaglia*, no. 1 for Luigi Dallapiccola (autograph)

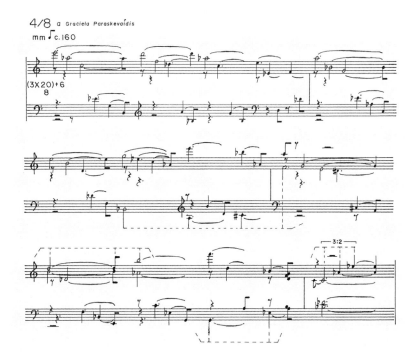

Ex. VII-3. Mumma, *Eleven Note Pieces and Decimal Passacaglia*, no. 4 for Graciela Paraskevaídis (autograph)

Ex. VII-4. Mumma, *Eleven Note Pieces and Decimal Passacaglia*, no. 9 for Linda Burman-Hall; no. 10 for Coriún Aharonián; no. 11 for Robert Ashley (autograph)

cluster of all eleven pitches released as two separate groups [ex. VII-4]. Thus, from their simple pedagogical origins as a private indulgence, the *Eleven Note Pieces* evolved in accordance with my concern with statistical pitch distribution at that time. The set closes with the "Decimal Passacaglia," a chromatic fantasy that warps the Baroque tradition of variations over a repeating ground bass. It earns its qualifier from its 10 × 10 proportional structure: the ten-note repeating bass line appears ten times, supporting a ten-chord chromatic progression with variations.

Than Particle (1985)

Than Particle is a collaborative work for acoustical and synthetic percussion. It combines a live percussion virtuoso in duo with digitally synthesized percussion sounds generated by a Yamaha CX5M computer from the first generation of such devices in the early 1980s. The computer part functions as a fixed platform for the live soloist, whose role includes fixed and improvised components. It was composed for percussionist William Winant, who premiered the work with me at the Arnold Schoenberg Institute on November 7, 1985, as part of the New Music America Festival in Los Angeles. Winant and I performed it widely on tours.

    Than Particle is performed from a fully notated score that includes traditional musical notation, special sonority notation, and passages of solo improvisation of specified position and duration. It is structured in ten one-minute sections connected by brief transitions of heightened rhythmic activity. Section 8 of the autograph score [ex. VII-5] provides a model for the notational and performance strategies of *Than Particle*. It shows six systems of two staves in standard five-line-staff format. The computer part is indicated in the upper of the two staves; it provides pitch and rhythmic information for the synthesized percussion console but displays only useful cues for the live percussion performer. The lower of the two staves contains choreographic performance information for the live percussionist. Each line of this lower five-line staff denotes a specific class of percussion sonority and rhythm, but *not* pitch. The staff, moving upward from the lowest to the highest line, indicates a progression of instruments from longer to shorter durations of sonority. The percussionist is free to choose the specific instruments that will fulfill each sonority class as specified, selecting at will from among metal, glass, wood, or string percussion instruments. The lowest line is for the instrument of longest duration, such as a tam-tam or gong, while the middle (third) line is for the central instrument of the ensemble, a high-pitched, shallow snare drum. Section 8 is accordingly an extended solo for snare. The computer part of section 8, by contrast, is more disparate, including the calm, the pedestrian, the lyrical, the banal, and the pugnacious. As is also seen elsewhere in this work, section 8 includes a disguised allusion to other music (few listeners have caught the inversion of Tchaikovsky's 5/4 scherzo theme from the "Pathétique" Symphony in mm. 228–30).

The passages of improvisation for the solo percussionist are indicated in the score by a large number under an arrow. The arrow specifies rhythmic placement and duration, while the number denotes the number of discrete physical gestures. All other musical choices are at the discretion of the soloist. The length and rhythmic saturation of these improvised passages increase as the work unfolds; thus section 8 has five brief improvisation areas, one of which (mm. 241–42) is especially vigorous. The ranges of dynamics (from loud to quiet) and durations (from long to short) are very wide. The tempo is generally regular except for developing accelerations, evident, for example, in the closing measures of section 8.

Than Particle is a practical work adaptable to touring and educational venues. The synthesized sounds require wide-frequency-range loudspeakers placed at floor level among the percussion instruments and arranged so that the performer hears the same sound balance as does the audience. The original Yamaha CX5M computer used for *Than Particle* still survives today, although it is now on the order of a "historical instrument." This synthesizer was based on a classic Z-80 8-bit CPU with basic "four-operator" FM synthesis algorithms as developed by John Chowning. Relative to the huge institutional mainframe computers of the 1980s, the CX5M was inexpensive and portable, but limited, and it could not be modified. In some respects it provided a more stimulating challenge than working with large computers that obeyed detailed commands. In composing *Than Particle* it was necessary to accept both the limitations of the CX5M and the numerous unpredictable software bugs that affected the music. For more recent performances my original computer-generated percussion sounds have been transferred to a digital compact disc accompanying the score.[1]

Composing the music and synthesizing the sounds required collaboration between composer and computer rather than a master-slave relationship. It involved embracing the quirky, "ersatz" voice of the CX5M in dialogue with the real percussion instruments. In live performance, the physical activity of the percussionist clarifies some of the intentional differences between the acoustically real and the computerized sonorities. In experiencing this work on recording without the visual cues of live performance, the differences of sonority in *Than Particle* may be humorously ambiguous. No less so is its title: "than particles" are short-lived surrogate phenomena, allegorically analogous to a fourteenth-century head-bashing game that typically involved facial laceration and rampant wagering.

GORDON MUMMA : THAN PARTICLE

Ex. VII-5. Mumma, *Than Particle*, section 8 (autograph)

From the *Sixpac Sonatas*, Sonata no. 6 (1991–97)

The *Sixpac Sonatas* began with an invitation in 1985 to contribute a short composition to a *Festschrift* for musicologist H. Wiley Hitchcock.[2] I determined that a short movement using Domenico Scarlatti's harpsichord sonatas as a formal template would be appropriate for this scholar of eighteenth-century music, and I composed it quickly. Its template idea took hold, however, eventually spawning a series of six sonatas, all using the classic ABA tripartite design. All are notated in 5/8 as a practical means of establishing pulse without the traditional metrical implications of rigidly accented downbeats. Each successive sonata took longer to compose than the previous one, as the template concept became increasingly complex and ambiguous due to the progressive expansion of developmental processes and layering of musical motifs. They are playable on any keyboard instrument of sufficient range, more often the harpsichord than others (dynamic markings were later added for the piano).

I took a long time in composing the Sixpac Sonata no. 6, with much rewriting and elimination of extraneous materials to create an intensely compact movement of significant musical density. The motifs or musical ideas in the Sixpac Sonata no. 6 have a clear identity. Some are very short rhythmic gestures of two or three notes, while others are relatively long melodic lines. As this sonata progresses, the shorter motifs are constantly varied, combined, and recombined with each other, with all literal repetition avoided. This sonata falls into fairly obvious sections with increasingly complex motivic variations as it develops.

The score of Sonata no. 6 is reproduced as example VII-6. Section A (mm. 1–28) contains three major activities: the punchy sixteenth-note introductory motif (A^1, m. 1), a legato "melodic line" in longer notes in the right hand (A^2, mm. 2–8), and short accompaniment motifs of two and three eighth-note groupings in the left hand, interspersed with the melody (A^3). In mm. 9–15 the melody A^2 and accompaniment A^3 exchange hands in what is traditionally called invertible counterpoint, retaining their character even though different pitch and register material is used. The texture is largely in three voices. A sustained pitch of A (mm. 16–17) provides a temporary point of arrival; this calming gesture recurs as a demarcation point later in the sonata (as in m. 36). Finally, the materials of the previous sections are recalled with variation and compression (mm. 18–28), the texture thickening to four voices.

Section B (mm. 29–53) is marked by a halving of the tempo and new material, a dragging theme B^1 with its triplet rhythm (mm. 29–33) and a jaunty rhythmic theme B^2 (mm. 34–35, r.h.), accompanied by variants of motives A^3. The rhythmic urgency of theme B^2 and its capacity for contrapuntal imitation

from the SIXPAC SONATAS
6

GORDON MUMMA

p.1

Ex. VII-6. Mumma, *Sixpac Sonata* no. 6. (© 2001 C. F. Peters Corporation, with permission)

Mumma: *from the SIXPAC SONATAS #6*

p.2

Ex. VII-6. Continued

p.3

Ex. VII-6. Continued

Mumma: *from the SIXPAC SONATAS #6*

p.4

Ex. VII-6. Continued

(see m. 40) and fragmentation (m. 42, r.h.) promote traditional development techniques and rising energy. Just before the close, a new thirty-second-note rising motif B³ appears fleetingly in the right hand (m. 49); it is developed in the closing coda.

The recapitulation is anticipated by a premature entry of motif A¹ in m. 52. The recapitulation proper (mm. 54–59) recalls motifs of the exposition section, now in four voices, with increasing variation and overlapping. In the coda, which is initiated by rhythmic transformations of theme B³ (upbeat of m. 60–61), the density of activity heightens and accumulates, with earlier themes driven to new metrical complexities. Though the tempo is roughly the same as at the opening, motivic saturation and time contractions seem to propel the movement headlong to its abrupt end.

These structural procedures achieve an underlying coherence because the varying motifs maintain their substantial identity even with the growing musical density. The formal design was only subconsciously planned, the outcome of my years of experience performing the standard classical repertoire in orchestras and ensembles.

From the Rendition Series (2006)

This composition is for a single pianist on one or two grand pianos, with an optional live-electronic component controlled by an additional performer. The macro-structure of *From the Rendition Series* is a construction set assembled by the performers from fixed, fully notated score units (or "ex Streams," as they are called). The score page of each ex Stream contains small notational groups separated by blank spaces, the micro-components of the composition. They are fully notated and performed as specified, separated in time and space by silences. The variable component consists in the performers' choice of which ex Stream segments will be performed and in which order. As a result the total duration of the ex Stream renditions is variable.³

Although optional, the live-electronic component is a significant addition to the work. In the premiere performance at November Music in s'Hertogenbosch, The Netherlands, in November 2006, I controlled small electronic audio devices placed inside the piano and containing pre-recorded sounds from various sources, including electronically processed piano sounds and a flock of noisy chickens. The entries of the supplemental electronic sounds were planned in consultation with the pianist, Tomoko Mukaiyama. The selection of sounds activated by the live-electronic unit was more or less random, sometimes occurring while the pianist was playing, and sometimes in the silences between the piano gestures, creating mysterious ambiguities of sound source like a phantom voice issuing from within the instrument.

Abrupted Edges for piano and string quartet (2011)

The technique of resonating sounds that vary slowly over time has been an aspect of my electronic music from the 1950s, including *Pontpoint,* parts of *Epifont* (1984), and *Echo-D* (1978). When transferred to my piano music as early as the final movement of the *Suite for Piano* (1958–60), the result is more that of a sound painting than of a momentum-driven music. In "Octet for David Behrman" from the *Sushi verticals* construction set, for example, eight distinctive chords, mostly widely spaced in register, sound for over a minute and a half. The sustaining pedal is depressed throughout, aggrandizing the resonating interactions of the chordal sonorities. The *Songs without Words* for Christian Wolff and David Revill also employ pedal-sustained sonorities as a context for motivic activity.

A comparable technique is central to *Abrupted Edges,* composed in honor of Alvin Lucier. It involves the cross-resonances of decaying piano chords with overlapping string quartet swells. This composition developed from a single basic idea: the limitation of sound materials within its developing structure. In this respect *Abrupted Edges* celebrates Lucier's poetic imagination in developing large-scale performance works from small ideas.

Another of its basic premises is the collision of tuning systems. The piano is tuned to equal-temperament ratios, while the string quartet performs within the "pure" tuning of simple whole-number ratios, mostly without vibrato. Thus its fundamental sound-making gestures combine and contrast those two tuning systems within the essential differences of articulation of piano and strings. In this sense, *Abrupted Edges* differs from the traditional performance practice of chamber music for piano with unfretted string instruments, in which the performers work to attenuate the very pitch discrepancies that are fundamental to the sonorities of this composition.

Abrupted Edges begins with a mundane reference to the tuning ritual, with the quartet calibrating its open string D to the center-point D of the piano keyboard. Besides setting the instruments at the same pitch reference and providing a theatrical signal that the performance is beginning, the tuning section also contributes a basic rhythmic motif for the entire performance: a short-long iambic gesture in the piano enlarged by the string quartet response. Thereafter, it unfolds somewhat like a group of threaded beads. The piano chord construction plays upon its physical configuration of black and white keys radiating symmetrically around two axes, D and A-flat. Beginning entirely with D, the piano initiates chord constructions, the pitch-intervals of which are vertically

Ex. VII-7. Mumma, *Abrupted Edges*, mm. 3–5

symmetrical around D, as seen in example VII-7 (mm. 3–5). Each piano chord decays naturally as it overlaps with a complementary string quartet sonority, upbowed to create a gentle timbral swell. My assigned pitch restriction allowed many choices of intervals that maintain this vertical symmetry, with the added variables of register and transposition. There are sufficient interval combinations that I could assign a further restriction: any interval pattern occurs only once in the entire composition. These substantial limitations allowed me to discover new micro-structural relationships within the macro-structure.

The lengthy central section incorporates the A-flat and its vertically symmetrical response, further exploring the implications of these disciplinary limitations and gradually supplanting the D. For the closing cadence I introduced new material: the pitch of A-flat in the entire ensemble, with the strings adjusting tuning for the first time to the piano and tempering the pitch with vibrato (ex. VII-8). The final gesture incorporates all twelve pitches of the chromatic scale, with the piano recalling its basic idea before yielding to open-string harmonics.

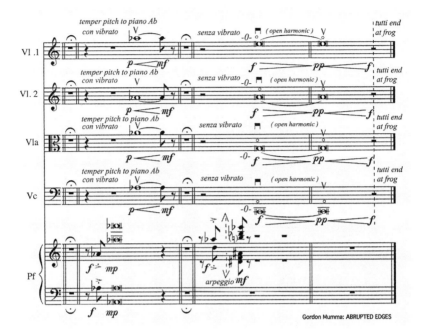

Ex. VII-8. Mumma, *Abrupted Edges*, mm. 55–58

Final Cadence: About Music

Aggregate replies to the recalcitrant question: "What is music?"

Often quoted, from Gottfried Wilhelm Leibniz (1646–1716): "Music is a hidden mathematical exercise of a mind unconscious that it is calculating."

Several of my replies:

Music is a network of ideas, interconnections, and creative decisions, presented in time as patterns and relationships of sounds.

Music happens when a sound (or silence) exceeds the character of itself and the meanings or implications of its origins.

Music is a human activity, not an object. It became a "thing" only with the mass-production of sound recordings as commodities.

Musics are streams in time and times of sounds and silences, with places in spaces.

SELECTIVE LIST OF GORDON MUMMA'S MUSICAL COMPOSITIONS

The following list of works is limited for the most part to those accessible in commercial recordings or cited in the text of this book. It is organized by genre and instrumentation. Within each category, the works are organized chronologically by date of completion, and within a single year, by date of premiere. Dates associated with each work denote the period of major compositional activity, in some cases two or more years in duration.

Abbreviations

chor	choreography
cyb	cybersonic(s)
mag	magnetic
prem	premiere performance
quad	quadraphonic
rec	recording(s): CD format unless otherwise noted:
	AC audiocassette
	VN vinyl recording
res	resource(s)/scoring
st	stereophonic
synth	synthesizer

I. Electro-Acoustic

A. STUDIO ELECTRONICS (WITHOUT SIGNIFICANT LIVE PERFORMANCE)

Vectors (1959) [a.k.a. Soundblock 5]
    Res: st mag tape
    Prem: Wayne State University, Detroit, MI, November 1961

Densities (1959)

    Res: st mag tape

    Prem: University of Michigan Creative Arts Festival, Ann Arbor, May 18, 1962

    Note: See also Retrospect (1982); rev. version of tape from *Sinfonia*
        (1958–60). See section II.B.

Mirrors for Milton Cohen (1960–61)

    Res: quad mag tape

    Prem: Manifestations in Light and Sound, San Francisco, CA, November 1961

Greys, electronic score for the film *Greys* by Donald Scavarda (1963)

    Res: st mag tape

    Prem: First Ann Arbor Film Festival, Ann Arbor, May 23, 1963

    Rec: NWR 80567-2 (ONCE Festival, December 3, 1963)

Music from the Venezia Space Theatre (1963–64)

    Res: quad mag tape

    Prem: 27th Venezia Biennale, Venice, Italy, September 11, 1964 (ONCE Group
        with dancers)

    Rec: (1) VN: Advance FGR-5 (mono); Lovely VR-1091 (st); (2) Lovely LCD
        1093

The Dresden Interleaf 13 February 1945 (1965)

    Res: quad mag tape, with live alcohol-burning airplane engines

    Prem: ONCE Festival, Ann Arbor, February 13, 1965 [at prem preceded by
        Small Size Mograph 1964 and followed by Medium Size Mograph 1963]

    Rec: (1) VN: Lovely VR-1091; (2) Lovely LCD 1093

Wooden Pajamas (1974)

    Res: st mag tape

    Prem: Musée Galliera, Paris, France, October 14, 1974 (Sonic Arts Union)

    Note: See also Retrospect (1982)

Echo-D (1978)

    Res: st mag tape; materials include harpsichord, Buchla synthesizer, and elec-
        tronics

    Rec: (1) AC: Slowscan 9; (2) Lovely LCD 1093

Cirqualz (1980)

    Res: acoustical tape montage of musical samples, Buchla synth, and noise

    Prem: Cirque Studio, Portland, OR, March 14, 1980, with choreography by
        Jann McCauley (Portland Dance Theatre)

    Rec: NWR 80632-2

Pontpoint (1966–80)

    Res: st mag tape; cyb modified materials from bandoneon and bowed psaltery

    Prem: Cirque Studio, Portland, OR, March 14, 1980, with choreography by
        Jann McCauley (Portland Dance Theatre)

    Rec: (1) VN: Lovely VR-1092; (2) Lovely LCD 1093

Stressed Space Palindromes (1976–82)
  Res: quad mag tape
  Prem: University of California, Santa Cruz, April 24, 1982
  Rec: Brainwashed 004B
Retrospect (1982)
  Assembly of four short pieces with fixed media:
    Densities (1959)
    Phenomenon Unarticulated (1972), live electronics; see section I.B
    Wooden Pajamas (1974)
    Spectral Portrait (1982)
  Res: st mag tape (second piece also includes live electronics)
  Prem: University of California, Santa Cruz, October 6, 1982
  Rec: Lovely LCD 1093
Epifont: Spectral Portrait in Memoriam George Cacioppo (1984)
  Res: synthesized and acoustical sounds on st mag tape
  Prem: University of Michigan, Ann Arbor, April 14, 1985
  Rec: (1) AC: Slowscan 9; (2) Lovely LCD 1093
Ambulare (1999)
  Res: quad electro-acoustic tape
  Prem: University of California, Santa Cruz, May 5, 1999

B. LIVE ELECTRONICS

Note: These works include substantial electronic materials performed in real time. They may also include other resources, such as live performance of acoustical instruments, recorded sound materials, motion-induced telemetry, and live cyber-sonic modification.

Meanwhile, a Twopiece (1961)
  Res: percussion and one or two additional instruments, with st mag tape
  Prem: ONCE Festival, Ann Arbor, February 10, 1962 (Robert Ashley and Mumma)
  Rec: NWR 80567-2
Medium Size Mograph 1963 (1963)
  Res: piano 4 hands, with cyb modification of live and pre-recorded piano sounds
  Prem: Richmond Professional Institute, Richmond, VA, April 9, 1964 (Ashley and Mumma)
  Rec: Tzadik TZ 7074 (Ashley and Mumma at ONCE Festival, February 13, 1965)
Megaton for Wm. Burroughs (1963–64)
  Res: live performers, pre-recorded magnetic tape, film soundtrack, clickers, and ten communication channels

Prem: ONCE Festival, Ann Arbor, February 28, 1964

Rec: (1) VN: Lovely VR-1091; (2) NWR 80632-2

Le Corbusier (1965)

Res: orch, organ, pre-recorded material on st mag tape, and cyb console

Prem: Southern Methodist University, Dallas, TX, February 13, 1965

Horn (1965)

Res: horn, voices, and two cyb consoles

Prem: St. Andrew's Episcopal Church, Ann Arbor, MI, March 29, 1965

Rec: [all of the prem] (1) VN: Aspen 4 (monaural); (2) AC: Slowscan 9; (3) Tzadik TZ 7074

Mesa (1966)

Res: bandoneon and cyb console

Prem: Fondation Maegt, Saint-Paul de Vence, France, August 6, 1966 (David Tudor and Mumma)

Rec: (1) VN: CBS Odyssey 3216 0157-8 (Tudor and Mumma), co-issued on CBS France S-346 1065; re-issued on VN Lovely VR-1092; (2) Tzadik TZ 7074 (re-issue of CBS recording, Tudor and Mumma); (3) NWR 80712-2 (Tudor and Mumma, Paris, November 9, 1966)

Chor: Merce Cunningham, *Place* (1966)

Diastasis, as in Beer (1967)

Res: two guitars and cyb console

Prem: Eliot House, Harvard University, May 14, 1967 (Mumma and Christian Wolff)

Hornpipe (1967)

Res: waldhorn, valve horn, reed horn, and cyb console

Prem: Pomona College, Claremont, CA, December 5, 1967

Rec: (1) VN: Mainstream MS-5010; (2) Tzadik CD TZ 7074

Note: Earlier concept titled *Hornpipes* (begun c. 1962), with resonating pipes (withdrawn)

Beam (1969)

Res: violin, viola, cyb console, and digital telemetry bow-arm sleeves

Prem: Crosstalk Intermedia Festival, Tokyo, Japan, February 5, 1969 (Yoko Hayashi, violin; Konusuke Ono, viola; Mumma, cyb console)

Conspiracy 8, collaboration with Stephen Smoliar (1970)

Res: 1–8 live performers, cyb console, teletype, and digital computer

Prem: MIT, Cambridge, MA, February 20, 1970 (Mumma, bowed musical saw with cyb; Smoliar, teletype console to PDP-6 computer)

Rec: NWR 80632-2

Communication in a Noisy Environment, collaboration with David Behrman, Anthony Braxton, Leroy Jenkins, and Robert Watts (1970)

Res: multi-level building with electronic audio and video intercommunica-
tions, variable instruments, cars, and machines

Prem: Automation House, New York, NY, November 19, 1970

Three Electronic Pieces (1967–70)

  1. Crosshatch, for Lowell Cross (San Francisco)
  2. Foreskin, for Barbara Lloyd (New York, NY)
  3. Stovepipe, for Richard Nelson (Harwich, Cape Cod, MA)

Res: three color television sets, nude dancer with current-limiting power supply, lasers, and stovepipe with mirrored dampers

Edition: Roger Johnson, ed., *Scores: An Anthology of New Music* (New York:
Schirmer, 1981), 203.

Loops, collaboration with Merce Cunningham (1971)

Res: dancer with telemetry unit and technician

Prem: Museum of Modern Art, New York, December 3, 1971 (Cunningham
and Mumma), with Jasper Johns's *Map (Based on Buckminster Fuller's Dymaxion Airocean World)* (1967/1971)

Chor: Merce Cunningham, *Loops* (1971) and *Loops and Additions* (1973)

Phenomenon Unarticulated (1972)

Res: variable live electronics

Prem: Brooklyn Academy of Music, Brooklyn, NY, February 1, 1972

Chor: performed with Merce Cunningham, *Landrover* (1972)

Telepos, collaboration with the Merce Cunningham Dance Company (1972)

Res: dancers with electronic accelerometer belts and telemetry

Prem: Brooklyn Academy of Music, Brooklyn, NY, February 2, 1972

Rec: NWR 80712-2 (live; Venice, September 12, 1972)

Chor: Merce Cunningham, *TV Rerun* (1972)

Ambivex (1972)

Res: cyb cornet or trumpet, with phantom myoelectrical telemetering system
and perf appendages

Prem: Pro Musica Nova, Radio Bremen, Germany, May 6, 1972 (Mumma, cyb
cornet)

Cybersonic Cantilevers, installation (1973)

Res: recorded sound materials, cyb console, loudspeakers, with public participation

Prem: Everson Museum, Syracuse, NY, May 19, 1973 (Sonic Arts Union)

Rec: (1) VN: Folkways FTS-33904 [excerpt]; (2) NWR 80632-2 [longer]

Some Voltage Drop (1974)

Res: live theater work with music, using pre-recorded tape materials

Prem: Musée Galliera, Paris, France, October 13, 1974 (Sonic Arts Union)

Film: Robert Ashley, *Music with Roots in the Aether*, program 4 (Lovely DV 7704)

The Ives Railroad (1974)
Res: musical saw, propane stove and teakettle, diapositives
Prem: Charles Ives Centennial, Yale University, October 21, 1974 (Mumma), under the subtitle Some Voltage Drop
Telepos-Foxbat, collaboration with Tandy Beal (1974)
Res: multi-sensor telemetry
Film: Robert Ashley, *Music with Roots in the Aether*, program 4 (Lovely DV 7704)
Than Particle (1985)
Res: solo percussion with digital computer-generated percussion sounds
Prem: Arnold Schoenberg Institute, Los Angeles, CA, November 7, 1985 (William Winant, percussion; Mumma, computer console)
Rec: Tzadik TZ 7074
Yawawot: Spectral Portrait (2003)
Res: solo violin with electro-acoustical soundscape
Prem: Merkin Concert Hall, New York, NY, March 18, 2004 (Conrad Harris, violin; Mumma, soundscape)
From the Rendition Series, with 8 ex Streams (2006)
Res: solo piano with internal electronics
Prem: Verkadefabriek, 's-Hertogenbosch, The Netherlands, November 18, 2006 (Tomoko Mukaiyama, piano; Mumma, electronics)
Rec: November Music NM 010 (prem)
Gambreled Tapestry (2007)
Res: solo piano with optional internal electronic resonances
Prem: Cunningham Dance Studio, New York, NY, November 19, 2007 (Mumma)

II. Instrumental

A. KEYBOARD

Suite for Piano (1959–60)

I. 76/104
II. 50/64
III. 96/104
IV. 52/72

Res: solo piano
Prem: ONCE Festival, Ann Arbor, February 25, 1961 (Ashley)
Rec: NWR 80686-2 (Daan Vandewalle)

Gestures II (1958–62)

    Res: 2 pianos

    Prem: ONCE Festival, Ann Arbor, February 16, 1962 (Ashley and Mumma)

    Recordings: 6 Selections: NWR 80567-2 (ONCE); Sections 7 and X: NWR 80651-2 (Tudor and Mumma)

Very Small Size Mograph 1962 (1962)

    Res: any number of pianos

    Prem: ONCE Festival, Ann Arbor, February 16, 1963 (Ashley and Mumma, 2 pianos)

    Rec: NWR 80651-2 (Tudor and Mumma; two versions for 2 pianos and 4 pianos, 4 hands)

Medium Size Mograph 1962 (1962)

    Res: any number of pianists at any number of pianos, with choreographic notation

    Prem: ONCE Festival, Ann Arbor, February 16, 1963 (Ashley and Mumma)

Large Size Mograph 1962 (1962)

    Res: solo piano

    Prem: ONCE Friends, Ann Arbor, December 16, 1962 (Larry Leitch)

    Rec: NWR 80567-2 (Leitch); NWR 80686-2 (Vandewalle)

Very Small Size Mograph 1963 (1963)

    Res: piano 4 hands

    Rec: NWR 80651-2 (Tudor and Mumma)

Small Size Mograph 1964 (1964)

    Res: piano 4 hands

    Prem: ONCE Festival, Ann Arbor, February 13, 1965 (as prelude to *The Dresden Interleaf*)

    Rec: NWR 80651-2 (Tudor and Mumma)

Medium Size Mograph 1964 (1964)

    Res: 2 pianos

    Prem: Mills College, Oakland, CA, November 22, 1981 (Robin Beloff and Mumma)

    Rec: NWR 80651-2 (Tudor and Mumma)

Eleven Note Pieces and Decimal Passacaglia (1978)

    1. à Luigi Dallapiccola

    2. à Durand Begault

    3. à Diane Carlson

    4. à Graciela Paraskevaídis

    5. à Padre Mugica

    6. à Jacques Bekaert

    7. à Pauline Oliveros

8. à Eduardo Bértola
9. à Linda Burman-Hall
10. à Coriún Aharonián
11. à Robert Ashley
12. Decimal Passacaglia, à Carolyn Cook

Res: solo keyboard [harpsichord, fortepiano, or piano]
Prem: March 16, 1979, Santa Cruz, CA, by harpsichordist Durand Begault
(selections)
Rec: (1) AC: Slowscan 9 (Mumma, harpsichord); (2) Musical Heritage Society
513988A (Linda Burman-Hall, harpsichord); (3) NWR 80686-2 (Vandewalle, piano)
Edition: *Soundings XVI* (Santa Fe, N.M.: Soundings, 1990)

9 Songs without Words (1990s)

for Christian Wolff (1996)
soprapensiero, for Dominic Gill
for Richard Felciano
for Younhie Kim (with two extensions)
for Jon Barlow
for MerrilLynn Taylor
for David Tudor . . . who went on ahead of us (August 13, 1996)
for George Exon (d. May 4, 1994)
for David Revill

Res: solo piano
Rec: NWR 80686-2 (Vandewalle)

Threesome (1995)

1 of a Threesome
2 of a Threesome
3 of a Threesome

Note: reworking of several movements from *Faisandage et Galimafrée* (1984; see
section II.B)
Res: solo piano
Rec: NWR 80686-2 (Vandewalle)

Four Pack Ponies, with three Interstices (1996)

1. Bay
2. Connemara
3. Dun
4. Chestnut dreams

Res: solo piano
Rec: NWR 80686-2 (Vandewalle)

Graftings (1990–96)

1. Scion
2. Recitative
3. Scion
4. Scion
5. Grafting and Slipwaltz
6. Scion

Res: solo piano
Rec: NWR 80686-2 (Vandewalle)

19 from the Sushibox (completed 1996)

5 Sushiverticals (1996)

1. for Merce Cunningham
2. Octet, for David Behrman
3. for Lou Harrison
4. for William Colvig
5. for C. T. Mumma

3 Perspectives (1966–96), in memoriam Jacqueline Leuzinger (d. 1966)

6. Perspective 1
7. Perspective 2
8. Perspective 3

11 Sushihorizontals (1986–96)

9. for Jackson Mac Low at 75
10. for Alexis at 22
11. for Agnes Martin
12. for James Klosty
13. for Jonathan at 12
14. Erdös number . . . for Paul Erdös
15. for Christopher at 15 (time flies like two arrows)
16. for Carolyn Brown
17. for Bun-Ching Lam
18. for Anatole Leikin
19. for Charles Shere

Res: solo piano
Rec: NWR 80686-2 (Vandewalle)
Edition: Material Press (Frankfurt)

Basket of Strays (1970–97)

> Treble Song (1996)
> Soft Saloon Song (1977), version for piano solo (see section II.B)
> Tearing off: A piece (2001)
> Clavichord at 18 (1997)
> Un bocado de tango (de los desaparecidos) (1970)
> Octal Waltz, for retuned harpsichord in 8-note equal temperament (1980)
>
> Res: variable keyboard
> Prem: Octal Waltz, University of California, Santa Cruz, April 9, 1983
>   (Mumma)
> Rec: complete set: NWR 80686-2 (Vandewalle); Octal Waltz: Musical Heri-
>   tage Society 513988A (Linda Burman-Hall, harpsichord)

Jardin for Michelle Fillion (1958–97)

> 1. Poplars
> 2. Tricycle and fence
> 3. Coulisse pour Michelle
> 4. Lunar asparagus, d'après Max Ernst
> 5. Planted song 1
> 6. Planted song 2
> 7. Planted song 3
> 8. Planted song 4
>
> Res: solo piano
> Rec NWR: 80686-2 (Vandewalle)

Sixpac Sonatas (1985–97)

> 1. for H. Wiley Hitchcock
> 2. for Julia Wilson Jones
> 3. for Homer Keller
> 4. for David Bernstein
> 5. (no dedication)
> 6. (no dedication)
>
> Res: solo piano (or fortepiano or harpsichord)
> Rec: NWR 80686-2 (Vandewalle)

Tapizdos (2008)

> Res: piano 4 hands double-mobile
> Prem: Casa Encendida, Madrid, Spain, March 14, 2008 (Vandewalle and
>   Mumma)

Construction 4 hands (2012)
    Res: piano 4 hands
    Prem: Haus der Berliner Festspiele, Berlin, Germany, March 23, 2012 (Vandewalle and Mumma)

B. OTHER INSTRUMENTS

Etude on Oxford Changes (1957)
    Res: solo violin
    Prem: Nordwestdeutsche Musikakademie, Detmold, Germany, November 18, 1960 (Werner Grobholz, violin)
Sinfonia for 12 Instruments and Magnetic Tape (1958–60)
    Res: chamber orchestra; four untitled movements, with mag tape accompaniment in third movement
    Prem: ONCE Festival, Ann Arbor, March 4, 1961 (ONCE Chamber Orchestra)
    Rec: NWR 80567-2 (ONCE)
A Quarter of Fourpiece (1960–62)
    Res: 4 variable instruments
    Prem: Smith College, Northampton, MA, January 30, 1963
    Rec: NWR 80567-2 (ONCE, February 9, 1963)
Peasant Boy, collaboration with Bob James Trio (1964)
    Res: trio with piano
    Rec: VN: ESP 1009-2 (Bob James Trio), track 4 [incorrectly listed as track 1]
Swarmer (1967) [a.k.a. Swarm]
    Res: two or three folkloric instruments
    Prem: Cornell University, Ithaca, NY, February 1968 (Mumma, musical saw, and Cage, concertina)
Schoolwork (1970)
    Res: one or more folkloric instruments (e.g., musical saw, psaltery, melodica)
    Prem: Radio Bremen, Germany, April 1971
    Rec: (1) AC: Slowscan 9 (Stockholm, 1972); (2) Orange Mountain Music 0015-1 (live at The Kitchen, New York, NY, 1979)
    Film: Robert Ashley, *Music with Roots in the Aether*, program 4 (Lovely DV 7704) (Mumma, musical saw)
Equale—Internal Tempi (1975)
    Res: 3 horns, 3 snare drums
    Prem: Warner Arts Center, Oberlin Conservatory of Music, Oberlin, OH, February 8, 1975
    Edition: Material Press (Frankfurt, Germany, n.d.)

Equale: Zero Crossing, for seven instruments (1976)

    Res: flute, clarinet (B-flat), tenor sax/horn (F), bassoon, violin, cello/contra-
bass, bandoneon

    Prem: San Francisco Conservatory Ensemble, April 20, 1976 (conducted by
John Adams)

    Edition: Material Press (Frankfurt, Germany, n.d.)

Soft Saloon Song (1977)

    Version for bandoneon and piano (originally piano solo; see section II.A)

    Prem: Portland Dance Theatre, Portland, OR, September 9, 1977 (Mumma
and Tom Robbins)

    Chor: Jann McCauley, *Earheart: Flights, Formations, and Starry Nights*

    Edition: Material Press (Frankfurt, Germany, n.d.)

Fwyyn: Lament for a Princess Enchanted into Death, from *Fwyynghn*, co-composed
with Pauline Oliveros (1979)

    Res: two bandoneons

    Rec: VN: Lovely VR-1092

    Edition: Material Press (Frankfurt, Germany, n.d.)

Faisandage et galimafrée, divertimento in eight movements (1984)

    Fanfare
    March Waltz
    Romanza
    Hommage
    Scherzo
    Minuetto al rovescio
      Trio extruduto
    Notturno
    Bagatelle

    Res: variable instrumental trios
    Prem: New Music Works, Santa Cruz, CA, June 10, 1984
    Rec: VN: Opus One 129 (Leta Miller, flute, with Ensemble Nova)

Aleutian Displacement (1987)

    Res: chamber orchestra

Orait (1987)

    Res: vocal solo and ensemble with mouth/body percussion
    Text: Melanesian Pidgin text by Gregory Bateson
    Prem: University of California, Santa Cruz, May 1988

Ménages à deux, variable duos (1989–90)

    Res: variable combinations of violin, vibraphone, marimba, or piano
    Prem: Freeman Musicale, Los Angeles, March 31, 1991 (Winant, vibraphone;
Mumma, piano)

Phaedrus Laterals (1991)

    Res: percussion, horn, and calculated sounds

        Prem: Freeman Musicale, Los Angeles, March 31, 1991 (Winant, percussion; Mumma, piano)

Comitatus 2 (2009)

    Res: violin and piano

        Prem: Ostrava Festival, Czech Republic, August 30, 2011 (Harris, violin; Vandewalle, piano)

Abrupted Edges, for Alvin Lucier, "a diamond among . . . " (2011)

    Res: string quartet and piano

        Prem: Crowell Concert Hall, Wesleyan University, Middletown, CT, November 6, 2011 (West End String Quartet; Neely Bruce, piano)

—Gordon Mumma and Michelle Fillion

NOTES

Introduction by Michelle Fillion

1. The premiere of *Medium Size Mograph 1963* took place at the Richmond Professional Institute, Richmond, Virginia, on April 9, 1964. See the appendix to this book for a selective list of Mumma's musical compositions.

2. The name "Cybersonics" was legally registered by Mumma and Ribbens in the State of Michigan according to the Certificate filed on June 4, 1965 (GMC). The early years of the firm are summarized in "Firm Produces Electronic Music Equipment," *Ann Arbor News,* November 9, 1965, 6.

3. Adapted from Mumma, interview by Vincent Plush, 88.

4. "Composer's Notes," in Mumma, *Electronic Music of Theatre and Public Activity* (NWR 80632-2), 11–12.

5. This performance is released on Tzadik TZ 7074.

6. The rare research writings by Mumma, notably his readily available "Sound Recording" in the *New Grove Dictionary of American Music*, have been omitted from this collection (see Works Cited). Likewise omitted are peripheral or popular publications deemed to be of lesser historical value, among which are "What Is a Performance? How the Idea of Playing Music Is Changing" and "Northwest November Notes"; "Electronic Resources in the Music of Roger Reynolds," which Mumma deemed insufficient to the subject; and items that duplicate previously published material, such as "Electronic Music for the Merce Cunningham Dance Company."

Preamble by Michelle Fillion

1. Mumma spoke of Archie Mumma in his May 1982 interview by Vincent Plush.

2. Mumma, "Reflections on the Life of a New Englander."

3. Ibid.

4. Mumma, interview by Vincent Plush, 47.

5. This story is recounted in Miller, "ONCE and Again," 22–23.

6. Rascher and Tudor recorded a program of virtuoso arrangements (Concert Hall Society LP CHS-1156).

7. Dewar, "Handmade Sounds," 95.

8. Mumma, interview by Vincent Plush, 44–45. Miller, "ONCE and Again," 33, provides additional documentation of Gerhard's significance from interviews with Mumma, Reynolds, and Scavarda.

9. Violinist Werner Grobholz's performance of the *Etude on Oxford Changes* at the Nordwestdeutsche Musikakademie, Detmold, on November 18, 1960, was the first of Mumma's works to be performed in Germany. The remainder of his music for traditional ensembles from before 1959 has been withdrawn from his catalogue, including Variations for piano (1957), String Quartet (1957), Trio for flute, english horn, and bass clarinet (1958), and Chamber Symphony (1958).

10. This statement is adapted from Mumma, interview by Vincent Plush, 88.

11. Mumma, "To Portray Man within His Society" and "Lady Chatterley in America."

12. According to Mumma, the title "Sonic Arts Group" may have been the suggestion of Benjamin Patterson, a bass player with whom he had performed in the University of Michigan Concert Band and Orchestra in the 1950s. The first known use of this title was in a mixed concert program at the Library and Museum of the Performing Arts of the New York Public Library at Lincoln Center on November 7, 1966. Only Behrman and Lucier were present, joining an ensemble with Patterson, Takehisa Kosugi, and Max Neuhaus.

13. It reunited most recently in Berlin in 2012, as documented in Schröder and Straebel, *Cage and Consequences*.

14. See also Dewar, "Handmade Sounds," 77–78.

15. Mumma, interview by Vincent Plush, 157.

16. Composers Chris Brown and Daniel Wolf have written appreciatively of their studies with Mumma in Santa Cruz; see Brown, "Frisch, lebendig und überraschend" and Wolf's "Renewable Music" blogspot, http://renewablemusic.blogspot.com/2011/01/mumma-in-musiktexte.html.

Part I. Editor's Introduction

1. See Miller, "ONCE and Again," 96–104, for an inventory of ONCE Festivals and related events.

1. Music's Avant-Garde

1. The term for this process more commonly used today, "spatial music," has been substituted in all subsequent references.

2. That recording has been re-released on Naxos CD 8.557530-31.

3. The term "tape music" is now commonly applied to this genre.

4. Scherchen's death in 1966 dealt a blow to the promotion of contemporary music.

5. An example is his "Musikalisches Würfelspiel" [musical dice-game], K. 516f (1787).

6. Carter, String Quartets nos. 1 (1951) and 2 (1959).

2. *Manifestations: Light and Sound*

1. On the Space Theatre, see Hejmadi, "Dome of Light"; Ashton, "Art," 7; Cohen, "Space Theatre," 10–11; Manupelli, "Films and Photography," 28–32; Kuh, "Fascinating Rhythms," 30; James, "ONCE: Microcosm of the 1960s," 363–68; and Miller, "ONCE and Again," 22–26.

2. The 1962–63 studio performances of *Manifestations: Light and Sound* would include tape music by Lejaren Hiller, Toshi Ichiyanagi, Philip Krumm, Richard Maxfield, Ramon Sender, and Morton Subotnick.

3. According to Pauline Oliveros, Cohen's public concerts at San Francisco's Sacramento Street firehouse provided her first contact with the music of Ashley and Mumma, after which they "began to correspond and exchange tapes" (Oliveros, "A Theater Piece Book," manuscript, Oliveros Papers MSS 102, box 10, folder 8 [Mandeville Special Collections Library, University of California, San Diego]), with thanks to David Bernstein for this information.

4. Mumma and Ashley developed their four-channel recording technique privately; quadraphonic tape was not yet commercially available.

5. Mumma commented in his 1982 interview by Vincent Plush: "I can't recall anything that I was ever involved in beforehand that was so energizing, so fruitful in terms of ideas and production as [the Space Theatre]" (60).

3. An Electronic Music Studio for the Independent Composer

1. Prieberg, *Musica ex Machina*, 9–47.

2. Schaeffer, *À la recherche d'une musique concrète*; LeCaine, "Electronic Music," 474–76.

3. Eimert and Stockhausen, "Electronic Music."

4. Hiller, *Report on Contemporary Experimental Music*; Tall, "Music without Musicians," 56–57.

5. Olson, Belar, and Timmens, "Electronic Music Synthesis," 311–19; Olson and Belar, "Electronic Music Synthesizer," 595–612; Mathews, "Acoustical Compiler," 677–94.

6. Hitchcock, "Current Chronicle," 244; Yates, "Music," 8; Boucourechliev, "Tone Roads—Fin," 75–76; Kasemets, "Current Chronicle," 515–19.

7. The composers Ramon Sender and Morton Subotnick established the San Francisco Tape Music Center [Sender, "An Overview of the Tape Music Center's Goals, Autumn 1964," in Bernstein, *San Francisco Tape Music Center*, 47–49]. In Cambridge, England, the composer Roberto Gerhard has a busy schedule of electronic music commissions for the BBC. Henry Jacobs established his own studio with filmmaker Jordan Belson for the "Vortex" series at the Morrison Planetarium, San Francisco.

8. See Mumma, "*Manifestations: Light and Sound*," in this part.

4. The ONCE Festival and How It Happened

1. Complementary to this article are Mumma's extended letter to the editor (Peter Yates) in *Arts and Architecture*; James, "ONCE: Microcosm of the 1960s"; Miller, "ONCE and Again," and the 7-CD "Music from the ONCE Festival, 1961–1966" (NWR-80567) that her essay accompanies; Holmes, "ONCE and Future Innovators: Robert Ashley and Gordon Mumma," in *Electronic and Experimental Music,* 187–210; and Dietrich, "ONCE and the Sixties."

2. The revised figures derive from the accounting documents in GMC.

3. Toshi Ichiyanagi was to have shared the program with Young, as advertised in the festival brochure. Ichiyanagi was unable to return from the Tokyo Festival in time and was replaced by Jennings for the February 9 opening concert, with resulting program changes.

4. The name ONCE had stuck, quelling all talk of changing it to TWICE, THRICE, or ONCE AGAIN. In quiet moments we collected playful alternatives: ONCE TOO OFTEN, ONCE IS ENOUGH, and SO WHO ONCE IT? [original note].

5. Absent from this article is the final ONCE Festival of February 8–10, 1968, given by the ONCE Group and the Sonic Arts Group and held at the Michigan Union Ballroom.

6. In 1972 Mumma commented in an interview by Barney Childs: "We were doing things which really would be impossible now, not only because of the cost, but somehow our innocence about what we were getting into then gave us a great protection" (6).

7. This paragraph is excerpted from Mumma's unpublished "Equipment for the Independent Electronic-Music Studio" (1965; GMC), submitted by invitation from Hermann Scherchen to *Gravesaner Blätter,* suspended on Scherchen's death in 1966.

8. Reviews include Hitchcock, "Current Chronicle"; Kasemets, "Current Chron-

icle"; Boucourechliev, "Tone Roads—Fin"; Sheff and Slobin, "Music beyond the Boundaries"; and Yates, "A Ford to Travel 4: ONCE."

9. See Mumma, "*Manifestations: Light and Sound*," no. 2 in this book.

10. See Mumma, "An Electronic Music Studio for the Independent Composer," no. 3 in this book.

11. Ashley, *Kittyhawk (An Anti-Gravity Piece),* in "Three Pieces," 192–95.

12. Ashley's *Crazy Horse,* Cacioppo's *Time on Time in Miracles,* Mumma's *Music from the Venezia Space Theatre,* and Scavarda's *Landscape Journey* were released on Advance FGR-5, now a collector's item.

5. The ONCE Group's *Unmarked Interchange* and *Night Train*

1. A film of the 1965 ONCE AGAIN performances was made by Ed Emshwiller for the United States Information Agency. When Emshwiller died in 1990 it was still illegal to mention such "cold war" projects in print, and thus this documentary is not included in his official list of creative works. Access to USIA projects in the United States remains prohibited.

Part II. Editor's Introduction

1. "Composer's Notes," in Mumma, *Electronic Music of Theatre and Public Activity* (NWR 80632-2), 11–12.

6. Creative Aspects of Live-Performance Electronic Music Technology

1. So portable was the sound box that it was stolen from under Mumma's eyes during the question period after a performance, suspending the performance life of *Medium Size Mograph 1963.*

2. This paragraph has been expanded with details from Mumma's program note to "Live-Electronic Music," in Tzadik TZ 7074.

3. Although this work is referred to as *Hornpipe* in the original article, the presence of the resonating pipes (the source of its title rather than the sailor's dance) identifies this work as the preliminary concept-piece *Hornpipes.* The cursory description of *Hornpipes* in the original presentation required additional clarification from manuscript notes and interviews with the composer. *Hornpipes* was never realized; it was supplanted by the more sophisticated portable circuitry of *Hornpipe* (1967), a major live-electronic touring solo for Mumma into the early 1970s (the latter discussed in "Two Cybersonic Works: *Horn* and *Hornpipe*," in this part of the book).

4. On the structure and production of Cunningham's choreography for *Place*, see "From Where the Circus Went" (no. 15 in this book, especially its sidebar).

7. Alvin Lucier's *Music for Solo Performer 1965*

1. The physical premise of the work, as explained by Lucier (*Music for Solo Performer 1965*, typescript score, GMC), is deceptively simple: "It is well known that the alpha rhythm of the brain has a frequency of approximately 10 cycles per second, and if amplified enormously and channeled through an appropriate transducer, becomes audible. It is also known that the alpha rhythm can be blocked by such things as visual attention with the eyes open, mental activity with the eyes closed, and so forth, and that it returns when the subject is in a resting state with the eyes closed. . . . The activity of the subject consists simply in the alteration of thought content, for example a shifting back and forth from a state of visual imagery to a state of re-laxed resting." Its first performance took place at the Rose Art Museum, Brandeis University, on May 5, 1965. A 2007 recording of *Music for Solo Performer 1965* was issued by Lovely Music (CD 5013); the original 1965 recording accompanied this essay in *Source* 1, no. 2 (July 1967).

8. Two Cybersonic Works

1. "Creative Aspects of Live-Performance Electronic Music Technology," no. 6 in this book, reflects a transitional stage in the evolution of *Hornpipes* to *Hornpipe*. In the 1970s Bill Colvig, Lou Harrison, and I also discussed the acoustical properties of resonant metal pipes in conjunction with their gamelan constructions.

2. The original release of this recording of *Hornpipe* (Mainstream MS 5010) warped its structure because of cuts in the first part to accommodate the limited time-span of that LP disc. These excisions are restored in the Tzadik CD version (TZ 7074).

10. A Brief Introduction to the Sound-Modifier Console and *Sun(flower) Burst*

1. Klüver, Martin, and Rose, *Pavilion*, xi, xiii.

2. The design process for the sound modification system is outlined by Nilo Lind-gren in ibid., 48–58.

3. Tudor's recordings of these works on the Osaka Pavilion system are released on Tudor, *The Art of David Tudor, 1963–1992* (NWR 80737–2). The technical data contained in this essay provide insight into the creative process Tudor used in these works.

4. The final sentence is adapted from Mumma, interview by Barney Childs, 21.

11. What We Did Last Summer

1. Thompson, *June 1st 1974*, includes an extended memoir of ICES 1972, extracted online as "ICES 72: The Woodstock of the Avant Garde," http://davethompson books.wordpress.com/2013/03/24/ices-72-the-woodstock-of-the-avant-garde/.

2. Davies, *International Electronic Music Catalog*.

3. She is now known as Annea Lockwood. Matusow, KPFA radio interview by Charles Amirkhanian (March 15, 1972), http://archive.org/details/AM_1972 _03_15_2.

12. Two Decades of Live-Electronic Music, 1950–70

1. Early sources on the application of computers to musical composition include Hiller and Isaacson, "Musical Composition with a High-Speed Digital Computer" (1958) and *Experimental Music* (1959).

2. Much of this paragraph was adapted from Mumma and Smoliar, "Computer as a Performing Instrument."

3. This is discussed in "David Tudor the Composer," no. 18 in this book; thus the segment dealing with Tudor (Appleton and Perera, *Development*, 297) has been omitted here.

4. All three have been recorded by the Sonic Arts Union, re-released on CD by Alga Marghen (B5NMN.020).

5. The following section on the MIT premiere of *Conspiracy 8* is an addition adapted from Mumma and Smoliar, "Computer as a Performing Instrument," and from notes and interviews with Mumma.

13. Witchcraft, Cybersonics, and Folkloric Virtuosity

1. The resulting *Sushumna Jam (PowerFlick #13)* is available online, http://www .lightbuilders.com/pfl.html.

2. Tesla, *Lectures, Patents, Articles*; Mumma's personal copy (GMC) is signed by the entire cast and musical ensemble of *Canfield*.

3. This involves a process reminiscent of that used for Alvin Lucier's *Music for Solo Performer 1965*; see no. 7 in this book.

Part III. Editor's Introduction

1. For historical readings on Cunningham's choreography in the 1960s and early 1970s, see Cunningham, *Changes*; Klosty, *Merce Cunningham*; individual essays in Kostelanetz, *Merce Cunningham: Dancing in Space and Time*; Vaughan, *Merce Cunningham: Fifty Years*; C. Brown, *Chance and Circumstance*.

2. On May 14, 1960, was a lecture titled "Indeterminacy" with *Concert for Piano and Orchestra*; May 16, 1960, included *Music Walk*. See Dunn, *John Cage*, 32, 42.

3. Dunn, *John Cage*, 13, 32; Mumma, ONCE inventory (1961–63), GMC.

4. See "Tramway" from "Twenty-Five Minutes with John Cage," no. 21 in this book.

5. The extraordinary beginnings of the Cunningham milieu in the 1950s have virtually no known film or video documentation. In the 1960s the first eleven films

of live performances by the Cunningham Dance Company were made, seven of which were from European tours.

6. Mumma, interview by Barney Childs.

7. Vaughan, "Retrospect and Prospect," in Kostelanetz, *Merce Cunningham: Dancing in Space and Time*, 124.

8. In its emphasis on musical process, this essay differs from other writings of the same time that focus solely on the visual component, such as Don McDonagh's "Merce Cunningham," in Kostelanetz, *Merce Cunningham: Dancing in Space and Time*, 1–14.

9. Vaughan, *Merce Cunningham: Fifty Years* (1997); C. Brown, *Chance and Circumstance* (2007).

10. Curated by the Merce Cunningham Trust, http://dancecapsules.merce cunningham.org/?8080ed.

15. From Where the Circus Went

1. On Tudor and the bandoneon, see Goldman, "Buttons on Pandora's Box," 30–60, including a substantial account of the origins and performance history of *Mesa* (46–50).

2. Anne Opie Wehrer (1929–2007), actress, writer, and wife of University of Michigan professor of architecture Joseph Wehrer, was an Ann Arbor friend and supporter of the ONCE Festivals; see Miller, "ONCE and Again," 36.

3. This is a reference to Cunningham's "Space, Time and Dance (1952)," in Kostelanetz, *Merce Cunningham: Dancing in Space and Time*, 37–39.

4. Cunningham, "Choreography and the Dance," 52–53; Banes, "Dancing . . . the Music," 3–22.

5. Wolff's work was initially billed as *Untitled*. The aptly named *Suite by Chance* was the first choreography that Cunningham created by chance procedures; see Beal, "Short Step along the Way," 25–26.

6. The original Barron disc transfers of the *Symphonie pour un homme seul* and Wolff's *Music for Magnetic Tape I* are in GMC. Both show significant wear from repeated use in early Cunningham performances. On the development of magnetic tape, magnetic recording, and tape editing, see Mumma, "Sound Recording," 4:268–69; Holmes, *Electronic and Experimental Music*, 77–99.

7. For an extensive account of the choreography of *Antic Meet*, see Vaughan, *Merce Cunningham: Fifty Years*, 103–9.

8. For Cunningham's account of the 1964 tour, see his "Story Tale of a Dance and a Tour," 14–21; Carolyn Brown, *Chance and Circumstance*, 375–446.

9. The conceptual component of Cage's published score of *Variations V* is captured in its subtitle, *Thirty-seven Remarks Re an Audio-Visual Performance*, and its preparation after the Lincoln Center premiere. Cage would complete the cycle with *Variations VIII* (1978).

10. The sound and technical equipment are amply demonstrated in the NDR-Hamburg film of Cage and Cunningham, *Variations V* (August 1966).

11. The *Indeterminacy* stories are published in part in Cage, *Silence*, and were released on a Folkways recording called *Indeterminacy*, reissued on CD by Smithsonian Folkways in 1992 (SF40804/5). Later performances of *How to* added stories from *A Year from Monday* and other sources (Vaughan, *Merce Cunningham: Fifty Years*, 294).

12. Some segments were, however, included in later Events, as reported by Vaughan, *Merce Cunningham: Fifty Years*, 293.

13. The technical processes of *Mesa* are discussed in "Creative Aspects of Live-Performance Electronic Music Technology," no. 6 in this book.

14. See "Robert Rauschenberg in the Creative Fields," no. 16 in this book.

15. The commentary by Mumma in the top margin of the cue sheet, "Brandeis 21:55 + error" and a listing of audio equipment, refers to the timing and resources for his solo performance there of the music for *Place* on January 14, 1967.

16. Mumma's *Mesa* had a vigorous independent life during these years as a touring ensemble work with Tudor or—more often—with members of the Sonic Arts Group. It was recorded by Tudor and Mumma at the CBS studios in New York in August 1967 (Tzadik 7074) and was performed by them at Mills College during the First Festival of Live-Electronic Music in December 1967. Tudor also brought the *Mesa* equipment to Europe in 1968 for two concert performances of the work in Sweden in February 1968, apparently with Mauricio Kagel replacing Mumma (thanks to Jonathan Goldman for providing this information on the basis of Tudor documents at the Getty Research Institute).

17. Director Klaus Wildenhahn and a German documentary crew filmed the preparation of *Scramble* at the Cunningham Dance Studio in New York in the spring of 1967; see Wildenhahn, *498 Third Avenue*.

18. The May 1968 live-performance recording of the music for *Scramble* is released on *Music for Merce* (NWR 80712-2).

19. Cunningham's choreography is *RainForest*, while Tudor's music for it is spelled *Rainforest*.

20. The audio recording of Cunningham's Rio de Janeiro *RainForest* is released on NWR 80651-2 (2006).

21. Mumma's 1968 live-performance recording of Tudor's electronically enhanced version is released on *Music for Merce* (NWR 80712-2).

22. *Assemblage* was withdrawn at Cunningham's request and was never televised. The rediscovered and newly digitized film was screened at Electronic Arts Intermix, New York, New York, on January 15, 2014.

23. The piece was recorded in February 1966 at the Rose Art Museum, Brandeis University, but not commercially released until 1972 (Mainstream MS/5010, reissued on CD by Wergo as WER 69402); an extended version of this iteration appears on NWR 80604-2.

24. Lucier's note to the original recording describes the sondol ("*sonar dolphin*") as a "handheld echolocation device which emits a fast, sharp, narrow-beamed click whose repetition rate can be varied manually." The performer uses it to orient himself in the dark "by means of scanning the environment and monitoring the relationship between the outgoing and returning pulses." The sound output thus creates a sonic map of the performance space.

25. Johns is shown at work on *Map* in his Houston Street Studio, New York, in the 1990 film by Hans Namuth and Judith Wechsler, *Jasper Johns: Take an Object* (http://www.judithwechsler.com/films/jasper-johns-take-an-object).

26. They appeared, for example, in *Event no. 128* at UCLA (April 6, 1975), in which Mumma participated.

27. *Mureau* was reprinted in 1973 in Cage, *M*, 35–56.

28. On the compositional process and first performances of *Burdocks* (1970), see Hicks and Asplund, *Christian Wolff*, 46–49. Excerpts of Wolff's July 1972 Darmstadt lecture with comments on the work are summarized in Beal, "Christian Wolff in Darmstadt," 26–28.

29. Cunningham wrote the following explanatory note for inclusion in programs for Events: "Presented without intermission, [the] Event consists of complete dances, excerpts of dances from the repertory, and often new sequences arranged for particular performance and place, with the possibility of several separate activities happening at the same time—to allow not so much [for] an evening of dances as the experience of dance" (*Merce Cunningham Dance Capsules*, http://www.merce cunningham.org/index.cfm/choreography/dancedetail/params/work_ID/84/). Events proved so successful that they continued until 2012, the final tour year of the Cunningham Dance Company, and numbered in the hundreds.

30. In 2011 it reopened as the 21er Haus. The numbering of the Events is not yet standardized. The numbers used in this essay derive from the typescript partial inventory that Mumma made in 1973 (GMC), which coordinates with the numberings in most of the original Cunningham programs of the time. Several Events, however, are missing in this inventory. Dates are supplied to assist identification.

31. Sections of this performance were filmed by Wildenhahn; see his *John Cage*.

32. Klaus Wildenhahn and his NDR film crew were on hand; some of these scenes appear in Wildenhahn's documentary *498 Third Avenue* (1967). The event merited a lavish spread in *Vogue.*

33. See Carolyn Brown's devastating description of the event in a letter to Earle Brown in *Chance and Circumstance*, 492–93.

34. Mumma is referring to an unreleased sound recording in GMC.

35. Klosty's color photo of this Event is provided in Vaughan, *Merce Cunningham: Fifty Years*, 184–85.

36. For Carolyn Brown's account of the emotional toll of her resignation, includ-

ing Mumma's first-hand account of Cage's distress, see her *Chance and Circumstance*, 585–86.

37. Brook, *Empty Space*, 57.

16. Robert Rauschenberg in the Creative Fields of the Cunningham Dance Company

1. A 1954 performance by Cage and Tudor has been released on *Music for Merce* (NWR 80712-2).

2. Tomkins, *Off the Wall*, 49.

3. He had previously developed combine paintings, to which external objects were appended, inserted, or attached to the wall-mounted painting surface.

4. Table 2 is adapted from Rauschenberg's draft, reproduced in Cunningham, *Changes,* n.p.

5. Several of John G. Ross's exquisite color photographs of the original production of *Minutiae* (GMC) are accessible in multiple sources, especially Cunningham, *Merce Cunningham Dance Capsules* (http://dancecapsules.mercecunningham.org/overview.cfm?capid=46080), and Vaughan, *Merce Cunningham: Fifty Years*, 82–83.

6. C. Brown, *Chance and Circumstance*, 368–69, describes the choreography and sound, including a dramatic photo (facing p. 550). Archival footage of an excerpt of *Pelican* is accessible on the San Francisco Museum of Modern Art's "Explore Modern Art" website: http://www.sfmoma.org/explore/multimedia/videos/37.

7. Program note to the New York City performances in May 1965, GMC.

8. C. Brown, *Chance and Circumstance*, 455.

9. October 4, 1974, in Klosty, *Merce Cunningham*, 83.

17. With Tudor the Organist

1. Holzaepfel, program essay to *David Tudor and Gordon Mumma*, NWR 80651-2 (2006), 3.

2. Tudor, interview by Bruce Duffie (1986).

3. Oliveros, *Duo for Accordion and Bandoneon, with Possible Mynah Bird Obbligato* (1964); Lunetta, *Piece for Bandoneon and Strings* (1966); and Mumma, *Mesa* (1966).

4. These recordings were issued in the "Music of Our Time" series on CBS 32160157-8 (USA), and concurrently on CBS 34-61065 (FR).

18. David Tudor the Composer along the Path to *Rainforest*

1. These Cybersonics units are now housed in the David Tudor Collection at Wesleyan University.

2. This performance is available on *The Art of David Tudor,* NWR 80737 (disc 1).

3. A short film excerpt of this performance is available on the website of the

Daniel Langlois Foundation, http://www.fondation-langlois.org/html/e/page.php?NumPage=583.

4. The recording was released on NWR 80651-2. Cunningham's choreography for *Rainforest* was also presented by the Cunningham Dance Company during the Cornell University residency, March 7, 1969.

Part IV. Editor's Introduction

1. Mumma had served as technician for Cage's and David Tudor's May 1960 Ann Arbor performance of *Indeterminacy* and witnessed many Cage readings from the widening collection in conjunction with Cunningham's choreography *How to Pass, Kick, Fall, and Run* (1965).

19. Cage as Performer

1. Personal communication by Tudor to Mumma.

2. Cunningham was completing the *Socrate* choreography while Cage was at work on the extravagant multimedia *HPSCHD* (1969), a compositional collaboration with Lejaren Hiller.

3. This was notoriously the case in his Charles Eliot Norton Lectures at Harvard University in 1988–89, published as *I–VI*.

4. Redgrave's ensemble with Sting, Ian McKellen, and the London Sinfonietta conducted by Kent Nagano was released in 1987 (Pangea CD-6233).

5. The work is also known as *Swarm*. The impromptu performance was likely in conjunction with the Cornell University appearance of the Cunningham Dance Company on February 9, 1968.

6. The specific intervallic vocabulary was limited to m3, P4, m6, M7, M9, and P12. Among the syntactical restrictions, each of the two simultaneous pitches had to be different from the pitch or pitches sounded just previously by the other player. Further, a player could not use any pitch from the immediately previous choice, and not more than one pitch from the two previous choices.

20. John Cage, Electronic Technology, and Live-Electronic Music

1. Cage's radio debut is described in Revill, *Roaring Silence*, 25–27, 30.

2. Cage made an appearance in Maya Deren's *At Land* (1944, silent) and contributed music to Hans Richter's *Dreams That Money Can Buy* (1948) and Herbert Matter's *Works of Calder* (1950) (with appreciation to Dr. Julia Schröder for these details).

3. Idiophones are self-sounding percussion instruments that vibrate to produce a sound when "struck, shaken, scraped, or made to sound by friction, such as a bell, gong, or rattle" (*Grove Music Online*).

4. By the 1970s electronic music technology had caught up with Beyer's advanced

ideas, and *Music of the Spheres* was recorded by the Electric Weasel Ensemble (re-issued on NWR 80653).

5. The procedure of direct action on the piano string(s) was used by Cowell in his *Piece for Piano with Strings* (1923), *Aeolian Harp* (ca. 1923), and *The Banshee* (1925). On Cowell's string piano music see Nicholls, *American Experimental Music*, 159–66.

6. *Imaginary Landscape No. 1*, Edition Peters 6716 (1960).

7. An interesting exception is the 1942 recording of Kenneth Patchen's radio drama *The City Wears a Slouch Hat*, with music by Cage. This live-performance broadcast made in Chicago and re-broadcast at later hours by Columbia Broadcasting was permitted as a distraction from the war effort.

8. It was not Cage, however, but Christian Wolff who had first provided electronic music for the Cunningham Dance Company: Wolff's *Music for Magnetic Tape I* for the choreography *Suite by Chance* (1952), discussed in "From Where the Circus Went," no. 15 in this book. Cage participated in the splicing and editing of Wolff's tape samples (Hicks and Asplund, *Christian Wolff*, 28).

9. This live performance of February 17, 1963, was released on NWR 80737.

10. Miller, "Cage, Cunningham, and Collaborators," provides a recent perspective on the topic, incorporating copious interview materials, including communications with Mumma.

11. For a short time the Thereminvox was marketed in the United States under this name by RCA.

12. Cage-Cunningham, *Variations V* (Mode 258).

13. On the Events, see "From Where the Circus Went," no. 15 in this book.

14. Cross, *"Reunion,"* 35–42, provides a first-hand account of the event; Kubota, *Marcel Duchamp and John Cage,* provides extensive photo documentation.

15. When *Reunion* was performed at the Electric Circus in New York on May 27, 1968, by Cage, Tudor, Mumma, Behrman, and Cross (with John Kobler replacing the absent Duchamp), the visuals were provided by Stan VanDerBeek and Beverly Emmons.

16. These included Martin Kalve, Takehisa Kosugi, and Michael Pugliese. From the 1980s onward musician-technicians such as John Fullemann, Rob Miller, John D. S. Adams, and D'Arcy Philip Gray also toured with the group. Other composers who used electronic resources in their music for the Cunningham Dance Company include Maryanne Amacher, Robert Ashley, Larry Austin, Jon Gibson, John King, Ivan Tcherepnin, Yasunao Tone, and Christian Wolff.

17. This work is reproduced in K. Brown, *John Cage Visual Art*, 52–53.

18. The shift to video began in 1974, according to Grossman, "Talking with Merce Cunningham," 56–68.

19. The DVD release (Mode 174) features the choice of two orchestral performances: that by the WDR Symphony Orchestra of the German Radio in Cologne or that by the Spoleto Festival Orchestra.

21. Twenty-Five Minutes with John Cage

1. Cage, *Silence*, 260–73.

2. Performances of Cage's *Variations V* at the Saville Theatre took place on November 23–26 and December 1–3, 1966, in all cases partnered with Mumma's music for the choreography *Place*.

3. Revill, *Roaring Silence*, 194–96, recounts Cage's appearances on *Lascia o Raddoppia*, which left him six thousand dollars richer.

4. In an unpublished letter of August 29, 1968, from Finney to composer Roberto Gerhard (Cambridge University Library, Roberto Gerhard Archive), Finney would refer to Mumma as "doing well" with the "Cunningham ballet" (thanks to Gregorio García-Karman for providing this information).

5. This recording was released in 1993 on Newport Classic (NPD 85547).

Part V. Editor's Introduction

1. Recent research on this music includes Dal Farra, "Journey of Sound through the Electroacoustic Wires," and his "Latin American Electroacoustic Music Collection," accessible online from the Fondation Daniel Langlois.

2. For additional information on the Cursos, see Paraskevaídis, "Presencia de compositores argentinos"; Aharonián, "Resumen de los quince primeros cursos latinoamericanos."

3. Mumma, letter of November 26, 1971, to Coriún Aharonián and Héctor Tosar (GMC).

4. This is what Mumma called himself in a telegram to Aharonián of January 14, 1975, following the Fourth Curso (GMC). Translations during the courses were provided on an ad hoc basis by the participants. As noted with irony by Tosar in a letter to Mumma of November 17, 1971 (GMC): "It's not very necessary to speak another language when you have the imperial metropolitan one."

22. Innovation in Latin American Electro-Acoustical Music

1. Reasons for the decline and closure of the Di Tella Institute are explored by King, "El Di Tella," 107–11.

2. For additional information, including generous color photo documentation of his handmade instruments, see the Joaquín Orellana website (http://joaquin orellana.org/).

3. See De la Vega, "Avant Garde Music." The two-disc set issued by JME (ME 1-2) includes Latin American composers as well as Cage (*Variations II*), Earle Brown (*Four Systems*), and Mumma (*The Dresden Interleaf 13 February 1945*), GMC.

4. For an inventory of the Cursos, see Aharonián, "Resumen de los quince primeros cursos latinoamericanos."

5. Tacuabé E3, 4, 7, 8, 11, 12, 13, and 14, GMC.

23. Briefly about Conlon Nancarrow's *Studies for Player Piano*

1. Novaro, *Sistema natural de la música.*

2. In the late 1970s in the United States, the music of the now celebrated Nancarrow (1912–97) was little known.

3. Autograph facsimiles of a large sampling of the studies have been issued in Nancarrow, *Selected Studies for Player Piano and Study no. 41 for Player Piano.*

4. The candid comments that Nancarrow made about Julián Carrillo during Mumma's interviews with him in late December 1974 may provide some context for Nancarrow's isolation in Mexico City: "Carrillo was a big self-promoter. He wrote a book on his music once. I was translating things at the time, and his secretary asked me if I'd like to translate it into English. . . . I didn't want to have anything to do with it. He used to have articles about himself in the paper every week. It was ridiculous. You should hear some of his music . . . it's really awful" (Mumma, "Mexico City and Montevideo, 12.1974–1.1975").

5. Quartet no. 1 received its premiere in Saarbrücken, Germany, by the Saarbrücker Streichquartett on May 20, 1982, according to Hocker, "Chronology: Nancarrow's Life and Work." The quartet is published by Sonic Art Editions (Baltimore: Smith, 1986).

6. For a more detailed survey, see Tenney, "Conlon Nancarrow's *Studies for Player Piano.*"

7. The more recent pianos in Nancarrow's Mexico City studio were used for the October 1968 recording of twelve of the studies issued by Columbia Records in 1969 (MS 7222), out of print by 1973. His complete *Studies for Player Piano* have since been issued on 5 CDs by Wergo (WER 69072).

8. The mandolin attachment consists of pieces of plastic, wood, or metal mounted on a rail, which, when activated between the hammer and the piano string, alter the piano tone to sound sharper or more "tinny."

9. This paragraph is adapted from Mumma, "Nancarrow Notes," 247.

24. Uruguayan Diary

1. On Bértola (1939–96), see Paraskevaídis, "Eduardo Bértola." Carlos Pellegrino (b. 1944) is a poet, novelist, composer of electro-acoustical music, and agronomist (Ph.D., Universidad de São Paulo) who published his second collection of poetry, *Versatorio,* in 1973.

2. *La Plata* refers to the area surrounding the river basin dividing Uruguay and Argentina, noted for its sharp verbal humor.

3. On Ediciones Tacuabé, see Aharonián, "Technology for the Resistance," 195–205.

4. Born in Montevideo, Uruguay, in 1944, Graciela Figueroa is a major Latin American dancer, choreographer, pedagogue, and dance therapist. In 1965 she

received a Fulbright Fellowship to study at the Juilliard School in New York. For the next five years she danced and choreographed for the Lucas Hoving Dance Company and the Twyla Tharp Dance Company, associated with the Merce Cunningham studio, and taught at Connecticut College. In 1970 she returned to Latin America and a distinguished career in Uruguay, Chile, and Brazil. Her many distinctions include a Creative Arts Fellowship in Choreography from the John Simon Guggenheim Foundation in 1984. Among her students was dancer Gregorio Fassler (Chile, 1951–97).

5. See Aharonián, *Héctor Tosar.*

6. Clozier (b. 1945) and Barrière (b. 1944) co-founded the GMEB in 1970, later to become the Institut International de Musique Electroacoustique de Bourges (1995–2011). The GMEB would prove an important resource for many Latin American electro-acoustic composers.

7. Before its performance, the words that Salvador Allende spoke to a newspaper reporter from the day before his assassination are read: "De aquí sólo me sacarán en pijama de madera" (they'll have to carry me out of here in wooden pajamas).

8. Armando Albuquerque (1901–86), Brazilian composer, pianist, violinist, and professor of musicology, was one of the founders of the Brazilian Society of Contemporary Music. See Chaves, "Piano Works of Armando Albuquerque."

9. Documentation of Orellana's life and works, including photographs and sound samples of his self-made instruments, is available online at http://joaquin orellana.org.

10. The work described here is surely Clozier's recently completed *Symphonie pour un enfant seul*, a four-movement concrète piece realized at the GMEB in 1972–74.

11. In spite of Mumma's response, Clozier would again represent the GMEB at the 7th Curso in Brazil in 1978.—Ed.

27. Good Times Up on the Farm

1. The friends for both occasions were David Behrman, John Nash, Frederic Rzewski, and David Tudor, with Mumma and Christian Wolff (Wergo LP 60063, reissued on CD as WER 67772).

29. On the Ives Railroad

1. Rossiter, *Charles Ives and His America*; Crunden, "Charles Ives' Place in American Culture."

34. Crossings with David Behrman

1. Our 1968 recording of *Wave Train* has been reissued on Alga Marghen CD B5NMN.020.

35. Becoming Alvin Lucier

1. Lucier's recording with the members of the Brandeis Chamber Chorus, *Extended Voices: New Pieces for Chorus and for Voices Altered Electronically by Sound Synthesizers and Vocoder* (Odyssey 32 160156), was released in 1968.

36. Working with Pauline Oliveros

1. The performance was filmed by Randall Packer (unreleased).
2. The score of *Fwyyn* is also reproduced on the sleeve of Lovely Music LP VF 1092.

37. Notes on My Creative Procedures

1. The score and disc are available from the composer (www.brainwashed.com/mumma/).
2. Crawfort, Lott, and Oja, *Celebration of American Music*, 473.
3. Mumma has avoided all public comment on the speculative connection of this terminology to controversial U.S. interrogation practices.—Ed.

WORKS CITED

Aharonián, Coriún. *Héctor Tosar: Compositor Uruguayo*. Montevideo: Ediciones Trilce, 1991.

———. "Resumen de los quince primeros cursos latinoamericanos de música contemporánea" (2007). http://www.latinoamerica-musica.net/informes/cursos .html. Accessed July 3, 2014.

———. "Technology for the Resistance: A Latin American Case." *Latin American Music Review* 23, no. 2 (2002): 195–205; reissued on *Latinoamérica música*. http://www .latinoamerica-musica.net./frames/en.html. Accessed July 3, 2014.

Appleton, Jon H., and Ronald C. Perera, eds. *The Development and Practice of Electronic Music*. Englewood Cliffs, N.J.: Prentice-Hall, 1975.

Ashley, Robert. "Three Pieces: The ONCE Group." *Tulane Drama Review* 10, no. 2 (1965): 187–202.

Ashton, Dore. "Art." *Art and Architecture* 78, no. 3 (1961): 7.

Austin, Larry, Douglas Kahn, and Nilendra Gurusinghe, eds. *Source: Music of the Avant-Garde, 1966–1973*. Berkeley: University of California Press, 2011.

Banes, Sally. "Dancing [with/to/before/on/in/over/after/against/away/from/without] the Music: Vicissitudes of Collaboration in American Postmodern Choreography." *Journal of Choreography and Dance* 1 (1992): 3–22.

Beal, Amy C. "Christian Wolff in Darmstadt, 1972 and 1974." In *Changing the System: The Music of Christian Wolff*, ed. Stephen Chase and Philip Thomas, 23–47. Burlington, Vt.: Ashgate, 2010.

———. "'A Short Step along the Way': Each-Thingness and Music for Merce." Program essay for *Music for Merce, 1952–2009*, 9–99. New World Records NWR 80712-2 (2010).

Bekaert, Jacques, ed. *John Cage*. Brussels: Algol, 1971.

Bernstein, David W., ed. *The San Francisco Tape Music Center: 1960s Counterculture and the Avant-Garde*. Berkeley: University of California Press, 2008.

Boucourechliev, André. "Tone Roads—Fin." *Preuves* (July 1964): 75–76.

Brook, Peter. *The Empty Space: A Book about the Theatre; Deadly, Holy, Rough, Immediate*. New York: Touchstone, 1968.

Brown, Carolyn. *Chance and Circumstance: Twenty Years with Cage and Cunningham*. New York: Knopf, 2007.

Brown, Chris. "Frisch, lebendig und überraschend: Studieren bei Gordon Mumma." *MusikTexte* 127 (December 2010): 62–63.

Brown, Kathan. *John Cage Visual Art: To Sober and Quiet the Mind*. San Francisco: Crown Point, 2000.

Cage, John. *I–VI*. Cambridge, Mass.: Harvard University Press, 1990.

———. *Imaginary Landscape No. 1*, Edition Peters 6716; New York, C. F. Peters, 1960.

———. *M: Writings '67–'72*. Hanover, N.H.: Wesleyan University Press, 1973.

———. *One¹¹: A Film without Subject* (1992). A film by Henning Lohner, Van Carlson, and Andrew Culver. Mode DVD (Mode 174).

———. *Silence: Lectures and Writings*. Middletown, Conn.: Wesleyan University Press, 1961.

———. *Variations V: Thirty-seven Remarks Re an Audio-Visual Performance*. New York: Henmar Press and C. F. Peters, 1965.

———. *A Year from Monday*. Middletown, Conn.: Wesleyan University Press, 1967.

———, and Merce Cunningham. *Variations V*. Film. Co-production of Norddeutscher Rundfunk Hamburg [NDR] and Sveriges Radio Television (August 1966). Filmed at NDR Studio, Hamburg, Germany, August 1966. Mode DVD (MDE 258).

———, and Lejaren Hiller. "HPSCHD." *Source* 4 (1968): 10–19.

Celant, Germano, ed. *Merce Cunningham*. Milan: Charta, 1999.

Chaves, Celso. "The Piano Works of Armando Albuquerque." D.M.A. diss., University of Illinois, 1989.

Cohen, Milton J. "Space Theatre." *Arts and Architecture* 79, no. 8 (August 1962): 10–11.

Cohen, Robert P. *Choreographers/Composers/Collaboration*. New York: Routledge, 1992.

Cope, David H. *New Directions in Music*. 5th ed. Dubuque, Iowa: Brown, 1989.

Crawford, Richard, R. Allen Lott, and Carol J. Oja, eds. *A Celebration of American Music: Words and Music in Honor of H. Wiley Hitchcock*. Ann Arbor: University of Michigan Press, 1990.

Cross, Lowell. "*Reunion*: John Cage, Marcel Duchamp, Electronic Music and Chess." *Leonardo Music Journal* 9 (1999): 35–42.

Crunden, Robert Morse. "Charles Ives' Place in American Culture, in *An Ives Celebration*, ed. H. Wiley Hitchcock and Vivian Perlis, 4–13. Urbana: University of Illinois Press, 1977.

Cunningham, Merce. "Choreography and the Dance." In *The Creative Experience*, ed. Stanley Rosner and Lawrence E. Abt, 52–62. New York: Grossman, 1970.

———. *The Dancer and the Dance: Merce Cunningham in Conversation with Jacqueline Lesschaeve*. Rev. ed. New York: Marion Boyars, 1991.

———. *Merce Cunningham Dance Capsules*. Web site administered by the Merce Cunningham Trust. http://dancecapsules.mercecunningham.org/?8080ed. Accessed January 22, 2015.

———. *Changes: Notes on Choreography*. Edited by Frances Starr. New York: Something Else, 1968.

———. "Story Tale of a Dance and a Tour." *Dance Ink* (Spring 1995): 14–21; rpt. in Celant, *Merce Cunningham*, 113–21.

Dal Farra, Ricardo L. "A Journey of Sound through the Electroacoustic Wires: Art and New Technologies in Latin America." Ph.D. diss., University of Quebec, Montreal, 2006.

———, curator. "Latin American Electroacoustic Music Collection." Web site administered by the Fondation Daniel Langlois. http://www.fondation-langlois.org/html/e/index.php. Accessed May 17, 2013.

Davies, Hugh. *Répertoire International des musiques électroacoustiques; International Electronic Music Catalog*. Paris: Groupe de recherches musicales; New York: Independent Electronic Music Center, 1968.

De la Vega, Aurelio. "Avant Garde Music at the American Art Biennial of Cordoba." *Anuario* 3 (1967): 85–100.

Dewar, Andrew Raffo. "Handmade Sounds: The Sonic Arts Union and American Technoculture." Ph.D. diss., Wesleyan University, 2009.

Dietrich, Ralf. "ONCE and the Sixties." In *Sound Commitments: Avant-Garde Music and the Sixties*, ed. Robert Adlington, 169–86. New York: Oxford University Press, 2009.

Dunn, Robert, ed. *John Cage*. Edition Peters Catalogue. New York: Henmar Press and C. F. Peters, 1962.

Eimert, Herbert, and Karlheinz Stockhausen, eds. *Die Reihe*, 1: "Electronic Music." Bryn Mawr, Penn.: Presser, 1958.

Gann, Kyle. *Robert Ashley*. American Composers. Urbana: University of Illinois Press, 2012.

Goldman, Jonathan. "The Buttons on Pandora's Box: David Tudor and the Bandoneon." *American Music* 30, no. 1 (2012): 30–60.

Grossman, Peter Z. "Talking with Merce Cunningham about Video." *Dance Scope* 13 (1979): 56–68.

Hejmadi, Padma. "The Dome of Light." *Michigan Daily Magazine* (May 24, 1959); *Illustrated Weekly of India* (October 2, 1960).

Hicks, Michael, and Christian Asplund. *Christian Wolff*. American Composers. Urbana: University of Illinois Press, 2012.

Hiller, Lejaren A., Jr. "Report on Contemporary Experimental Music, 1961." Technical Report. Urbana-Champaign: University of Illinois, 1962.

———, and Leonard M. Isaacson. *Experimental Music: Composition with an Electronic Computer.* New York: McGraw-Hill, 1959; rpt, Westport, Conn.: Greenwood, 1979.

———. "Musical Composition with a High-Speed Digital Computer." *Journal of the Audio Engineering Society* 6 (1958): 154–60.

Hitchcock, H. Wiley. "Current Chronicle." *Musical Quarterly* 48, no. 2 (1962): 244–48.

Hocker, Jürgen. "Chronology: Nancarrow's Life and Work, 1912–1997." http://www.nancarrow.de/chronology.htm. Accessed July 4, 2014.

Holmes, Thom. *Electronic and Experimental Music.* 2nd ed. New York: Routledge, 2002.

James, Richard S. "ONCE: Microcosm of the 1960s; Musical and Multi-Media Avant-Garde." *American Music* 5 (1987): 359–90.

Johns, Jasper. *Jasper Johns: Take an Object* (1990). A documentary film by Hans Namuth and Judith Wechsler. http://judithwechsler.com/films/jasper-johns-take-an-object. Accessed February 27, 2013.

Kasemets, Udo. "Current Chronicle." *Musical Quarterly* 50, no. 4 (1964): 515–19.

———. "Space Theatre at Ann Arbor." *Literary Times* (September 1964): 8–11.

King, J. "El Di Tella and Argentine Cultural Development in the 1960s." *Society for Latin American Studies* 1, no. 1 (1981): 105–12.

Klosty, James, ed. *Merce Cunningham.* New York: Dutton, 1975; rpt, New York: Limelight, 1987.

Klüver, Billy, Julie Martin, and Barbara Rose, eds. *Pavilion by Experiments in Art and Technology.* New York: Dutton, 1972.

Kostelanetz, Richard, ed. *Merce Cunningham: Dancing in Space and Time.* Chicago: Chicago Review Press, 1992; rpt, New York: Da Capo, 1998.

Kubota, Shigeko. *Marcel Duchamp and John Cage.* N.p.: Takeyoshi Miyazawa, c. 1970.

Kuh, Katharine. "The Fine Arts: Fascinating Rhythms in Sculpture." *Saturday Review of Literature* 44 (July 1961): 30.

LeCaine, Hugh. "Electronic Music." *Proceedings of the I.R.E.* [Institute of Radio Engineers] 44, no. 4 (1956): 457–78.

Manupelli, George. "Films and Photography." *School Arts* 62, no. 7 (1963): 28–32.

Mathews, Max V. "An Acoustical Compiler for Music and Psychological Stimuli." *Bell System Technical Journal* 40 (1961): 677–94.

———, Joan E. Miller, and others. *The Technology of Computer Music.* Cambridge, Mass.: MIT Press, 1969.

Matusow, Harvey. KPFA Radio Interview by Charles Amirkhanian (recorded March 15, 1972). http://archive.org/details/AM_1972_03_15_2. Accessed June 18, 2013.

Miller, Leta E. "Cage, Cunningham, and Collaborators: The Odyssey of *Variations V.*" *Musical Quarterly* 85, no. 3 (2001): 545–67.

———. "John Cage's Collaboration." In *The Cambridge Companion to John Cage*, ed. David Nicholls, 151–68. London: Cambridge University Press, 2002.

———. "ONCE and Again: The Evolution of a Legendary Festival." Program essay for *Music from the ONCE Festival, 1961–1966*, 13–108. New World Records 80567-2 (2003).

Mumma, Gordon. "Conlon Nancarrow." *Neuland: Ansätze zur Musik der Gegenwart* 1 (1980): 123–30.

———. "Cunningham Company Notes" (April 1971). Typescript, GMC.

———. "Decade 6 and Decade 7, tour process." Typescript, GMC.

———. "Electronic Music for the Merce Cunningham Dance Company." *Choreography and Dance* 4, no. 2 (1996): 51–58; corrected reprint in Celant, 202–6.

———. "Electronic Resources in the Music of Roger Reynolds." In *Roger Reynolds: Profile of a Composer*, ed. Don C. Gillespie, 38–40. New York: C. F. Peters, 1982.

———. "Four Sound Environments for Modern Dance." *Impulse: Annual of Contemporary Dance 1967: The Dancer's Environment*, ed. Marian Van Tuyl, 12–15. San Francisco: Impulse, 1967.

———. Interview by Barney Childs. N.d. [1972]. Barney Childs Collection, University of Redlands, California. Typescript GMC.

———. Interview by Vincent Plush (May 17, 1982). Yale University Oral History of American Music. Typescript, GMC.

———. "Lady Chatterley in America." *Generation* 9, no. 3 (1958): 42–47.

———. Letter to the Editor [Peter Yates]. *Arts and Architecture* 83, no. 2 (1966): 45–47.

———. "Mexico City and Montevideo, 12.74–1.75." Journal, GMC.

———. "Nancarrow Notes." In Zimmermann, *Desert Plants*, 247–52.

———. "Northwest November Notes." *Numus* 5 (1974): 51–53.

———. ONCE inventory (1961–63). Typescript, GMC.

———. "Reflections on the Life of a New Englander" [November 1949]. Typescript, GMC.

———. "Sound Recording." In *The New Grove Dictionary of American Music*, ed. H. Wiley Hitchcock and Stanley Sadie, 4:267–72. New York: Macmillan, 1986.

———. "To Portray Man within His Society: Observations on Certain Achievements in World Cinema." *Generation* 9, no. 1 (1957): 38–44.

———. "What Is a Performance? How the Idea of Playing Music Is Changing." *Selmer Bandwagon* 13, no. 5 (1965): 12–13.

———, and Stephen Smoliar. "The Computer as a Performing Instrument" [February 20, 1970]. *Artificial Intelligence Memo* 213 (MIT Artificial Intelligence Laboratory, February 1971): 1–11.

Music for Merce, 1952–2009. 10 CDs. New World Records NWR 80712-2 (2010).

Nancarrow, Conlon. *Selected Studies for Player Piano*. Edited by Peter Garland. Soundings Book 4. Berkeley, Cal.: Soundings, 1977.

———. *Study no. 41 for Player Piano*. Santa Fe, N.M.: Soundings, 1981.

Nicholls, David. *American Experimental Music, 1890–1940*. Cambridge: Cambridge University Press, 1991.

Novaro, Augusto. *Sistema natural de la música*. Mexico City: By the author, 1951. Available online from the Augusto Novaro Society. http://www.anaphoria.com/novaro51.pdf. Accessed April 20, 2013.

Olson, H. F., and H. Belar. "Electronic Music Synthesizer." *Journal of the Acoustical Society of America* 27 (1955): 595–612.

———, H. Belar, and J. Timmens. "Electronic Music Synthesis." *Journal of the Acoustical Society of America* 32 (1960): 311–19.

Paraskevaídis, Graciela. "Eduardo Bértola." *Revista del Instituto Superior de Música* (Universidad Nacional del Litoral, Santa Fe, Argentina) 8 (2001): n.p.; reissued in abridged form as "Eduardo Bértola: Un retrato del compositor argentino (1939–1996). *Latinoamérica música,* http://www.latinoamerica-musica.net/compositores/bertola/paras-es.html. Accessed July 4, 2014.

———. "La presencia de compositores argentinos en los cursos latinoamericanos de música contemporánea." *La Revista Argentina de Musicología* 14 (2014): 53–76.

Payne, Maggi. "The System Is the Composition Itself [Landscape with Gordon Mumma]." In *Music with Roots in the Aether: Interviews with and Essays about Seven American Composers*, ed. Robert Ashley, 109–24. Cologne: MusikTexte, 2000.

Prieberg, Fred K. *Musica ex Machina: Über das Verhältnis von Musik und Technik*. Berlin: Ullstein Verlag, 1960.

Revill, David. *The Roaring Silence: John Cage; A Life*. New York: Arcade, 1992.

Rossiter, Frank R. *Charles Ives and His America*. New York: Norton, 1975.

Ruble, Gary Aro. *Sushumna Jam (PowerFlick #13)*. http://www.lightbuilders.com/pfl.html. Accessed May 24, 2013.

Schaeffer, Pierre. *À la recherche d'une musique concrète*. Paris: Editions du Seuil, 1952.

Schröder, Julia, and Volker Straebel, eds. *Cage and Consequences*. Hofheim, Germany: Wolke Verlag, 2012.

Sheff, Robert, and Mark Slobin. "Music beyond the Boundaries." *Generation* 17, no. 1 (1965): 27–65.

Tall, J. "Music without Musicians." *Saturday Review* 40 (January 26, 1957): 56–57.

Tenney, James. "Conlon Nancarrow's *Studies for Player Piano*." In Conlon Nancarrow, *Selected Studies for Player Piano*, ed. Peter Garland, 41–64. Soundings Book 4. Berkeley, Cal.: Soundings, 1977.

Tesla, Nikola. *Lectures, Patents, Articles*. Compiled by Vojin Popović, Radoslav Horvat, and Nikola Nikolić. Belgrade: Nikola Tesla Museum, 1956.

Thompson, Dave. *June 1st 1974*. E-book. Amazon Digital Services, 2013. Extracted online as "ICES 72: The Woodstock of the Avant Garde." http://davethompson books.wordpress.com/2013/03/24/ices-72-the-woodstock-of-the-avant-garde/. Accessed June 8, 2014.

Tompkins, Calvin. *Off the Wall: A Portrait of Robert Rauschenberg*. Rev. ed. New York: Picador, 2005.

———. "On Collaboration" [1974]. In *Merce Cunningham: Dancing in Space and Time*, ed. Richard Kostelanetz, 44–47. Chicago: Chicago Review Press, 1992.

Tudor, David. *The Art of David Tudor, 1963–1992*. 7 CDs. New World Records NWR 80737-2 (2013).

———. Interview by Bruce Duffie at the Blackstone Hotel, Chicago (April 7, 1986). http://www.bruceduffie.com/tudor3.html. Accessed March 3, 2013.

Vaughan, David. *Merce Cunningham: Fifty Years*. Edited by Melissa Harris. New York: Aperture Foundation, 1997.

Wildenhahn, Klaus, dir. *John Cage* (1966) and *498 Third Avenue* (1967). Film documentaries. Re-released on DVD as *Klaus Wildenhahn: Dokumentarist im Fernsehen*. Hamburg, Germany: Absolut Medien, 2010.

Wolf, Daniel. "Renewable Music" (blogspot). http://renewablemusic.blogspot .com/. Accessed February 14, 2014.

Yates, Peter. "A Ford to Travel 4: ONCE." *Arts and Architecture* 82, no. 9 (1965): 8–9, 33.

———. "Music." *Arts and Architecture* 80, no. 6 (1963): 8.

Zimmermann, Walter, ed. *Desert Plants: Conversations with 23 American Musicians*. Vancouver, B.C.: Aesthetic Research Center of Canada, 1976.

INDEX

100, 116, 125; *Sixteen Dances for Soloist and Company of Three*, xxix; *Story*, 113–16; *Suite by Chance*, xxix, 111; *Suite for Five*, 99, 111, 161, 162; *Summerspace*, 143, 161; *Tread*, 106, 115; *TV Rerun*, 96, 115, 126–29, 265; *Variations V* (with John Cage), 100, 112–13, 116; *Walkaround Time*, 115–16, 121–22, 162; *Winterbranch*, 113–14, 141

Mercenier, Marcelle, 160

Messiaen, Olivier, 144, 245

Milhaud, Darius, 80

Monk, Meredith, 96–97

Moog, Robert, 112, 170–71

Moore, Peter, 184

Moroi, Makato, 80

Morris, Robert, 115–17

Mother Mallard's Portable Masterpiece Company, 87–**88**, 134–35

Mumma, Adamae, xxvii

Mumma, Archie A., xxviii

Mumma, Colgan T., xxvii

Mumma, Gordon, xxi–xxiv; on audience reactions, 266; on collaboration, 265–66; collaboration with Ashley, 10–11, 13, **20**, 33, 43, 55, 152; collaboration with Behrman, xxxii, 255–56, 286–87; collaboration with Cage, xxxii, 55, 99–100, 109, 164–65, 174, 178, 183–84; collaboration with Cunningham, 126; collaboration with Oliveros, 258–59, 294; collaboration with Rauschenberg, 26, 152; collaboration with Tudor, 40, 55, 99–100, 109, **118**, 122, 129, 154, 156; on composing, 263–65; conceptual scores, 236, 240; development of cybersonic console, 55–59, **58**; on electronic music studios, 14–21; Expo '70 and, 65–72; influence of Cunningham on, 101–2, 265; on Ives, 242–44; on listening to music, 266–67; live-electronic music and, xxx, xxxiv, 43–49, 54–61, 65–72, 89–90, 265; meeting with Cage, xxix, 99; ONCE Chamber ensemble and, **31**; ONCE Festival and, 1–2, 23–35, **26, 37**, 300n6; ONCE Group and, 36–38; as performer, 52, 56, 89, 178, 263; photographs of, **10, 20, 21, 26, 31, 56, 62, 66, 104, 108, 118, 178, 253, 259**; relationship with Cage, 157–58,

189–91; teaching career of, xxxii–xxxiii; use of computers by, xxxiii, 41, 56, 60–61, 89–90, 271–72; work with Merce Cunningham Dance Company, xxxi–xxxii, 96, 99–102, **104**, 105–6, **108**–10, 116–19, 122–33, 171–73, 181, 265; work with Space Theatre, **10**, 30, 299n5

Mumma, Gordon, works by, 283–95; *Abrupted Edges*, xxxiv, 280–82, **281–82**, 295; *Aleutian Displacement*, xxxiii, 294; *Ambivex*, xxi, xxxii, 100, 287; *Ambulare*, xxxiv, 285; *Basket of Strays*, 292; *Beam*, xxxii, 286; *Cirqualz*, 264, 284; *Comitatus 2*, xxxiv, 295; *Communication in a Noisy Environment*, xxxii, 286; *Conspiracy 8*, 41, 89–**90**, 102, 286; *Cybersonic Cantilevers*, xxi, 40, 287; *Densities*, 284, 285; *Diastasis, as in Beer*, 45–46, 286; *The Dresden Interleaf 13 February 1945*, xxxi, 2, 28, 284; *Echo-D*, xxxiii, 284; *Eleven Note Pieces and Decimal Passacaglia*, xxxiii, 268–71, **270–71**, 289; *Epifont*, 264, 285; *Equale—Internal Tempi*, 293; *Equale: Zero Crossing*, xxxiii, 294; *Etude on Oxford Changes*, xxx, 293, 298n9; *Faisandage et galimafrée*, xxxiii, 294; *Four Pack Ponies*, 290; *From the Rendition Series*, xxxiv, 279–80, 288; *Fwyyn: Lament for a Princess Enchanted into Death* (with Oliveros), 258–60, **259**, 294; *Gambreled Tapestry*, xxxiv, 288; *Gestures II*, xxx, 289; *Graftings*, xxxiii, 264, 291; *Greys*, 284; *Horn*, 54–55, 286; *Hornpipe*, xxi, xxxii, 40, 54–61, **56**, 96, 100, 237, 286, 301n3; *Hornpipes*, 45, 55, 286, 301n3; *The Ives Railroad*, 288; *Jardin*, xxxiv, 292; *Large Size Mograph 1962*, 267–**68**; *Le Corbusier*, 286; *Loops* (with Cunningham), 287; *Manifestations: Light and Sound*, 8–13, 30, 299n2; *Meanwhile, a Twopiece*, xxxi, 285; *Medium Size Mograph 1963*, xxi, xxx, 44–45, 285, 289, 297n1, 301n1; *Megaton for Wm. Burroughs*, 2, 32, 34, 285; *Ménages à deux, variable duos*, 294; *Mesa*, xxi, xxxi, 40, 46–48, 100, 102, 117, **118**, 146, 153, 286, 305n16; *Mirrors for Milton Cohen*, 2, 12, 284; *Music from the Venezia Space Theatre*, xxxi, 2, 32, 284; *Orait*, xxxiii, 294; *Peasant Boy* (with Bob James Trio),

GORDON MUMMA worked for twenty years as a professor of music at the University of California. In 2000, he received the John Cage Award from the Foundation for Contemporary Arts. His wife **MICHELLE FILLION** is a professor of musicology at the University of Victoria, British Columbia, and the author of *Difficult Rhythm: Music and the Word in E. M. Forster*.

MUSIC IN AMERICAN LIFE

Live Fast, Love Hard: The Faron Young Story   *Diane Diekman*
Air Castle of the South: WSM Radio and the Making of Music City   *Craig P. Havighurst*
Traveling Home: Sacred Harp Singing and American Pluralism   *Kiri Miller*
Where Did Our Love Go? The Rise and Fall of the Motown Sound   *Nelson George*
Lonesome Cowgirls and Honky-Tonk Angels: The Women of Barn Dance Radio
     Kristine M. McCusker
California Polyphony: Ethnic Voices, Musical Crossroads   *Mina Yang*
The Never-Ending Revival: Rounder Records and the Folk Alliance   *Michael F. Scully*
Sing It Pretty: A Memoir   *Bess Lomax Hawes*
Working Girl Blues: The Life and Music of Hazel Dickens   *Hazel Dickens and*
     Bill C. Malone
Charles Ives Reconsidered   *Gayle Sherwood Magee*
The Hayloft Gang: The Story of the National Barn Dance   *Edited by Chad Berry*
Country Music Humorists and Comedians   *Loyal Jones*
Record Makers and Breakers: Voices of the Independent Rock 'n' Roll Pioneers
     John Broven
Music of the First Nations: Tradition and Innovation in Native North America
     Edited by Tara Browner
Cafe Society: The Wrong Place for the Right People   *Barney Josephson,*
     with Terry Trilling-Josephson
George Gershwin: An Intimate Portrait   *Walter Rimler*
Life Flows On in Endless Song: Folk Songs and American History   *Robert V. Wells*
I Feel a Song Coming On: The Life of Jimmy McHugh   *Alyn Shipton*
King of the Queen City: The Story of King Records   *Jon Hartley Fox*
Long Lost Blues: Popular Blues in America, 1850–1920   *Peter C. Muir*
Hard Luck Blues: Roots Music Photographs from the Great Depression   *Rich Remsberg*
Restless Giant: The Life and Times of Jean Aberbach and Hill and Range Songs
     Bar Biszick-Lockwood
Champagne Charlie and Pretty Jemima: Variety Theater in the Nineteenth Century
     Gillian M. Rodger
Sacred Steel: Inside an African American Steel Guitar Tradition   *Robert L. Stone*
Gone to the Country: The New Lost City Ramblers and the Folk Music Revival
     Ray Allen
The Makers of the Sacred Harp   *David Warren Steel with Richard H. Hulan*
Woody Guthrie, American Radical   *Will Kaufman*
George Szell: A Life of Music   *Michael Charry*
Bean Blossom: The Brown County Jamboree and Bill Monroe's Bluegrass Festivals
     Thomas A. Adler
Crowe on the Banjo: The Music Life of J. D. Crowe   *Marty Godbey*
Twentieth Century Drifter: The Life of Marty Robbins   *Diane Diekman*
Henry Mancini: Reinventing Film Music   *John Caps*
The Beautiful Music All Around Us: Field Recordings and the
     American Experience   *Stephen Wade*
Then Sings My Soul: The Culture of Southern Gospel Music   *Douglas Harrison*

The University of Illinois Press
is a founding member of the
Association of American University Presses.

Designed by Jim Proefrock
Composed in 10.25/13 Marat Pro
with Franklin Gothic display
at the University of Illinois Press
Manufactured by Sheridan Books, Inc.

University of Illinois Press
1325 South Oak Street
Champaign, IL 61820-6903
www.press.uillinois.edu